The Scout: *The Bobby Dinnie Story*

I asked my wife, Betty, if she would like to go to the United States for our honeymoon. Naturally she was ecstatic. What I didn't tell her at the time was I was taking 18 players with us… to play in a football tournament.
Bobby Dinnie MBE

The Scout: *The Bobby Dinnie Story*

The Scout

The Bobby Dinnie Story

Bobby Dinnie MBE

Club Books

The Scout: *The Bobby Dinnie Story*

First published in the United Kingdom 2006.
Re-published in 2014.

Copyright © Bobby Dinnie MBE.
All rights reserved.

No part of this book may be reproduced, stored in a retrieval system or transmitted by any other means, without prior and express written permission by the author/publisher.

A catalogue record of this book is available from the British Library. ISBN 978-1-907463-99-0

Cover Art © Plan4 Media

All photographs are from private collection unless otherwise stated.

Bobby and Her Majesty photograph courtesy of © BCA Films

© Copyright Bobby Dinnie MBE

© The Scout 2006 edition special appreciation to Braveheart Promotions

www.bobbydinnie.com

CONTENTS

INTRODUCTION	9
THE BEGINNING	16
HITLER GOT US A HOUSE IN POSSIL	21
THE HUMBLE BOYS	33
THE HANDS THAT BUILT A LEGACY	46
THE CALL	59
THE BEAUTIFUL GAME	69
THREE KINGS AND A QUEEN	74
AN INTERVIEW WITH A LEGEND	77
THE WORKING YEARS	89
MY CROWNING GLORY	96
NO MEAN CITY	100
FROM THE DRESSING ROOM AND BEYOND (PART ONE)	110
THE FUNNY THINGS WE SAY	127
FROM THE DRESSING ROOM AND BEYOND (PART TWO)	135
IN CONVERSATION	159
FROM THE DRESSING ROOM AND BEYOND (PART THREE)	170
BOBBY'S BOOK PROJECT IN WORDS	263
TRIBUTES	284
DOWN MEMORY LANE	286
REMEMBERING	297
MY ACKNOWLEDGEMENTS	301
FINAL WHISTLE	308
VERNACULAR INDEX	310

Only in a lifetime, a truly great individual is sent to greet us,

to become the guide in our lives.

They have that spirit,

that aura,

that sheer angelic form,

almost too difficult to describe,

and they touch us in such a way with their greatness;

that we cannot help but become great ourselves.

RESPECT

DURING THE MAKING of this book we were deeply saddened to learn of the passing of Archie Leven and George Best.

To the people of Possilpark

INTRODUCTION

BOBBY DINNIE IS ONE OF THE MOST respected gentleman ever to grace the beautiful game; as many from inside and outside the game have testified. Raised from humble origins – he found his love-affair with football amidst Hitler´s dust and the crunching rubble underfoot of World War Two.

He soon learned the lessons of survival but didn´t tuck away the map of contents of his kit and compass: he used that spirit from the air-raid shelters, the bond and the importance of togetherness and spread what is arguably the most difficult gospel to reach the masses: honour, honesty, dignity, loyalty, courage, discipline, consideration, tolerance, acceptance and respect for others.

When all around us were too concerned about building walls; Bobby was busy building bridges. When many refused or didn´t have the courage to combine religions, colour, class or creed; Bobby mixed the very pot with the ingredients of respect for others no matter who one was. He stamped the very mark of what a good honest human being should be made of. We have learned from him and that can only be for the good of the game and for humanity as a whole.

Aside from scouring the local parks in search of talented footballers, Bobby Dinnie started out his own football career in 1948. No slouch himself as a player; he played through all the age groups at Possil YMCA. In 1958 Bobby took over at the helm of the club and only a couple of years later Possil YMCA became the feeding ground for Arsenal FC.

A succession of young talent continually flowed towards Highbury from the North Glasgow institute before Bobby linked his academy to other clubs in the English league; with Aston Villa, Sunderland and Coventry City becoming beneficiaries of the famous Possil YMCA production line.

His very own talent – in finding talent itself – has taken his scouting expertise from the small lesser-known clubs to the elite of the Scottish and English premium heights. Working under managers and coaches like Rangers´ greats Jock Wallace, John Greig, Tommy McLean, Graeme Souness and Walter Smith. Legends in the English and International scene with household names such as Tommy Docherty, Bob Stokoe and Billy Wright.

The early 80s was to see a prominent change in Bobby´s scouting life. The then Rangers manager John Greig invited Bobby to set up a youth policy at Ibrox where it reaped rewards with young players coming through the scheme with the likes of John Spencer, Sandy Robertson and Gary McSwegan. The big money first-team spending arguably put paid to this type of project when clubs – not only Rangers – were forced to buy would-be instant success.

Bobby´s own father was a useful footballer; turning out in the junior ranks before an injury in the First World War scuppered any chances of a professional career. Bobby is also related to the great Scottish athlete Donald Dinnie, who many still say to this day was the greatest Scottish athlete ever. For avid Iron Brew (Irn Bru) enthusiasts, Donald Dinnie was a famous iconic figure and for many personally, a childhood visual brand; his image was used on the bottle labels.

On the 1st of July 1998 Bobby Dinnie was honoured by Her Majesty for his services to his profession. The title MBE sits proudly after a name, not short of fame already, in a distinct history of the proud Dinnie clan.

The Scout: The Bobby Dinnie Story honours a truly great Scot for his legendary work amongst the community of Possilpark and beyond. For the marvellous achievements he accomplished in the game. For giving belief and hope to others to enable them to go on in life – for themselves to achieve – not only in the football world but to achieve good citizenship in other environments. For the countless years and boundless energy he gave to shape some of the greatest players in the British game. For his teachings of tolerance and acceptance of others and for spreading the importance of discipline. For giving us the true meaning of life…and all without even as much as a raised voice in his command.

Great peers have called him the 'Godfather of amateur and youth football', the 'Guardian for the working-class' and the 'Philanthropist in Possilpark'.

If Bobby had been a scientist they'd have labelled him a genius. If he'd opted to work in the political world they'd surely nominate him for the Nobel Peace prize but Bobby is a humble man from humble origins with a great desire to give, to encourage; who broke down any barriers that divided the rich from the poor. He instilled self-belief in the not so confident and not only did he rise from the ashes of a smouldering city; he took everyone with him, never leaving a soul behind. The 'Dalai Lama' of Scottish football?

To leave this book entirely at the dispense of Bobby would mean wrestling with his own humility; such is the man's humbleness. This is why we have combined both an autobiographical and a biographical project where Bobby allows himself the great opportunity to thank all who have played a major role in his life and in turn we have the stage to say our thanks to him for his incredible work not only in the football world but in all worlds around us.

The most difficult part in writing *The Scout: The Bobby Dinnie Story* was trying to think of a title. Of the thousands of words in this book it is amazing to learn that no-one could come up with a title that could capture the characteristics and persona of one of Glasgow's greatest sons.

It was ironic that during the planning for the title of this book there were clear similarities between the Scout movement founded by Robert Baden-Powell and the work that Bobby is synonymous with. Scout's law states: to promote the development of young people in achieving their full physical, intellectual, social and spiritual potential, as individuals, as responsible citizens and as members of their local, national, and international communities: A very nourishing recipe that bakes healthy citizens.

Bobby has mastered and executed such laws without having any connection whatsoever to Baden-Powell's organization but it is quite remarkable how Bobby, perhaps unknowingly or subconsciously, used such humanitarian values to bond unique community achievements amid the hard-working class area of Possilpark and surrounding areas. He is also known as one of the finest talent scouts in his, or any other generation.

What started out as The Bobby Dinnie Story soon adopted 'The Scout' as a brand to what is already a grand name.

Possil YMCA is perhaps more famously known for producing top international players but behind the scenes and away from the training, the grooming and holding cups aloft there were magnificent people who worked effortlessly to help keep the club afloat. Administration work is paramount and like professional clubs; amateur organizations require a good backroom staff. Members of the community of Possilpark and surrounding areas have played an invaluable part in the history making of Possil YMCA. Fund-raising events, tireless work with important duties like managing kit, organizing the logistics of the game and for giving young men from the hard-working class area the unique opportunity to visit and play in tournaments in America, England and Europe. They gave undoubted support for those young members and the rare chance to broaden their education via travel and bonding with other youngsters from other countries around the globe.

The people of Possilpark have all-but-sealed their place in history and formed their own legacy.

This book would not have been possible without the following people: Bobby Dinnie, for giving me the great opportunity to work with him on his book. It has been a long journey but one of great enjoyment. For trusting me with the key to his address book which includes legends after legends. For believing in me that I could pull off a book that he would be pleased and proud of. For the treasure chest he entrusted me to look after that contained his great personal documents including items from Pele, Sir Stanley Matthews, George Best, Her Majesty the Queen and Kenny Dalglish among many others. Martina Lenz for her support and for her encouragement and for having faith in my ability to work on a book of this magnitude. She was also the one who kick-started this book project. Chic Charnley for his work and for helping our team with many of the contributors that are involved in this book. Without Chic I believe this project would have taken a different road. There are many who can make a fortune in football but few can truly make a name. Chic is one of that few.

Special gracious and warm thanks to the following for donating their time and effort in making this book come alive: Neil Leven, Allan Fleck, Clark Brown, Sir Alex Ferguson, Bertie Auld, John Woodward, Bert Paton, Robert Caven, George Adams, Frankie Anderson, Kay McMillan, Allan Moore, Norrie McKay, Derek Robertson, Charlie Rae, Billy Whyte, Robert Carrenduff, Albert Monaghan, William Smith, William Harte, Chic Charnley, Alex McMillan, Allan Dinnie, Bobby Briggs, Davie McKnight, Mae Walker, Donny Chisholm, Graham Diamond, Hugh McColligan, Ian McConachie, Ian McLean, Ian Ramsay, James Fisher, John

McColligan, Katie MacDonald, Stewart Graham, Tommy Douglas, Tommy Gormley, Tommy Young, Wes Greer, William Smith, Grant Reid, Gerry Collins, Jimmy Smith, Jim Duffy, John Thomson, Alex Forsyth, Danny McBryan, Kenny Dalglish MBE, Billy Reid, George Gray, Ian Ross, Graham Smillie, Gordon Chisholm, Gerry Walker, Jim McCLuskey, Kenny Hope, Steve Marley, Stuart Girvan, Gus MacPherson, John Clarkson, Jim Hay, Jimmy Dinnie, John McCartney, Jim Murphy, Tony Fitzpatrick, James Hutchison, Bill Shedden, Jim Donald, John Wyles, Malcolm MacDonald, Ian Birkens, Gordon Speirs, James McGill, Jim Mullin, Harry Robertson, Norrie McLeod, David Moyes, Alex Robertson, Ian Grey, Niall MacTaggart, Gary McSwegan, Brian McGinlay, Ian Steedman, Ross Caven, Dougie Canning, Alastair MacColl, Sammy Smith, Garry Robertson, John Greig MBE, Joe Gaughan, Father Francis Meagher, Alan Harris, Alex McEwan, Gilbert Baird, John Willock, Alex Totten, Baillie Allan Stewart, Ian Taylor, Murray MacDonald, Sammy Johnstone, John McKelvie, Alex Tulloch, Danny Murray, Robert Russell, Alister Rutherford, Ian Doyle, Jim Pyott, Jim Torrance, Jimmy McGill, Jimmy Ross, John Hendrie, John Rice, John Wales, Norman McAllister, Ricky Roughan, Robert Morris, Sadie Gordon, Willie McDougall, Bill McMurray, Raymond Stewart, Alex Hosie, Eddie McCulloch, Bob Smith, Robert W. Reid, Douglas Eadie, Tommy Scoullar, Jack Steedman, Ronnie Patrick, Bertie Rhodie, Junior Hemple, Jimmy Eccles, Matthew Eccles, Jim Taylor, Bobby Brown, George White, Allan Granger, Colin Granger, Jimmy Granger, Bob Marshall and sons Colin and Robert, and Billy Shedden.

Special thanks to all the staff at the doctor's surgery: Dr Reid, Dr Crawford, Dr Connell. Nurses Ruth Campbell and Ame Harvey. Reception staff: Carin Hamilton, Lynsey Fitzpatrick, Margaret Butterly, Claire Hayburn. Practice manager, Alisdair

MacDonald.

My gratitude to Alex McEwan Snr for his tracing help. My sincere thanks to all the contributors to this book. Without them we couldn't possibly have written a book with such variation. All the phone conversations, interviews, letters, faxes and E-mails have been greatly appreciated.

Thanks to Dougie Canning for sending me material in relation to Günter Netzer, the German legend. Sadly it was a bit late but very ironic. I pass Herr Netzer's studio on my many scouting missions and believe me I would not have hesitated to pop in and try my luck for an interview.

Finally, to the people in the north of Glasgow who gave up their time to offer me an insight from their perspective as to how their environment has changed over the decades. Too often the sprawling housing areas are stigmatized for the wrong reasons and I did not need any reminding that we only hear the bad things that come from these areas. We rarely hear the positives – and there are many positives – but they're so often ignored. We hope we have portrayed that positive side of humanity in this book and it's all thanks to people like you.

This book is about the life and times of Bobby Dinnie. Many of you have played a part in his life and in those times so this book is yours. It's about you, the people that matter to Bobby. Without you there may never have been a Bobby Dinnie; the one we know and certainly not one with a title after his name. To be honoured by members of Parliament or the Monarchy is a tremendous feat and to be honoured by your own people is a touching moment to behold.

THE BEGINNING

1933 WAS TO BECOME SIGNIFICANT for Great Britain, Europe and across the Atlantic. It was the year the construction of the Golden Gate Bridge in San Francisco first took place, Hitler became German Chancellor, Lone Ranger began a twenty-one year run on ABC Radio, King Kong premiered, the first sighting of Loch Ness monster was reported and the chocolate chip cookie was said to be invented…Oh! and yes! It was also the year I was born…a mixed bag of events and emotions; as if my parents didn´t have enough to digest…

My parents were incredible people; they raised offspring just a couple short of a full football team: I was the baby of the litter. My sister Catherine and brother John sadly died at a very young age. Two other brothers are no longer with us: Hugh passed away in his mid-sixties and my other brother George departed from this world in his late sixties. I am survived by my blood-family of sisters Agnes and Betty and my brother Jim.

Our home, although small and slightly over-populated by today´s calculations – had enough space for love and a bonding closeness that kept away the harsh winter chills that crept unwelcome up the stairhead close. Our abode was a typical Glasgow room-and-kitchen style, which, as you can imagine, often meant the weans sharing one bed. Our family and playing environment were secure, nevertheless; our grandparents, aunts and uncles all lived in the same street – which wasn´t handy for getting into trouble as there was always a watchful eye on all of us keen to indulge in rare boyish moments of mischief.

Most families lived the same way back then. Glasgow was a

growing city and housing was not nearly as spacious as it is today; in fact, not much of what we had can be found in today's society. We didn't have much in the way of material possessions but we had a great sense of community spirit and boundless respect – which sadly seems elusive at present.

Dad worked for the roof slater and builder's firm and mum – ever the industrious leader of the family – worked constantly just to keep our heids above watter. As dad would come sauntering home from a hard day's graft, mum would be off to clean the houses of the *better off* types of Maryhill. She had an enormous task with her day-to-day homely duties looking after us kids and a hungry man but no-one complained in our house. Dad also worked for himself as the local chimney sweeper to bring in some much needed extra cash: if it wasn't for having just the twenty-four hours on the clock I'm sure they'd have worked more. The police would call my dad at all hours in the morning in the harsh winters to go out and attend to the dangerous chimneys that were damaged due to winter effects and corrosion.

Our house was basic but had all the necessary belongings required to house, feed and nurture a large family. Washing involved ceremonial-like activities where mum would pull the zinc bath from underneath the bed – which was recessed in the living-room – and continuous kettles of boiling water would be heated on the stove: no soft-scented bath oils and definitely no central heating. We didn't have modern bathroom facilities as such but this was our bathing luxury. For most families a weekly and sometimes fortnightly pilgrimage to the local baths was a pre and post war ritual among the core of the city's dwellers. That's right! Once-a-week or twice-per-month was indeed a very common bathing time schedule. Hot water cost money to burn and not everyone had money never mind some to burn so the more necessary things like eating was first on the to-do-list. Again, no-one complained, we just got on with it. It was the way it was in those days and as most people lived the same way there wasn´t much anyone could do or say about it…there was no point, it wouldn´t get you anywhere.

We all took it in turns to get a bath before mum would put us all into bed. Mum´s work never ended there, not in the slightest; she would be up for most of the night attending to other duties like darning, sewing, cleaning, washing and preparing for the next day ahead. Socks would be pulled over empty milk bottles, almost anvil-like, to allow mum to fix holes in them. The tools and templates we used back then were part hand-me-down tips and part survival instinct.

I am proud to come from such a family; the size, the siblings I was blessed with, my parents, of course, and they were all hard-working and good people. We were also of mixed religion, which didn´t bother any of us and it certainly didn´t hinder our upbringing – my parents would never allow such a thing.

Dad was a great footballer. He was considered to be one of the best junior players at this time. He turned out for Benburb Juniors and there was strong talk of him joining the famous Partick Thistle. An eye injury during the war put paid to his football career when he lost the sight in one. It didn´t deter him from the game as he was a successful trainer with Kilmun Thistle – who were Scottish Cup winners having lifted the trophy in the late 1930s at Hibs´ ground, Easter Road.

Working hard always merits a small moment of pleasure and dad was no different from most hard-working men; he enjoyed a pint and company away from the rigours of industry. In those days the pubs closed at 9pm to 9.30pm. Dad´s ritual would be the bookies – where he´d punt – and then a couple of pints before heading back home. He loved talking to people, he was communicative that way and was very well-liked. Cowboys were his passion; he often sang 'Ragtime Cowboy Joe'.

Dad was taken captive during the First World War whilst serving as a corporal with the Royal Scots Fusiliers. He spent a total of four years as a Prisoner of War under German control. He never spoke about his time as a POW but one can only imagine the torment he, and all of the other brave soldiers were going through during their captivity. My greatest respect will always go to those brave men and women who served the country.

My father never once complained or had a bad word to say about his time under German detention. He never raised his voice. In fact, when any of us weans were mischievous my mum would warn us: "Wait 'til yer father gets home." I was quite alright with this as my mum wore a harder shell than my dad…God love him!

Of all the harsh and difficult winters up on those roofs fighting off storms and winds it was on ground level where he succumbed to a painful injury: he slipped on ice just outside the close and broke his hip. He lived to the ripe old age of eighty-eight. Without my parents I could not have become the boy, the youth or the man that I am today.

My complete family. Back row: George, Betty, Jim, Hugh and Agnes. Front row: Dad, Mum, and myself. Taken in the 1950s.

Dad (front row, centre) during his POW days, First World War, Germany.

HITLER GOT US A HOUSE IN POSSIL

WHEN NEVILLE CHAMBERLAIN made his famous war declaration radio broadcast little did we knowthat the city of Glasgow was about to enter a facial and characteristic change; that would shape the dear green city for generations to come. For all of Great Britain it would mark the beginning of an era of a then unknown chapter in the book of many lives of families; across the length and breadth of the nation.

No-one could foresee the extent of the catastrophic measures the cities and towns would endure; we didn´t have anything to compare; we had no TV so we didn´t have the advantages we have today where we could at least have a visual of what an attack may look like. We prepared for the unknowns but the probables through our constant announcements and warnings from our radios – or wireless as it was more commonly known; it was our most prominent source of immediate information in those difficult times; and the surviving people who lived in the First World War would tell us about their times during the 1914-1918 conflict: not a very pleasant bedtime story, let me tell you. Families would gather, huddled beside warm fireplaces, to hear the crackly airwaves and leadership tones: Britain was heading to war!

My own family were very close-knit and experienced those nights in front of the wireless. We lived in a typical Glasgow tenement building in 26 Kilmun Street; consisting of four houses in each block. My immediate family lived in the first house on the right-hand side of the close. Granny Hamilton,

Aunt Agnes Nicol, old Annie Smith and Mrs Garvie lived up the stairs from us. Hugh Hamilton resided at No 16 Kilmun Street. Aunt Nan Kennedy stayed up the other close; her daughter, Margaret, died at the age of twelve having suffered diphtheria. Aunt Jeanie Nicol lived next close.

Maryhill is a suburb (a residential area, if you like,) that lies in the North of Glasgow. The name Maryhill originates from Mary Hill, who once owned the Gairbraid Estate. The Charles Rennie Mackintosh Queen's Cross Church (which of course is home to the Charles Rennie Mackintosh Society), and the Ruchill Church Hall are located within the Maryhill constituency. Another architectural piece of history is St Agnes' Chapel, in Lambhill. St Agnes' was designed by the legendary Pugin, circa 1893. Pugin was very much involved in the design and building of the Palace of Westminster; that includes the House of Lords and the House of Commons. Monumental landmarks were probably not first on Hitler's list; although a great morale crusher if targeted – it was the area's industrial compounds that the Germans sourced to slaughter.

Very shortly after the announcement, all became more clear as children were taken away for evacuation. We were all allocated gas masks; which we carried in cardboard boxes transported by string-straps. The gas masks – or respirators as they were known – were often uncomfortable and to us children, quite scary looking, but they were a much required commodity and a reassuring piece of apparatus. The very young children had different kind of respirators; their respirators were cradle-like and air was hand-pumped through a filter at the side to ensure the babies did not inhale gas.

For months after the war declaration we were taught air-raid drills. Very seldom were our gas masks out of sight. The school bell would ring and we had to put on our masks very quickly and get to the floor. In real time action I guess we'd have hidden under the school desks, which in hindsight could well have provided us with greater protection: the school desks in those days were often made from solid oak and iron. We hurried our masks on which inevitably the visor would form a hazy mist. Fortunately the drill duties were never put into real practice during our school schedules.

We were pre-warned that it would be likely we were going to come under heavy air attack from the Luftwaffe. As it turned out, the city of Glasgow suffered great damage and more importantly, suffered enormous death toll and casualties. Street lights now dimmed, windows – often the gateway to a brilliant roar of gossip – were taped with sticky rolls of paper in a crisscross fashion to cushion any blast damage thrown to us from the enemy attack. Sticky adhesive paper would be stretched across the horizontal area of the window, tacking it inside each frame reveal, repeating the process vertically; perhaps looking like a cross that would give protection to the darkest vampire of them all: Der Führer. The tape would then be stretched across the furthest away points from top left to bottom right and vice-versa, by now starting to look more like a Union Jack… iconic! For more added security and assurance more tape would be tacked across the whole window – now resembling basket weave.

Two devastating evenings stand out in the horrifying war calendar of events: March the 13th and 14th were two dates that will never be forgotten for those who can remember. We were accustomed to blackouts and disdain quite but on one particular evening a bright moon may have given the overhead enemy a better glimpse of their intended targets. The moon shone down on the river Clyde offering a glimmer to German bombers that hovered the city looking for her prey. The Clydeside was targeted due to its industrial status and had set about their preparations for such an occasion but the extent of the devastation was quite overwhelming. Damage was huge and in many respects nearby Clydebank never really recovered from her injuries and mighty blows.

John, Ellen and Jack Geddes lived a few closes up the street from us and when the sirens sounded their warning wail they'd come down to our house. On one particular evening John was fed up, he said, "There's nothing happening, it's too quiet, I'm away up to my own house." My mother tried to get John to stay, offering both Ellen and John a place of rest for the night at our house. John wasn't having any of it and troddled up to his own place. Just a few minutes later we were bombed. Sadly, John was killed in the explosion. Our house was hit and both my parents managed to get us all out of the house. There were no severe casualties in our home…thank God! What saved us or what reduced the impact may have been down to the fact that a few months prior to the devastation, the local authorities erected steel poles in the tenement closes to aid the building should they suffer any impact; which of course there was. Those poles really saved our lives. I was the only one that was injured. A part of the ceiling came down on top of me resulting in a slight head injury.

My brother George, who was twelve-years-old at the time, rescued our Aunt Margaret Hamilton. This was not a normal rescue. Taking George's age into account was significant enough but Margaret was blind. It's amazing, even to this day, how young George managed to get Margaret to safety through the bombings. Almost buried in the debris George helped Margaret through the dark and the dangerous rubble underfoot. Poor Margaret was stunned by the whole experience. Her moans and groans allowed her to be guided, with young George at her every delicate step. George finally got Margaret out onto the close-mouth where she gained enough strength to proceed what seemed like an endless journey of a half-a-mile walk to the nearest rest centre.

Margaret wanted George to leave her and to look after himself but George gripped her to his arm, never letting go, and thinking only about the safety and well-being of his dear aunt.

George's brave stint was recommended for the George medal but nothing came of it. George did receive his moments of fame, however, when the Daily Express ran the story including a photograph of the brave and very proud George Dinnie.

My other brother, Jim, was at the dancing in Sandbank Street on the evening of the bombing of our house. When he heard the drones and the whistling of dropping bombs he hid for shelter in the cellars that housed coal. There was nothing he could do at this moment other than to hide and try to remain safe. When the all-clear sounded he quickly made his way to Kilmun Street. Jim got the shock of his life. His house was destroyed and the police had cordoned off the area, open only to the Emergency Services.

My mother went back to the house the next morning during salvage to retrieve some valuable items (against police orders) and found our budgie Joey, still alive. He lived a further seven years: one of the few moments of happiness during a torrid and harrowing period of carnage.

My sister Betty recalls her experience of that evening on March14th: "I remember the night we were bombed out of our house. Someone woke me up, I can't remember who it was but I was dragged out the house at a hurried pace; obviously there was a great need to get out of the building. We all managed to get out of the close and out onto the street. The building across the street from us was on fire. Two bombs hit us causing great destruction. We scrambled our way to a nearby field for safety away from buildings and anything that could collapse and cause harm. The field turned out to be Maryhill Harps' football ground; which is quite ironic; football even at this early stage in Bobby's life was to play a significant role. Later on that evening the police came and took us down to the foot of Kilmun Street at the junction of Maryhill Road and stopped some passing cars and instructed the drivers to take us to the school in Shakespeare Street where we received a much needed shelter for a short period. I was eight-years-old but can still remember some of those terrible times quite vividly."

Let's not forget the devastation in other cities across the UK. Many large English cities, too, suffered extensive damage on large scales. It is estimated that over two hundred bombers were responsible for the destruction of the Clydeside. In Kilmun Street, my place of birth, and the street that housed a lot of my family, suffered severe loss and casualties due to the attacks on our tenement buildings. Whether those bombs were headed for industrial outlets and possibly strayed their course is irrelevant; they were brutal blows to civilians.

Nearby Clydebank took a few heavy blows as incendiaries and bombs bombarded the town with great ferocity. Yoker Distillery was hit with force, Singers' timber yard – which was holding a full stock of ware at the time – was savaged to say the least and Auchentoshan Distillers was also rocked by the enemy's brutal attacks; the warehouse sparked an inferno which resulted in whisky produce spewing into the burn; the fire spread quickly expanding to the close-by Clyde. John Brown's shipyard and Arnott Young's were just some of the industrial landmarks to find themselves on the receiving end of what became known as the *Clydebank Blitz*.

Rescue departments struggled through the night to cope with the casualties and the devastation. The town's water main was also cut down in the raids resulting in fire crews fighting fires on a handicap and rescue attempts being carried out at a battle. For hours on end the Germans reigned continuous waves of attacks on Clydebank. As the night became wee small hours the toll of destruction mounted and more deaths accounted for. As first light dawned, the fortunate survivors rose from the smoking debris and crumbling homes to another new town completely…a smouldering town at that.

Some reports say as many as 48,000 refugees dispersed, scattered and spread; a great many depleted citizens would never return to the town; even years later. Hundreds died under a violent sky and to make matters worse: the German bombers returned to complete their mission at a neighbouring town. Thousands of houses destroyed as were schools and Churches. If the Germans intended to destroy the moral of the population they were clearly mistaken. In a way, the war brought people closer together. The higher the pitch of the air-raid sirens – the more organized we´d become; the lower the Luftwaffe flew over our heads – the tighter our grip for security and the louder the bombs that fell on us – the more we protected not only ourselves but each other. As Glasgow and her neighbouring towns and dwellings suffered some severe Third Reich blows; it made us even stronger: as a country, as a city, as people and as a community.

The constant wail of sirens that pierced the black night were really quite eery. The drones of the German bombers after the sirens were definitely not a welcome tone. Sounds that no-one who was there could easily forget. In truth, the war pictures you see on history channels may give us insight to what it was like to live or be involved in the war but you really had to be there to understand what it was really like. It´s an experience that will always be fresh in our minds.

It didn´t get any easier just because the sirens stopped and the city dusted itself off after Hitler´s hangover. News soon broke out about the Italians siding with the Germans during the war. Now, as many will know, Glasgow, like a lot of cities in the UK, had a fair share of families hailing from Italian origin. The Italians were prominent in the chip shop business and ice cream parlours – and very good ones, too. Apparently some Italians were taken away and put into camps for safety measures. Windows of these Italian business establishments were trashed by some of the locals who took umbrage to them and their country's political standings beside the Germans. As family folklore would tell you; our very own Granda Hamilton was responsible for some of the spraying shards.

Granda Hamilton was a character. The local Parishioner came to his house as his absence from Sunday worshipping was imminent to the good man of the cloth. On questioning Granda Hamilton about his non presence Granda Hamilton replied, "Ah huvnae got a suit to wear, it's in the pawn." The man from the house of God presented Granda Hamilton with the money to retrieve his suit from the pawn shop to enable him to attend prayer. Needless to say he squandered the money that was given to him in good faith. He was seen in a pub, intoxicated and stripped to the waist challenging fellow drinkers and the occasional onlookers.

Food products became a much sought after necessity. Just when we thought that life was tough wearing those horrid gas masks we were then stripped of luxuries like caramel dainties and liquorice. The government devised a plan, implementing food rationing. Of course, rationing didn't just include food; petrol and clothing were also on the programme. The whole country had to curb what we would deem today as 'available luxuries'. What started as the essentials like butter and sugar soon included products like meat, dairy produce, canned fruit and sweety stuff like jam and biscuits. Fish wasn't on the ration list as such but was very difficult to source. Each family were allocated ration books that contained token-like coupons where they had to register with the local grocers and butcher shops. At Christmas time it was chaotic at these outlets as crowds of people gathered for the rich pickings of dried fruit and baking material for the Christmas cakes.

If you ran out of coupons – even sweety coupons – that was it! You couldn´t get bread for love nor money. There would be queues of people in long lines waiting impatiently to get their hands on bananas; that was how scarce everything was. A relative of ours would send us the odd parcel containing delicious luxury items like fruits and other bits-and-pieces to keep us going. I suppose being so young made for some adventure but it must have been hard on the parents and especially the older generation. And talking about Christmas: old socks hanging at the fireplace, excited children (and adults), and in the morning Santa had been and placed a sixpence and sour sweets…what an occasion!

Saturday afternoons at the cinema gave us rare flashes of sweet Scottish moments. If I could rewrite the script for those times I´d give it some Braveheart input with my clenched fist, raging towards Germany, yelling, "You may take our tenements but you can never take our sweeties!"

Even basic hygiene items like soap became hard to get a hold of (literally) and if you managed to get a bar it most likely wasn´t scented soap. Saccharine replaced sugar and powdered milk became an accepted substitute for a sweetener.

We had virtually nothing in those days but we had certain qualities that can be so hard to find in the modern world today. Respect was boundless. The need for survival got us out of bed quicker, and often there would be the size of half a football team huddled under Camberwick and jackets-for-blankets. Times were often hard but we all just got on with it. There was nothing anyone could do, it was no use in complaining.

My mum was taken into hospital and dad had to look after six of us until she recovered. Dad coped great. He´d get up early in the morning and light the fire; then get us ready for school before he'd go to work. He would attend to all the chores in the house and make sure we were all very well-looked after: a real champion.

George helped, he was domesticated. I was too busy running around daft and playing fitba. When mum got well she went out to work, cleaning all the toffs' houses. Most women did that. Mum left to work at the munitions factory, making shells for the war effort; enduring very long shifts. Father would get us up before mum came home and she'd get a few hours kip before resuming her household chores and shopping errands. It was a constant flow of work; get some shut-eye before it all started again and having both parents alive and together made it easier than a lot of families who weren't so fortunate but nevertheless, a very demanding and industrious time. I don't think anyone had time for stress, you couldn't afford to be stressed, it was all survival, survival and more survival.

> *My country that I served*
> *…she did employ me*
> *The unit that I ranked*
> *…he did deploy me*
> *The enemy that was sent to greet me in the trenches*
> *…was sent to destroy me*
> *But not once did I fall into the arms of evil.*
> *The more dark blue uniforms I slaughtered*
> *…made me feel a lesser man*
> *The more I aimed my weapon and hit my human target*
> *…the more strange I felt on this foreign land*
> *But not once did I fall into the arms of evil.*
> *My shell lies empty less inside a polished wooden coffin*
> *…my nation's proud flag drapes neatly creased and folded*
> *and under the white cross,*
> *poppy flowers swaying to the tune of bugles and bagpipes…*
> *lies an Unknown Soldier.*

When peace was declared it took some time for the country and its people to get back on their feet. I remember the little luxuries slowly but surely coming back to us. The simple things like street lights were a huge form of entertainment and a comforting relief that the nation was at last on the way to freedom. A crowd of us would walk into the town – which was a fair travel by foot, and we'd all sing the song: When the lights go on again all over the world. It was a magical moment and one that I'll treasure forever.

The city of Glasgow faced post war problems with housing and health issues. Prior to the hostilities of the war the city had embarked a rebuilding phase culminating on the clearing of slums. The breakout of war put paid to any plans. A staggering 400,000 (plus) houses across Scotland had no proper toilet facilities and an average of three out of five city dwellings had no bathroom. It was refreshing to live in peace time but on a whole, the city (and the country) had a massive renovation project on their hands. Some say that it wasn't until the 60s that families started to enjoy a more acceptable level of living standards. Rail and road networks were not overlooked and although it took some time, Glasgow became a bustling and vibrant city again. Today the city of Glasgow is one of Europe's top tourist destination spots.

In 1941 we moved to Bardowie Street. A three close tenement building that thankfully had a concrete shelter. Before we arrived in Possil a bomb dropped in a school across the road from where we were but without casualties. A great relief to all. I remember going down Saracen Street to the sawmills during the war where the captured enemy were kept and made to work. Across from the sawmills was St Theresa's Chapel grounds. Quite a small Church and it stood itself. At that time it was used as an R.A.F camp, mainly Police R.A.F. were there to guard it, presumably. And at the old Mecca cinema were centurion tanks – ready to be sent to war.

There is something to be said about the balance of life and the difference between having too much of something and not having enough of anything. I was born into humble origins where wartime struggles, fears and deprivation were common hand but I spiritually believe that, amidst Hitler´s dust, rations, evacuations and gas masks we had this inner-built community spirit: it grew instinctively. We certainly found our harmony amongst the blackouts and air-raid shelters…and in a terrible twist of fate: Hitler got us a house in Possilpark.

And onto the beaches they came
And into the villages they marched
And in through the city streets trampling over crushed rubble and debris
and tell me
…who cast the first stone?

THE HUMBLE BOYS

A HUMBLE CHILDHOOD can sometimes set the tone for a fruitful and balanced adulthood. My childhood was very humble; simple in other words, but I am the better for having been brought up the way I was. Just about everyone I knew lived exactly like me: with hard-working parents, sometimes with large families and just getting by was the cry of the masses.

Our living conditions could not be further from today´s more sophisticated urban developments. Our tenement was basic but solidly built. The toilet facilities were located at the rear of the close (outside) and we quickly learned the importance of going to the toilet last thing at night before heading to bed. I doubt if anyone enjoys having to get up in the middle of the night but when you do, just think about the previous generations who had to walk the cold stairwell in the dark and outside to the toilet. Glasgow is a very cold place in the winter but more so when you are in sleeping kit and having to trawl the tenements right slap-in-the-middle of dark O´clock. The toilets were basic cubicles with Western saloon-type doors and the draught that came underneath the gap was most uncomfortable. The outside toilets were also a place for the 'imaginary' and the 'haunted' tales: definitely not a place you wanted to go to in the middle of the night! And just for good measure; we didn´t have soft inviting toilet roll in those days. Post dated newspapers were tied to the back of the cubicle door hanging on string. Sometimes a nail hammered to the door panel would pierce the papers to secure their position. On many trips to the toilet you were advised to take your own loo paper with you! Sometimes there were other surprises waiting for you lurking behind the solid saloon doors: no newspapers!

If the basic toilet facilities have the present generation grimacing wait 'til I tell you about the heating in our house. Thankfully it wasn't a big house to heat and just as well. Coal was the main fuel for the open fire. To some households coal was delivered and bought on delivery but coal was often scarce and when we couldn't get coal delivered my sister and I would take a pram, or in the winter we'd sledge it, all the way to Maryhill Gasworks to buy a bag of coal and transport it all the way back home; it was some jaunt. Half-a-crown for a sack and this gave us heating for about one week. In harsher times when we couldn't source the coal, or charcoal in some cases, we'd rip up linoleum, wax cloth as it was known, to feed the fire. Winters were terribly cold, it was just a means of surviving at times. But again, everyone I knew all lived the same way so we didn't know any better and it certainly didn't stop us from living a meaningful life.

At the rear of the backcourt we had the wash-house. This was a small building made from concrete and it's where the mothers would go to wash our clothes. Neighbours actually had a rota where washing duties were executed on that basis. This was just one of the meeting points where mothers, grandmothers and daughters would converge to trade gossip and enjoy their moments of a traditional Glasgow chin-wag.

Strangely enough, considering the strict environmental laws we have today, it's worth pointing out that the wash-house was directly next to the middens. For readers outside our dialect region the 'middens' were a place that housed the garbage cans (or for readers inside our dialect zone: the rubbish bins). They were small concreted areas which were separated by small compartments. It was nothing fancy but were indeed well-kept. I don't recall rubbish having segregation issues back then like we have today; we certainly didn't have colour coordinated bins, that's for sure.

The middens were not only a place to dump your rubbish, they were mythical. Stories would often unfold about 'lucky middens'. It was thought that people in richer areas would frequently throw out their unwanted belongings into their middens. This obviously arose curiosity among the young and eager who would scour the area in search of fortune. Truth be known, everyone threw out unwanted belongings or articles that clogged up what was already a small living space. In our own back yard there would be old books, comics and interesting stuff that people didn't want or had exhausted the need for. Kids would go around under false pretenses in their quest for someone else's abandoned riches. Midgey-raking was almost a national pastime. The middens being close to one another were useful for our fitness activity; we played 'jumps' where we'd hop and jump from one bin shelter to the next. Le Parkour hardly not but it did give another dimension to our childhood playtime. It was dangerous and one slip would mean you had to pull yourself from the residents' throw-outs and other unsavoury items.

When I was four I remember playing with my pals at the top of our street, Kilmun Street, which was quite a short street. We were playing in Morten's farm. We were just being typical wee boys playing in the haystacks when someone shouted, "Here's the polis coming!" We naturally tried to bolt ourselves out of the equation. I got my head stuck in the barbed wire fence. The police were fine with me, they took me down the street to my house to inform my mother. It was clear I required stitches. The police instructed my mother to get her coat and they took us to Oakbank Hospital. It was a journey no-one had anticipated. Here I was, me, my mother, and this big polisman on a tramcar ride to the hospital. He gave me a penny because I didn't cry. Nothing more was said of this incident but for many years later my mother always told this story.

Maybe we needed safer games to play. This is when we discovered one of the most enjoyable toys ever invented for a humble Glaswegian child: The Peerie. My mother bought one for me. A peerie was made from wood, about one-and-a-half inches at the top which tapered to a point. At the bottom was a steel stud. We used coloured crayons and start with, for example, a red circle, a blue circle and a green circle which we'd finish off with a white one. We had great pleasure from the simplest of things back then; the object of this toy was to spin the peerie to watch the colours spin; giving off great effect. The spinning motion was done by hand but for better effect we often used a piece of cloth which was twisted to a rope-like instrument but more often or not a piece of chord was used to spin the peerie. When the peeries slowed down we would spin it again and chased it. We'd tow it behind us and continue the process until we got tired. Such a simple but valuable part of our entertainment. There were many elements to this amazing toy that probably wouldn't be as entertaining today; giving into the technological world we live in but the *Whip and Peerie* was a fascinating toy enjoyed by many many kids.

Children love toys, it's an important part of their childhood and we were no different to the modern kids of today but we were also just like the children who lived generations before us; we loved to play. Any opportunity we had to get outside we'd snap at it. There was a whole world out there waiting to be discovered and all the kids in our area would be outside in all weathers. Small-sided games of football were played on concrete – if any proper fields and spare ground were occupied.

When I was a young boy growing up in Possil, most of my closest friends stayed in the same building, which consisted of three closes. The older friends of mine were only two years older than the rest of us. We had set rules which meant no swearing and every time we went home for a bite to eat we had to brush our teeth.

There were three air-raid shelters in our backcourt and our friends all had meetings in the shelter in my backcourt, as I always managed to get the key. There were no lights in any of the shelters (which were approximately about twenty yards long and about fourteen yards wide). There was no seating arrangements either but we sorted that out with a few builders' bricks; which were uncomfortable and cold but offered a steady place to park ourselves.

We arranged little boxing tournaments and the four poles in the backcourt – that were purposely for our mothers to hang out the washing – improvised as our boxing ring. One of the boys had a sister, who lived in London, brought real boxing gloves to the occasion. She was very good at bringing him items from London; some of the goods she brought we hadn't even seen before in our lives. I won a tournament, becoming the proud owner of ten marbles for my troubles. I think I did well partly because I was fast and managed to dodge swinging punches. You had to be quick in those days just to get away from the polis!

The boxing was just part of our own entertainment. It was mostly improvisation but was a lot of fun. It was noble and we adhered to all the rules but we were kids. Some of the boys were good and in some cases you could find yourself so far behind in points you'd have had to knock your opponent out just to get a draw! I think my speed in ducking and diving gave my opponents the flu with all the draft he was causing with his missed swipes! Jimmy Shearer and Jimmy Berry, the older guys, played the judges.

The railings in the backcourts were taken down and the material melted for the war effort. Those railings divided the three courts but being chopped down actually allowed us to have the three courts to ourselves to form our very own speedway track, which was enormous fun for all the kids. Speedway was and still is a fast and exciting sport; dangerous, mind you, but a very enthralling experience whizzing about in our bikes. Now, speedway riders use proper motorbikes but again, in our humble little world of improvisation, we didn't need the real thing; we made do with our own pedal bikes; if you were lucky enough to own one. If you were not one of the fortunate owners of a bike there was always someone willing to lend you theirs…usually some bribing went on like, "I'll lend ye a shot of ma bike fur a poke of liquorice." Yes, it all went on, all the hustling and the bustling just to get a few magical moments of fun on a wee bike…very humbling times but very enjoyable.

My bike came from my late sister-in-law. She lived in Anderston Cross, a fair distance from Possilpark (by foot). The bike needed a bit of work to it so I had to humf it from Anderston Cross to Possilpark, where a couple of minor repairs were carried out to the bike. Most of the other boys secured their wee bikes from other sources. At the end of the day some of us had no shoes left. They were scraped, scored and faded into oblivion. This didn't please our parents one single bit as in those days coupons were allocated for clothing. Most of the families didn't have much money and clothing and shoes were purchased sparingly – if at all!

Big Gordon Shearer won most of the races. He was a strong boy and superb athlete. In all, everyone was a winner as it was really great fun. In those days the kids used their own imagination and from a young mind of improvisation it can often blossom great creativity. I suppose in a way this is where the great footballers from former times come into this mindset. We didn't have TV so we couldn't really see the great players in action; unless you were lucky enough to have an older relative who would take you to any of the big league games. In Glasgow we are very fortunate to have so many teams in such a small area. In Glasgow alone we have three national stadiums and it isn't unrealistic to say you could walk from one stadium to the other. The young boys in our times practised their moves on the streets. When you think about the surfaces back then you can then imagine how difficult it was to control a ball. Ah! yes, the ball; let's forget about the streets for a moment and concentrate on the ball. It was rare that anyone owned a proper leather football in those days; as I said before, just getting by was the number one factor in our lives and no-one dared think about being able to buy a real leather football. It did occur but very rare.

Back to the speedway. My whole family used to go to the real speedway every Tuesday night at the local Ashfield football stadium. The speedway team was called the Ashfield Giants. Around twenty thousand people would flood the stadium to watch the speedway racing on those evenings. The star then was a guy called Ken Le Breton, who sadly died whilst riding in Australia. After his untimely passing the speedway crowds at the stadium began to diminish, to the disappointment of my family and many others and the speedway at Saracen Park sort of died with him.

Those speedway nights were great fun and very inexpensive for the entrance fee considering the high level of entertainment you got for your money. Adults were charged about half a crown for the entrance fee. Today, you can find speedway at the same grounds. Just look out for The Glasgow Tigers.

Our close in Bardowie Street was well-placed for many other ventures us young boys would find ourselves immersed in. We found old bicycle wheels and motor tyres and race round the streets with them. In a way it was very physical activity but we were so engrossed in those games you didn't want to stop and take a breather in case you missed some action. We'd run round to the next street with our circular friends; Carbeth Street was the next street then left into Sunnylaw Street and left again into Balgair Street and a further left which took us back into Bardowie Street. It was incredible stuff, all very thrilling and when you hear about kids getting into trouble today because there's nothing to do, it makes you wonder because our entertainment cost nothing, absolutely nothing…except for some imagination and a long walk from Anderston Cross: a small price indeed for an awful lot of fun and activity.

Another common game for us was peever – most commonly known as 'hopscotch' (a popular game from Victorian times). Peever in Glasgow was a game most girls played but boys were known to have joined in. The girls had their own games like skipping ropes and bounce-the-ball. The girls were very creative and often sang songs that were past down from previous generations. Often they'd make up their own words but I suppose that's how language and fresh ideas evolve. I don't know how they did it but they would have two rubber balls and bounce one off the ground, catching it, and the other one would be bounced against the wall, again, this ball would be caught and the whole motion continued in a nice rhythm. Some smart girls would use three balls and if you could bounce with three balls you were considered a very talented participator and you could draw crowds.

"One, two, three O'Leary" was a very recognizable lyric as it reverberated in the back greens. As was the popular *"My Maw's a Millionaire"*.

Rounders was a great game for the streets, weather permitting of course. This was one of those games that involved both boys and girls. We drew our own lines and circles on a large concreted area (usually the street). The ball was a tennis ball and bats were makeshift or tennis rackets. Definitely no protective equipment…who needed it?

Those were just some of the games and pastimes we got up to during our days growing up in humble surroundings. It was very interactive and kept you fit and occupied.

My mother – like most mums in those days – would look out for any kids in the street to run an errand for them. It was common practice if the mother was busy attending to her home duties and had little or no time to go to the shops. I was always difficult to find as I was always playing football and oblivious to her wishes. She would hang a line out of the window with money and the message at the end of the line for the kids. Instructions with the type of goods they needed to be brought back from the shop were scribbled on small bits of folded paper. Often, the kids would never return, they would just take the money and the note from the hanging line and disappear into thin air; never to be seen again.

School was never my favourite place to go to. I´d much rather have spent my time playing football and being with my pals. Of course, school is vital and necessary and an important part in any young life. I just didn´t like school. Partly because it took me away from the fitba but most likely it was the classrooms, in that dull brown paint job…it shudders just to think about it. I do have fresh (excuse the pun) memories of our daily quarter pint of milk!

When I was a boy at Possilpark Junior school I was reading my comic under the desk, totally oblivious to the classroom events and thinking the pupils were busy with the teacher when all of a sudden I heard a crashing sound and a blow to my desk from a wooden waste paper basket. The teacher yelled to me, "You can bring yer mother up, yer father too, for I am a guid runner!" Mr Kilpatrick was his name. I´ll never forget him.

When I say these things about school I wouldn't want any youngster reading this thinking they should feel the same way as me. It was a different environment back in those days and school is extremely important. Even if you want to become a professional footballer it is still important to stick in at school. You can never go wrong with education, it's vital so always listen and learn and believe it or not it does make a difference to your own football or any other career if you pay attention and learn from the masters that teach you.

Of all the street games that I took part in it was football that I loved best. I would kick anything. Getting a hold of even the basic living elements in life like food and clothing were difficult enough but a real ball was like holding a gift sent by God. Makeshift balls were commonly improvised with rags, stuffed newspapers into rags or even just newspapers! Street games usually involved a used stuff bladder. This was probably where the great players came from. Creativity was most likely the key to the tanner baw player. The more difficult and more elusive the ball was; the more imagination was required to master a certain skill. If you could dribble, pass accurately and shoot on target with a small ball or as close as one could get to a ball, the youngster would find the real leather ball in a real match for his local team much much easier to handle and control. The game of football in our city was endorsed amongst the damp cobbled streets and back greens.

We played small side-up games in Bardowie Street and I remember two very prominent players would visit the Kane family at No 200 Bardowie Street. Billy McPhail of Celtic FC and John McPhail of Clyde FC would come out of the Kanes' home and would kindly spend some time with us youngsters. We were in awe of those players and little did I know that later in life I would have the privilege to be involved in the football world on a prominent level.

My friends and I grouped together to form our very own club

by the name of Bardowie Rovers. The team included the likes of Gordon Shearer, Jimmy Shearer and the late Bobby Shearer. Bobby was a fantastic player; he went on trial with Hibs. Jimmy Mann went to Sunderland. A lot of us were only thirteen. Frank Dorans did his secretary (I was too young). Frank got us the park at the top of the street; costing a shilling a week to hire out. His favourite phrase was, "I huvnae got a sausage." Which meant he didn't have any money, but we always managed to get our park money no matter what but what we didn't have was a place to change into our kit. Frank's mother allowed us to clear out a bedroom in their house where we placed chairs in it so that the opposing team and ourselves could change on match-days. It was hardly close to the black ash pitch but the 300 to 400 yards walk from the house was just testimony to the phrase 'fitba daft' and we lived by that phrase…we still do!

The gang included great friends: Frank, Bobby, Gordon, Jimmy, John McCoy and Francis Meagher. Francis came from Irish descent and lived in the same close as me. Joseph never bothered much with football opting to play the violin; he was a clever boy but I don't know if anything ever progressed regarding his musical career. The Meagher family moved away when I was on Army duty later on in our teenage days but when I came back, Frank and his family had flitted to pastures new. I didn't see Frank since those days and it wasn't until 2003 that we finally met up after many decades. It was great to see him and naturally refreshing to learn he had chosen his own path and became a Priest. He did great work for his faith and for the Parish, spreading the good word.

Bardowie Rovers were formed not long after the war so you can imagine we were extremely short on football equipment but we certainly made up for it with our passion for the game and our enthusiasm was infectious. Our first kit was made of white shirts (which my mother dyed yellow to give us some bright identity). Of course, Glasgow does rain (on occasions) and you guessed it: the dye would run off the shirts, trickle down bodies and our skin would turn a strange tint of…well…yellow. Your original tan-in-a-can.

We had so much fun with our little team and it set the tone (probably a yellow one) for what became a great football life for me for the next decades to come.

Oh Leerie, Oh Leerie!

through rain hail and snow,

Ye'd come traipsing up oor street in the dork

Jist tae light us up a glow.

Oh Leerie, Oh Leerie!

Ye must huv looked eccentric,

the saddest day of my life…

was the day we turned electric.

*Le Parkour is the art of movement. More notably famous within the extreme sports world for the unique spiritual art involving jumping from building to building, created in France.

1949 as a fresh 16-year-old.

THE HANDS THAT BUILT A LEGACY

IT'S FUNNY LOOKING BACK and how life can sometimes take a twist of fate. My career at Possil YMCA has been a long but very fruitful journey. I've had the most wonderful and interesting life at the helm of this incredible club. My proud association began in 1948 in Dougie MacDonald's house. Dougie was General Secretary of Possilpark YMCA, which was based in Denmark Street. Dougie ran the various YMCA leagues and was secretary of the Scottish YMCA Association; part of his remit was to arrange disciplinary meetings each month; a tremendous amount of work considering Dougie had a family and regular day job. He seemed to thrive on these positions of responsibility and enjoyed his work immensely.

The YMCA hall opened in 1936 by Archibald Sterling at a cost of £350. Dougie and Alex Glassford were founder members along with Alex's father Richard, who was president. Dougie worked in the local rent office in Bardowie Street; a short distance from my house.

After being trailed by Possil YMCA whilst turning out for Bardowie Rovers I finally gave into their persuasion and I turned up for training one Monday night. The boys there all made me feel welcome but I must admit I felt a tad uncomfortable; probably because some of the players were from what I would label as the 'better off areas' of the city; toffs, if you like. Players were ordered to attend bible classes on a Sunday afternoon or they were excluded from the team's selection the following Saturday. Some of my other friends persuaded me to join the club as they certainly had very good players in their squad. I was just a typical young lad who was football-mad and I nearly lost out on joining the YM as it meant missing my Sunday football. Between Dougie MacDonald and Tom Blair they succeeded in convincing me that the YM was the place for me – and how right they were.

It wasn´t long before Dougie MacDonald and I became very close friends which lasted until about nine years ago when Dougie unfortunately passed away after a long illness. What an incredibly courageous man, he never stopped working for the YM and the football association during his illness. Dougie´s committed stance came from within and his resilience was evident in his character but behind Dougie was his wife Kate, what a rock she was and I´m still amazed at how she coped with Dougie´s ailment when she herself had so many operations. Both Dougie and Kate were major influences within the community and the city in general for their courage, determination, organization and for the amount of time they gave to others.

For all who remember Dougie and Kate will tell you about the wonderful fund-raising nights we had at the club. It was much more than selling raffle tickets and playing bingo: musicians, singers and actors were all an integral part of those events and hard to believe they were actually known first and foremost as footballers; such was the spirit and talent amongst the community´s core.

Getting back to me joining the YM; I eventually did attend bible classes. There were usually over one hundred members each Sunday where we would recite passages from the good book as well as blethering on about our games the previous day. A wonderful speaker at these meetings was a former Prisoner of War who unfortunately endured treacherous times in a Russian concentration camp. Although he obviously survived, it made me think about the more important things in life and as much as I and all the other guys loved the beautiful game it does ring true that indeed there are more necessary things to life than football.

Later, on my return from the Army in 1953, I would turn out for Possil YMCA U-21s and soon moved up to the senior team. Most of the players had played through the various age groups so we were all a very close unit and one big happy family. Two of the fathers (who had sons playing for the U-16s team) had to step down from their managing duties due to pressures of business and therefore could not carry on running the team. This prompted me to propose to Dougie MacDonald that I´d be happy to take the team for a couple of weeks until they found a suitable candidate to take care of team affairs. As many know, they never did recruit anyone else and the team was left to me…my tenure at the club as manager began in 1958.

Dougie was instrumental during the whole process of my induction into the team as manager and he left me to my own devices to run the footballing side of the club whilst Dougie looked after the administration and the other duty things at the club – that often go un-noticed in clubs and organizations alike. Dougie´s work behind the actual football curtain was paramount and extremely important and without his help the club could not possibly have enjoyed the success the club would encounter in the years ahead. Indeed, had it not been for Tom Blair and Dougie MacDonald and the influence they had on me I very much doubt I would have enjoyed my life as much for they gave me the start, the grounding and the back-up to go on and achieve the ultimate in amateur and youth football.

Dougie´s passing left me absolutely devastated. It took a long long time to come to terms with his untimely departure. He was a great man, one of the finest the world had.

I believe I was put on this earth for a reason and the reasons have been all what I´ve been doing all those years and thanks to Dougie MacDonald I´ve loved every single minute of it.

*Douglas MacDonald was honoured at Glasgow City Chambers and was presented with a book, with a message, signed by every Scottish manager at that time. He was, and still is to this day, a monumental figure within the grassroots of the Scottish game.

In 1961 I was invited by the Scottish Councils of the YMCA to represent Glasgow YMCA at a world YMCA conference in Vienna, Austria. Indeed one of the highlights of my YMCA career. I was quite young, 28-years-old, and I met other members from around Scotland who were representing their own YMCAs. It was a thrill to be representing my YMCA and we met other YMCA members from around the world. They travelled from Brazil, America and neighbouring Germany.

We didn´t have any plans as such to produce professional footballers on an international scale, all we wanted was to have a simple game of fitba on our door step for our well-being and leisure activity. The club, Possil YMCA, or more affectionately known as the 'YM' was born long before the days of mobile phones, computer games and fadgey-gadgets. It was created out of a humble background and no-one at the club could have predicted what the future held in store.

Football is a great leveller. Glasgow, like most cities around the world, embraces the beautiful game; it´s like an addiction that has no cure for (and let´s face it, who would want to be rescued from it´s grasp?) The game is unique in many ways. It doesn´t matter what religious background you come from, what colour your skin may be or your social settings, even right down to one´s ability; football is for the masses, it is the greatest equalizer (to excuse the pun) anywhere on this earth.

It unites, it defeats (another pun, sorry) almost any political or economic situation: perhaps it´s the greatest human bonding activity ever to be discovered, who knows? There is, however, argument as to where football was invented; some say the Romans kicked it off (ye´ll need tae excuse these awful puns), fossil findings somewhere in China that date back to the B.C. years (that´s not Boys´ Club, that´s before the good Lord´s time), but wherever this incredible game was invented, discovered or thought of, there can be no arguments as to the importance of it. Whether it be founded by fossil or produced in Possil we are just grateful that the baw found its way onto our cobbled streets and back greens.

Possilpark is a suburb located at the north end of Glasgow, footing the Campsies that lead to the Highlands. Possilpark was laid out by Walter MacFarlane of the Saracen Foundry in Anderston, Glasgow, acquiring the Possil Estate in 1867. The area at that time was developed around a vibrant industrial growth consisting of coal-mining, railway engineering, pottery and iron-works. Many say it was almost ahead of its time and regarded as the best laid and planned out industrial area in the city of Glasgow, of that era.

The region was awash with employment and prosperity but post-war circumstances gradually seeped into the heart of what was once a proud and thriving district. In the 1950s and 60s, changes put paid to the industries and soon the area of Possilpark was heading towards economic and social decline; not a spiral as such, just a light-headed tail-spin.

As our hard-working citizens were fighting off the inevitable of unemployment and probable social decay; the game of fitba flourished. Perhaps a new desire and fighting spirit crept into our communities. Just like the disaster of the war; the more the Glaswegians were beaten the more they fought back. Prior to all the economic and social evolving, a legacy was born in Denmark Street. Right bang-in-the-middle of the constant changing from war to peace, from industrial boom to business closure and under a dark charcoal Glasgow sky was born a light of hope in the glimmering name of football.

The hall in Denmark Street injected some much needed fresh air. It´s purpose was mainly to cater for the local youth; who at that time were denied such social facilities for one reason or another. The YM gave refuge and shelter but just as importantly it gave hope, a boost of confidence and every youngsters´ right: the chance to excel as individuals. From there these groups of youngsters could get the chance to interact, take part in the assortment of games and pastimes where social bonding subconsciously would simmer from a boiling pot of optimism. No matter what generation we hail from, these attributes are a very important factor in the upbringing of young people. The men behind the origins of the YM: Alex Glassford, a group of enthusiastic participants and Archibald Stirling probably had no idea about the legacy they were about to create.

The club had surpassed all expectations as years later the YM, as a football team, produced top-class players with many enjoying international acclaim. Names that once appeared in the local press in small columns for their scoring exploits soon found their way onto FIFA´s World Cup official programmes and would become known around the world. Kenny Dalglish, the most prominent figure known internationally from our club, was just one of the many Possil greats who carved out careers for themselves: Eddie Kelly, Ian Ross, Johnny Hamilton, Alan Moore, John Hendrie, Robert Russell, Alex Forsyth, Jim Duffy, Tony Fitzpatrick, Gordon Chisholm, Jim McGill, Paul Kinnaird and Gary McSwegan are a mere fraction of many.

It is often said that through hardship comes great courage and success. You can´t really compare other areas in the world with each other as we have different cultures but in a sense many areas globally are linked with similar failings as well as similar success rates. Take the humble boxer for example: deprived of social activities, in some cases food and education but develops himself into a top Olympic medal winner, or even a world title belt holder. It is a kind of hunger that food cannot replace that has something to do with his rise to a better plain. Much can be said about the footballer growing up in the favelas of Rio de Janeiro, the sprawling housing estates scattered over Napoli and Buenos Aries. Glasgow had its inner city troubles too but we never considered the word poverty, rather opting for a place that had the heart of its industrial core pierced by economic circumstance; a mix of political change and business evolution.

To think that way back when the hall opened in 1936, the kids in the area were all presented with a banana to celebrate the opening. This is not exaggerated folklore, it really did happen and to round off with another pun: the £350 they spent developing the YM hall proved to be a very fruitful investment indeed.

It also didn´t take the club long to put in place the first set of silverware: only three years after its forming, Possil YMCA won the Scottish YMCA Cup. Willie Miller, an outstanding goalkeeper, represented Scotland, including turning out at Wembley against England, was just one of our early legends. Miller was regarded by many as the best post-war goalkeeper to play for Celtic. Davie Reid, was another early talent that tumbled off the conveyor belt of the famous Possil production line. He later went on to play for Rochdale and Crewe Alexandra.

In the early Possil YMCA years the war interrupted what was becoming a nice steady flow of freshly cut diamonds to the surface; the production line of talent was temporarily halted due to the war breakout and many members of the YMCA were soon on another field: the battlefields. Air attacks were no longer about whipping in corners but on a more dangerous scale.

Jack Steedman was another early great, perhaps the most famous icon at this time, to roll off the belt at Possil YM. Steedman has been an emblematic figure of Scottish football and still is, maybe not as active as he once was, nevertheless he is still held in high regard amongst his peers and the public in general.

Aside from the football aspect of things, Possil YMCA were maintaining a stronghold within the community. Sunday bible classes were popular. No pressure was forced on anyone to attend the classes but they were the centre point for the community and the club combined Sunday bible classes with team selection. If you didn´t turn up for Sunday classes you didn´t get a game on a Saturday; simple as that. Everything was noted, each member´s attendance record was always under the watchful eye of the senior members of the club. Not in a way where fear was instigated but with a strict code of discipline which certainly didn´t do any of the young men any harm.

The club moved forward at a graceful pace and soon found themselves invited to tournaments in England, Europe and the United States. The young players were no strangers to leaving home as many of them had spells and trial periods with some of the top English Division sides. The YM became the nursery club for Arsenal, Aston Villa, Coventry and Sunderland.

Our association with Arsenal seemed unique in those days. It was quite a coup when Arsenal showed interest in Possil YM. Quite unusual when you think that a top English First Division club would secure Possil YM, a Glasgow Juvenile side, as a feeder club for the London giants. It was the beginning of a golden era for us when we were approached by the then Arsenal scout for Scotland, the late Joe Hill; he connected our team to Arsenal and we secured a £500 sponsorship deal over three years. This allowed us to buy equipment for the club and just for good measure they threw in a mini-bus too. We did pretty well out of Arsenal but there again, they didn´t do too badly out of us: Eddie Kelly (one of our players) helped Arsenal to win their famous League and Cup double in 1971. Not such a bad deal, both ways it should be said.

It was a tight relationship and they ran the rule over us occasionally and were very much committed to our team. Arsenal´s manager in those days was Billy Wright, who frequented our district regularly. He was escorted by Ian Ure and Frank McLintock, both participating in training sessions with us. It was a great experience and one that proved to have substance with results to boot.

It´s sometimes difficult to remain humble. Here we were, some years down the line from our little club house which we were granted from Perthshire Juniors (the one with the leaky roof) to training with two Scottish Internationalists at that time and let´s not forget Billy Wright, not only the manager of the great Arsenal but an ex-England captain and married to none other than one of the Beverley sisters; at that time were topping the charts. Mere humble boys from Possilpark and surrounding suburbs were now intermingling with household legends.

Our status as a recognized club was evident all around the country. Not only were we looking good on the park but we were kitted out reminiscent of the stars from the great Milan sides. Blazers, sharp flannels and polished shoes soon became part of the YM uniform where the boys all took pride in wearing.

Possil´s association with the prominent members of the football world started to widen when the legendary FIFA referee, Brian McGinlay, soon played his role in the great Possil connection. Brian McGinlay's first ever refereeing duty after passing his examination, came in 1961. Ironically it was a game involving Possil YMCA and Sandyhills YMCA U16s at St Augustine's school in the North of Glasgow. Kenny Dalglish was also playing in this match. Just after Brian McGinlay was promoted to Class 1 he was invited to take part in a tournament just outside New York – a tournament in which Possil YMCA won, defeating a team from St.Louis to lift the prestigious international trophy. Brian also gained an award as the best referee in the tournament; a good time to be Scottish, in fact, a proud time to be a Glaswegian, albeit a humble one. This was the beginning of a long friendship with myself and Brian McGinlay which I am proud to say has carried on to this very day.

So, here we were, down so many roads, a bunch of humble guys from the industrial area, the tenements, the closes and the back greens all rubbing shoulders with global elite in the football, pop, and even the refereeing world. Our feet were always on the ground, however, there was still a lot of work to do before we could really say we achieved something. The club started to pour more and more stars from the production line on a regular basis. We remained humble throughout, after all, the club was designed and developed to cater for the young ones in the area all those years ago with the emphasis on giving those kids something to do. The Boys' Brigade was another organization that offered the same sort of service to the junior members of the community, but they had a short lifespan in terms of age. After a certain birth mile was reached there really wasn't much for the young ones to do – this is where the YMCA came in – and all round the region, spreading nationwide, the YMCA have played a magnificent part in the welfare and well-being of the younger members of their respected local communities.

Football was the main focal point by this time, and indeed had been for so many years. It brought us close, it gave us a stage on which we could perform; after much dedication and practice of course, and it was the vehicle to visit other lands, meet with other people of different backgrounds and cultures. To think that some of our team members hadn´t even ventured out of their own area, never mind see another country. On a trip to England we were only at the Round Toll, about five tramcar stops away, when one of the boys asked if we were in England yet: although quite cute and humorous it was certainly an indication of the innocence and humbleness from those young players.

The club was run superbly by respected members, coaches, trainers and the many hands of helpers but facilities didn´t match the stature of the club; although in the early days almost all the juvenile and youth teams played on black ash parks and red blaes; thankfully black ash is no longer available in and around the modern city suburbs. We trained in all weathers outside and when we did go inside for training, the hall was a shade too small to accommodate the quantity of players and staff we had. No complaints were heard about facilities back then as almost everyone and every team were sailing the same ship. Some of the parks we played in would be unthinkable in today´s more sophisticated environment but the players didn´t need flush greens or Wednesday night astro training: most of the boys who played for Possil YM from the early days right up until the 80s and 90s were all accomplished, had technical ability and some are still revered today by their respected clubs for their achievements in the senior game.

I´ve been asked who was the best player we had at the club and to be honest there are too many to single out. Sure, Kenny Dalglish became a Celtic, Liverpool and Scotland legend and what a tremendous player he was, a smashing player, but we had guys who never made the grade at senior level who were also capable of perhaps going on to achieve international status but for reasons best kept to themselves, or reasons unknown, it wasn't meant to be for a lot of the players but we had literally pile loads of players who came through the YM hall doors who could have gone on to much greater things. I honestly couldn't name any names as such because the list would be too long but many a young player who played for Possil YM were of the highest quality possible and would have fitted perfectly in the top flight of the professional game.

I am proud of the boys who were associated with the great YM; from before and during my time at the club; the ones who didn't make it as a top player actually did well in other walks of life. At the YM not only did we have International players on board but we can also count a European Champion boxer in the name of 'Cowboy' McCormick, highly regarded members of the constabulary, honoured and acclaimed community workers, honourable working class individuals whom many have gone on to do impressively well for themselves and we have Clergymen as ex-Possil YMCA members. The YMCA has been good and kind to many but praise must also go to those individuals who played a huge part in the life of the YM. It's been a two-way street where free-flowing traffic has certainly been in abundance.

Discipline was important, it needed to be to reach the very top and to stay at the very top. We insisted that players tuck their shirts inside their shorts (I think it's now mandatory) and shin-guards were compulsory at the club (which is definitely mandatory worldwide nowadays). Only one player, Tony Fitzpatrick, played with his socks at his ankles. It wasn't rebellious in any shape or form, he was just one of those players that socks didn't seem to stay up: the Paul Breitner of Possilpark, no doubt. And he got away with it! Tony was a great player and a terrific lad so his dress style in the way he wore his kit was not a problem for any of us at the club. It's one of the things you accept that goes along with the territory of great players.

So there you have it; Possil YM and of course, myself, have had the great fortune to have been involved in the beautiful game for many decades that has lived within the Scottish game; witnessing the highs and the lows. From just after the war where we had the tanner ba´ era (or the tanner baw as many would write) to the cusp of the Thatcher period. Many will recall the ankle-height football boots and many will have vivid memories of the Mitre Mouldmaster. In any case I hope all the players from all the generations have taken a bit of Possil YMCA with them on their own journey in life. From what I hear these days, many have, and it's encouraging and a blessing to know this.

We will always remember the great people who set the Possil YMCA wheels in motion. I'm sure they had no idea at the time but as we look back, they were indeed the hands that built a legacy.

A yellow brick house cuddles up alongside the beige and white path that is already dressed in the four different shades from the hot Tunisian sun.

There, a small boy in a white tunic, tries desperately to sell his last piece of bread and his left shoe.

Rain drenched kids howl and scream under towering street lamps of misty orange; the burning of November fire lingers the thick air creating nostalgia for years to come.

There, a used tyre hangs helplessly around a street pole.

THE CALL

WHEN YOUR COUNTRY CALLS you don't need to be asked twice to act to the command. I was just one of the many young men up and down the land who would be drafted up to National Service. I served mine with the Army. I was instructed to report to Dreghorn camp in Edinburgh, which was a complete shock to the system. As the youngest member from a large family it wasn't something I relished, when I'm totally honest. Serving one's country and responding to duties ordered by above is never a problem but leaving my family, my friends and my fitba is another issue altogether.

I was quickly advised by my friends to get a haircut before reporting for duty as stories were flying around about the Army coiffeur and how crude they conducted the crop. Right intae the wid is an understatement. I took their advice but didn't make any difference because the first thing that the officers did at the camp was send me to their own barber where he carried out a brutal attack on my follicles. Basic training would last for six weeks before leave was allocated so in all it wasn't too bad; the length of time was plenty to grow back the hair for weekend leave.

After Dreghorn we were sent to Glencourse barracks for a further ten weeks' training course with the Cameronian Rifles. The training was part of our preparation for jungle warfare in Kenya. The time passed relatively quick and before we knew it we passed as full squaddies. We enjoyed our leave after passing out but the leave also passed pretty quickly and before we had the chance to blink we were all presented with our supplies and jungle kit. Aboard the Empire where a long few weeks' journey would be endured before it would drop us off in Singapore. It's a long long way from Possilpark, let me tell you! Reinforcements were required for the King's Own Scottish Borders in Korea; so a change of plan and a change of gear was the cry and off we went to one of the most unpredictable countries in the world; and we're not just talking about the weather either!

To give the younger readers an indication as to why we were sent to Korea let me say it wasn't for the World Cup (although that would have been nice – but many many years later before that would take place). The peninsula of Korea was split into two after the Second World War: North Korea and South Korea. The North was ruled by the Soviets and their communist regime; the South was under the watchful eye of the United States. In the summer of 1950, June to be precise, the North invaded the South, the latter looked to the UN for a comforting assist. The UK, with Canada and other commonwealth countries, offered their part; this is as good an explanation if any as to how we ended up in Korea.

Prior to Korea we made a stop in Hong Kong to take part in hill exercises in the new territories. To be fair, although we were all like a million miles away from home, the camaraderie amongst the boys was really good and it wasn't long before we got used to the training in the hills; this prepared us for the next journey ahead; Korea.

Whilst training in the hills we were granted a rest day. We headed off into Hong Kong on the train when we came across big Bill Speakman, who had just received the highest award in the British Army: The Victoria Cross. Bill was on the train, partly intoxicated as he clearly had a few refreshments. He set the fire extinguisher off all around us. Bill was a big guy, scaling 6ft 4. He was awarded the VC for fighting off the Chinese *commies,* saving his colleagues. He laid into them with beer bottles (probably empty ones) when he ran out of ammunition. I noticed Bill on the TV last year at the Queen's Jubilee. He was in a VIP car. It was good to see him behaving! Big Bill was a character; once met, never forgotten.

It was another world we were in. Sometimes it's good to see other places that are pleasing to the eye as it just reminds you what a marvellous interior designer God must be but on the other hand it can also be a good experience to see other places that don't look too pleasant: if only to remind you that no matter what you think you don't have back home it's still a lot more than what others have elsewhere.

Korea wasn't a very pleasant place and the experience was a mix of apprehension and anxiety with a strange reflection for years to come. We were taken by the truck load to Seoul before boarding the train to our camp. The journey was exceedingly uncomfortable; the seats on the train were hard wood and in hindsight probably acted as a pretext for what lay ahead for us young men. The camp wasn't too bad, mind you, consisting of typical rows of tents and camp beds; nothing new really or surprising, it was basically what we expected. We settled for a few days just breaking into our rhythm and way of life so far away from our homes: in more ways than one. Later on, other boys would join us; these young men just came back from the frontline, a little battle weary you could say. Soon it was our turn to patrol and take our stance at the front and unless you have been in a position of near death then it's pretty hard to describe what goes through your mind. Naturally we were very apprehensive but we stuck together to make the duties as best as possible. We all clubbed in with our hard graft; digging out holes for our watch and station. Four guys to one hole was the ratio; we just made the best of what we could in a tense situation. Many of us became mates and we were spread out but still quite close to each other; in a way it gave us all some sort of comfort. We were beside older soldiers too so this was also a comforting factor among the young.

We took it in turns to do watch. Two hours on and four hours off. Watching the enemy certainly keeps you a wake and you really don´t have much desire to take a nap that´s for sure. At times we´d take turns to go out there to listen for any noises and to try and establish where our enemy was located. On one particular evening´s watch a young man by the name of Robert Marshall and I were doing our duties in the trench when all of a sudden there was a huge bang that rang in my ears, so close it was and I didn´t need to think about how near we both were to immediate danger. Robert and I had taken a hit, both of us ironically took one each to the neck. The jolt threw me on top of Robert. The medics were swift to act and at times of great emergency we can sometimes underestimate the importance of speed together with the professional way they conduct their precise work. Both Robert and I were carried off into the medical HQ to be treated. I can remember very clearly one of the medical staff telling one of his colleagues, "I´m afraid that´s Robert gone." It was a great shock to me as he had just joined our company days before. Robert was with the catering staff and wanted to be an infantry man.

This was tragic beyond belief. How would Robert´s parents feel receiving such news? So young and with a full life ahead of him it is unbearable to think of what those loved ones back home will go through when they learn that their child has been killed in action: tragic.

I was severely shocked by my injury but when I recovered I was quickly sent to the frontline again to join my unit.

Some time later there were discussions at a meeting with the military top brass. The end to hostilities was agreed and we found ourselves on a very welcoming trip back to Hong Kong and to safety. Korea was indeed a black hole of a place. I lost some young friends during the conflict in Korea, many were thankfully only injured and thankfully survived.

At just 19-years-old I brushed with death but swept cleanly by luck and of course, thanks to God, I am living to this day to tell of that awful time.

The trip back home was something to look forward to but none of us could forget what we left behind. The memories of those lost will never be erased from our minds. The sight of the docks at Southampton seemed so close yet so far away; our journey back home felt like eternity. Through the dreary grey clouds and drizzle the land of United Kingdom – and home – was a sight to be cherished. The Empire docked and we were greeted by the Duchess of Gloucester. The military band tunefully played us off the Empire: after gunshots and painful cries in the night; the homecoming tunes were sweet music indeed to our ringing ears.

Leave was earned but straight after our leave we were sent to N. Ireland. Some, including myself, were sent to Holyrood Palace later on to take part in the guard of honour for the Queen. This was a great honour for me and a truly momentous occasion. Dressed in smart uniforms of beautifully fitted navy tunic with the white gloves and cane. Dressed perfectly for such an event.

One of my friends from those times was Jock Rodden, from Melrose. Jock and I hadn´t seen each other for fifty-three years and I met up with Jock and his lovely wife Eleanor and some of their family members. It was like we were never apart.

I ended my Army career in N.Ireland on the 5th of July 1953 to return to my old job back at the White Horse Distillers.

Diaries of my National Service.
Friday 9th May 1952.

It began around the end of April when it was announced we were going to Korea. It came as a bit of a shock as some of us were just celebrating our nineteenth birthdays. We were due to meet up with the others on the 30th of April but that didn´t materialize so it meant five us in a billet all to ourselves, just waiting on the news of our departure. We packed, prepared and did what we pleased until we got the call again. The call came, 7th of May was our date given, which of course was my birthday.

The days flew in, approaching the big kick-off and the day before, on the 6th of May, we argued about wages and stuff when into the billet came our announcer: "The draft´s off until the 9th of May!" We all looked at each other, this surely meant no wages. The expression on some of the lads´ faces was quite funny, especially Patterson´s as that seemed to be the only thing he was worried about.

The day came, we made our way to the square, along the way just giving the rest of the boys our cheerios. I don´t mind saying this but this draft was the most mysterious, none of us had any clue where we were heading; it was the great mystery tour but sadly no fun at the end of the ride. At the square there was no-one there to see us off or to give us any instructions; the mystery continued. We jumped on our waiting truck, now eight of us on board and none of the boys had any idea as to our destination. Sure, we knew the purpose of our being there but no place to match the reason.

We instructed the driver to take us to the station hoping to meet someone who would put us right. We finally met an Argyll Officer but to our surprise he was neither there to offer us any confirmation or to see us off. He was there strictly to welcome a batch of National Servicemen from the Black Watch. Our wait at the station didn´t last too long and before we knew it we were on the train making ourselves as comfortable as possible. It wasn´t too long before we headed into Kowloon Station where we would meet the ninth member of our party. We weren´t the only draft to come off the train;

a few English boys from different regiments were also at the station. The English guys were very organized indeed. They were well-supported and we didn´t even have as much as a senior soldier accompanying us on the trip.

Another wait was looming, this time a full hour would pass before we were finally escorted to the harbour to embark the Empire. Before embarking we were quizzed about our kit, which hadn´t arrived yet, this took up another half hour; by this time the waiting was beginning to set in our nerves. The whole logistics of the trip certainly played havoc with our patience.

After boarding we welcomed the fact that the ship was indeed quite comfortable and very modern. It was refreshing to finally get our place of rest, however, we still didn´t know our destination. We finally got our berths sorted out and after tea and supper we decided to take in a Humphrey Bogart movie. The evening finished with a sing song before we all retired to bed.

Next morning, May 10th, we rose at 6.30am where we proceeded with our ritual wash and beds fit for inspection. Again, still no further in the knowledge of the whereabouts of our destination. Next day was Sunday, the day of rest and the sweet sound of the Church bells ringing. Those bells reminded us of the long walks we would take with our sweethearts back home on a Sunday; you can say as the bells rang there was a lot of reminiscing going on in many a young man´s head.

To be honest, after all the tracking, the shipping, the toing and froing we were still as wise to our destination as when we first set out on the journey: we still hadn´t received word about where we were going. Night time came round again and some of the boys passed the time away with a couple of drinks, some played cards and some guys just didn´t know what to do or how to entertain themselves; it can get that way on a ship and especially if it's a ship where you don't know where you are going. As for Jock and Patterson, they always had something comical to keep the spirits up.

To round off the unpredictability of the whole trip we were finally welcomed off the ship by a band that played the tune, "If I knew you were coming I'd have baked a cake". Really? I'd have baked a cake myself if I knew where I was going.

Me as a young soldier, Hong Kong 1951.

Training in Hong Kong before heading to Korea. I turned out for the Company Team.

THE BEAUTIFUL GAME

BILLY WRIGHT, MANAGER OF ARSENAL FC at the time, came to Possilpark to view an arranged game on a Sunday. Possil YMCA were now the feeder club for the great London giants. Billy Wright arrived with Frank McLintock and Ian Ure.

We only had one strip which was in use on the Saturday. There was a mad rush to get the strips home and washed for the next day's presentation before the London contingent. The strips were full of wintry wet football kleber and my mother immediately soaked all the strips in the bath to get rid of the residue and stains. A hard task. The strips were saturated for about an hour where my mother would scrub and scrub until they were ready for their normal wash. You have to remember that we didn't have a washing machine in those days, everything was done by hand. After a full wash and rinse programme (manually, of course) the strips spent some time in our gas boiler in the kitchen. Time was of the essence as mum had visitors that evening and she still had to prepare the dinner. After a successful wash the strips had to be dried. Automatic timers and technical heating systems were not the norm, the humble and simple coal fire was our source of keeping warm. There were sixteen shirts, sixteen pairs of shorts and sixteen pairs of socks all hanging from every conceivable apparatus in our living room: step ladders, chairs, sofa and anything else that could accommodate wet clothing; what a sight! Don't forget, mum still had to get dinner ready as our visitors were due any minute now.

The guests arrived but there was a problem, all the attention was on the importance of getting the strips prepared for our

Arsenal visitors that we forgot about the seating arrangements for our guests. We sorted this problem as we had good neighbours who kindly donated their furniture attachments but the heat and humidity in the room was giving us another concern. Our very kind and understanding visitors, who by this time were shipped out into the cooler hall area, had no real problem with this and in a way found it quite hilarious but you know? What a lot of re-arranging for a game of football...honestly!

My mum was incredibly supportive and after the evening of entertaining visitors she stayed up all night making sure the strips were well-presented for the next day´s game. She said it was no problem as she was used to more than just washing a set of strips; mum and dad raised a team of us weans so in a way it was routine for her, as she put it.

Sunday´s game was at Perthshire Juniors´ ground and the then Arsenal manager and his staff were most impressed by what they saw. They invited Eddie Kelly, Jackie Carmichael, John Woodward, Norrie McKay, John Corr and Jim O´Rourke down to Highbury for trials. The only one that didn´t sign for Arsenal was Norrie McKay. The Arsenal manager wanted to take Kenny Dalglish too but Kenny´s father said Kenny was his only son and preferred if he stayed in Scotland. Probably much to the delight of Celtic supporters and later, Liverpool would enjoy the expert services from 'King' Kenny.

In 1973 I decided that I would accept an invitation to take Possil YMCA to the United States to play in a major tournament. It was vital that we took part not only for football reasons but for spiritual well-being and to be involved in adventure that would surely be remembered for the rest of our lives. Education is paramount for young people and having the chance to give the young members of the community a once-in-a-lifetime experience; I couldn´t pass on it.

I was called to the YMCA headquarters in Bothwell Street, Glasgow. The Chief Executive was a man named Mr George Smith. He said, "I believe you are considering taking Possil YMCA to the United States?" I said yes but he questioned me again by saying, "Are you off your head? Do you realize the organizing that it takes to undertake a trip of this magnitude? You must arrange transport to the airport, passports and visas for everyone. Flights and accommodation and above all, how are you going to raise the finances for such a venture?" He also questioned the area where we came from stating that companies were closing down around us; perhaps the closure or even the threat of local businesses going belly-up would surely dampen any sponsor chances. I informed Mr Smith that we hadn't just thought about this in the last few weeks or so, it was actually on-going for some time with my committee and we have given it great thought.

We did have something unique in our favour in the fact we had a very strong Parents Committee and we all gave it careful consideration. After much planning and discussing we agreed we would go ahead with the project. We were, after all, the nursery club for Aston Villa by this time and the late Joe Hill was their Chief Scout in Scotland. Joe knew everyone; in the media and in other important circles where we had the chance to raise funds for our USA trip. Joe raised a substantial amount of money for us with his connections to Radio Clyde which gave us air-time publicity.

Our Parents Committee should have been re-named Parents Committed for their amazing work they put in with the dances they organized, race nights and jumble sales; all executed by hard work and thoughtful planning. Nothing seemed to bother or faze them. They were a remarkable part of the success of our club and without them it is difficult to think where we would have ended up.

We did go to America and met teams from England, Mexico,

Germany and Canada. Lo and behold this humble bunch from Possilpark and surrounding areas came back with a beautiful trophy. The biggest prize, however, was the friendship we bonded from this expedition and some remain friends and very much in touch to this very day. Why Mr Smith had any doubts about us as a team, a community or as people I´ll never know. All round the whole trip was a success…I never doubted it and neither did any of the community.

Discipline was paramount within Possil YMCA. It was something I believed in that would be an asset to shape good players. We didn´t rule at the club, heaven forbid! You have to understand that the club had so much talent and we wanted to streamline this talent, nurture it and to help with their progress and without discipline it couldn´t possibly work. Friday evenings prior to games, especially important cup ties, the lads would meet at the local Lido Café. This was a favourite haunt after training for some of the lads. I always believed in Friday night – early bed. Saturdays required great energy and the players would need to be at their very best levels.

I would trawl the cafés making sure no player was there after a certain time and I would phone their homes to make sure they were in. Actually, they had to answer the phone in order for me to be totally satisfied. If they weren´t at home they didn´t play on the Saturday.

Some time after I would visit the cafés and to my pleasing there was never a soul in there except for the regular customers…no YM players. They all answered their phones. So, it worked, which was beneficial to all concerned. This kind of discipline wasn´t that we didn´t trust the players; we just wanted to make sure they understood the importance of discipline…and they did!

I was shocked when John Greig – who was the Rangers manager at the time – invited me to Ibrox for talks. The top scout at that time was George Runciman, who approached me about the move. I told them there was no way I could possibly leave the YM. George came back to me and said there was no reason to leave Possil. I went to Ibrox and had talks with John Greig, Tommy McLean and Davie Provan. John Greig welcomed me and he made it clear he wanted me to set up a youth policy at Rangers combining the job with Possil YMCA. Possil YM was to become part of the set-up. I went back to Possil to discuss with my colleagues and Dougie MacDonald gave me his blessing. One problem for me was that Rangers were noted for not signing (many, if any) Catholic players. I spoke to close friends of mine and in one, the late Joe Hill, who I worked with in the 60s, 70s and 80s: Joe was a devout Catholic. We discussed the situation as I had no intention in asking any young prospects what religion they were. It was their football talents I was looking for – not their religion. Joe told me I must accept the job because it could be something I might regret for the rest of my life. You don´t get offers like that every day of the week.

Peter Gallately, another great man and friend of mine was one of the top scouts with Celtic at the time. He also played for Clyde – a great player. Peter was also a devout Catholic and gave me great advice. He said, "Bobby, don´t think twice about this job." After due consideration I accepted the position at Rangers on January 1983.

I enjoyed my time at Rangers and again, I was lucky to be a part of a great club and very proud to have joined the famous Possil YM to another large team. Many young players came through our youth set-up; enjoying first-team experiences with Glasgow Rangers. The very fact that the great and legendary John Greig had faith in me is something I´ll never forget. It is great to be back at Rangers and having John Greig around at the club makes it all that bit special.

THREE KINGS AND A QUEEN

I´VE BEEN BLESSED with the amount of great people I´ve been associated with throughout my life; football or otherwise. I am also proud and honoured to say I´ve met three Kings and a Queen.

King Kenny [Dalglish], George Best and Pele. Three Kings as far as I´m concerned and of course, Her Majesty the Queen when I received my MBE.

Kenny was a great servant for Possil YMCA and was a wonderful footballer, even at a young age Kenny was supremely talented. I don´t think anyone was surprised that he went on to become a great player of the highest standard. A lovely lad with great humour and a terrific man, too. It was an enormous pleasure to see Kenny blossom into the player he became.

George Best, sadly lost to us, was a genius. What can anyone say about Bestie? Super player and one of the greatest players ever to have played the beautiful game. Some say – and there are not many who would argue – that he was the greatest player of all time. For those who didn´t know George Best he was a very approachable guy. Although he was the genius and an unbelievable player, he was a gentleman, a truly one-off and it was sad to learn of his passing.

Pele is another legend; in my opinion the greatest ever player. When I met Pele I couldn´t believe how warm and open he was. A real gentleman and my goodness what a player he was. It was an honour to share the same room as him.

Her Majesty was lovely, she was extremely nice and although

it was a bit of a shock to be honoured with my MBE, Her Majesty made the event very comfortable indeed. It was another great moment in my life that I'll forever cherish.

The King & I. Kenny Dalglish was a great Possil YMCA servant. Terrific lad and he had the most wonderful technique. Photo taken by Bob McLaren.

George Best flanked by myself and George Gray.

AN INTERVIEW WITH A LEGEND

DURING THE PROCESS of our research and planning this book we came across many who wanted to ask Bobby questions about the game, about scouting and about life in general. We always said it would be a difficult book to write; I mean, how can you put almost six decades of uninterrupted service to football and the community (and that's not taking Bobby's own personal life into the equation either) into a few chapters? We encouraged anyone who knew or knows Bobby to come forward and be open with us as Bobby wanted his book to be about the people. In a way it's as much your book as it is his and so some questions that were thrown our way were not relegated to the archives. We've selected at random some questions from various sources.

You were lucky enough to have lived your life in arguably the best years football had to offer. Putting economics and commercial issues aside, what do you think the difference is today between the players at present and the players from your era, in terms of skill?

Players today receive more sophisticated training and coaches are certified with various levels of qualifications. In my time players were just naturally gifted. We taught ourselves subconsciously by playing hours on end until dark, sometimes after dark. Around my suburb we had great players who were skillful by default and not so much by design. Players like Tony Fitzpatrick, Tommy Ring, Frank McAvennie, Kenny Dalglish,

Ian Ross, Johnny Hamilton, and Billy and John McPhail, were all gifted players. They didn't need coaching as such and as it wasn't the way in those days, the players were left to express their creativity by themselves and then pitting them against each other.

Without question, Bobby, you have unearthed some shining stars throughout your scouting career. I know your modesty and your humility won't allow but who was the best player you ever had at any of your youth set-ups?
 I wouldn't and couldn't possibly single any one particular player because we have had the great fortune to have had so many talented players and some cracking individuals who actually never made it to the higher levels of the game for one reason or another. I've explained in another chapter and given my feelings on this subject. I've been asked so many times what Kenny Dalglish was like when he was a youngster. Kenny was superb but we had many great young players at the club.

What exactly is it that you look for when you are trawling the region in search of talented youth players. Is there any secrets or tips you can give to scouts and more importantly; is there something special you look for in a player that might give some young player reading this some insight – perhaps they could work on the certain skills you are looking for in them, to attract you to them?
 Well, scouts vary in their taste and requirements when searching for players. I personally look for players who have natural skills and ability. Two educated feet are a distinct advantage but overall I look for natural ability. I've had, on many occasions, an excited feeling when I see someone who really covers all the requirements; from my point of view. It is strange and sometimes hard to explain but I get an almost instinctive intuitive feeling when I see a great prospect.

What was Kenny Dalglish like as a young player when he played for your youth team. Did he have special skills that no one else had.

Kenny had a strong build, his vision was outstanding and he could see things others probably couldn´t see in the game. He was not a pacey player but he more than made up for it with all the other elements he had to his game. His positional sense was terrific, he had a great shot and scored some wonderful goals. He also had great awareness. I remember when we played Morriston YM, managed by the late John Scott, his players would all wait to see if Kenny would come off the mini-bus; they knew if he played they were in for a very difficult game. Such was Kenny´s ability. Yes, he was a magic player, a truly gifted and wonderful footballer.

What was the best game you ever saw live?

The European Cup final between Real Madrid and Eintracht Frankfurt. I was at that game. Puskas, Gento, Di Stefano, Santa Maria were all a joy to watch. I doubt if Real had a weak player in their team; everyone was exceptional.

In Glaswegian terms it was sheer fitba! Classy skills and great technique from both teams. Even the referee was brilliant. Fantastic game. Everyone applauded both teams at the final whistle. It was, and perhaps still is, one of the greatest games ever. To think that a European Cup final could produce the amount of goals it did is astonishing. The crowd were on top form and even now, when you look back at DVD footage of that game, it´s hard to believe it was so long ago.

You have rubbed shoulders with the greats of the game, who would you say impressed you most as a person?

Pele. He was so humble and nice. It was no big thing for Pele to talk to anyone.

Did you ever dream of becoming a coach or a manager with a top club?

I was; with Possil YM. That's a top club.

Who has influenced you the most in your football career and who would you say has influenced you the most away from football?

My father and brother Jim. Both were extremely influential. Joe Hill and Dougie MacDonald. The late Davie Morrison who ran the U-21s. All of those great guys have been tremendous for me. Life would have been different without them; I'm sure of that.

If you could live your life all over again, would you go through all that you have gone through, with the war and being shot on duty et cetera?

No, I would have studied more. As far as football is concerned, yes. As far as meeting all the people all over again, I would. Just the studying bit I would change if I had the chance to do it all over again. I have no regrets at all. I've enjoyed everything about my life. I wouldn't change it for the world. The only regrets one should have in life are the things you didn't do.

We hear your father was reported to have been a great player. Did you see him play, did you rate him?

My father worked a lot so I didn't really see him play much. It was all work and survival for parents in those days.

Did anyone teach you football skills or were you like most war boys, you learned them all by yourself on the streets?

By myself. I had a ball every minute. I played against air-raid shelters and practiced all the time. They say practice makes perfect; it's true. Back then we didn't have video analysis, we just made tricks and moves up in our heads. We'd often dream a move in our sleep and then perform it in real life action. That was how we did it. No coaching like we have now; just simple creativity and a wee object that resembled a ball! That's all you really needed…and some spare ground of course.

At this moment, who would you say is the best player in the world?
Henry and Ronaldinho stand out for me. Ronaldinho plays with a smile on his face and has some terrific skills. Henry is probably a more complete player. His work rate is better than Ronaldinho's and an important factor in Henry's game is he has a beautiful temperament. A good sporting guy.

Are you concerned with all the talk that the country does not have enough facilities for boys' and youth football?
Always have been.

Do you think a Scottish team will ever win a European trophy and when do you think Scotland will make its mark on the international stage like we used to in the good old days?
I would say; maybe in a few years time but it will happen. Celtic did well in recent years with their runners-up placing in the UEFA Cup. Scotland's national team will take time before we can make any kind of mark but I'm sure the time will arrive where we won't need to fear anyone. It's good to see the young Scottish players coming through their ranks and representing their first-teams. A lack of money in the game means the big clubs have to play their own young as opposed to pulling out the cheque book and importing foreign players of the higher priced bracket. It can only be good for the Scottish game that we now have young players playing first-team football at the big clubs in Scotland.

Do you think Scotland should model their infrastructure on any particular country, like Scandinavia for example or do you think we should adopt our own style that suits our culture?
Go with our own culture. We are who and what we are.

What was it like to be shot during combat?
Not a pleasant experience. Terrifying to say the least but I am thankful that I survived. Many didn´t so I am blessed to have taken a shot and lived to tell the tale.

Do you have any interests outside football?
Yes. I was keen on jazz music but I didn´t have too much time in my early football days to fully enjoy my music interests. Athletics was also a great interest of mine and boxing is another sport I like. A lot of people stop me in the street and want to talk to me about football but most people think that´s all I talk about or know but it couldn´t be further from the truth. I am very interested in politics and history is a great interest of mine. I also take great interest in other people´s interests too and I love to have a real good chat about what others are into. You can learn from everyone and it can be a really good experience sharing what other people have to say. I probably get my character from my father as he also enjoyed meeting people and having a right good blether.

Have you ever been in trouble through football?
My grandson Joe was in our house recently, he was born at Christmas 2005. He was rolling around on the carpet surrounded by plenty of soft covers. I was playing about with him when I mentioned to Russell and Gillian that Joe had great football legs and when he´s older I´ll be taking him to the football with me. My wife, Betty chipped in with, "Aye that´ll be right!" She reminded everyone that when Robert was about

three-years-old I took him to an amateur football match at Huntershill Park, which was quite a distance from where we lived. Robert was soon playing in a big sand pit next to the pitch. I was so engrossed in the game that when it ended I made my way home; without Robert. I was at the end of Colston heading into Ashgill Road in the Milton scheme. I didn't have a car in those days. I panicked, naturally, and raced back to the pitch. I was shattered with a mixture of anxiety and the belting pace I was running at. The groundsman at the park took Robert in to his house as he knew who the boy was and was expecting me to come back but the relief was evident on the groundsman's face when I did finally make it back. Young Robert had gone into the kitchen and found a gardening shovel. He was out in the garden digging up a number of the flowers at the groundsman's house. The next time I was at Huntershill the groundsman had a big notice up that read: **DINNIE'S BOYS BARRED!**

Needless to say it was many years before I was allowed to take any of my boys to the football...on Betty's orders.

Do you see a bright future in the Scottish game?

I do. I am sure we'll come good one day as I said earlier. Things maybe looking up but we still have a long way to go.

How many players have you nurtured, scouted, coached or managed in your career?

It's very difficult to keep track of all the players. A few years ago I wrote a list of players who either made the senior and junior grade. There's a lot of players missing because the list was compiled many many years ago.

I've often been asked who was the greatest player ever to dawn the Possil jersey and I can put my hand on my heart and say: they were all great players. Of course, the more famous ones like Kenny Dalglish – who is without a doubt one of the nation's greatest ever players; not just to come out of Scotland. Bobby Russell, a very fine player indeed, a terrific talent. The list is endless and I am very proud of those boys. I've had the privilege of watching the following players go on to great things after Possil YM. Players like: Eddie Kelly, Ian Ross, Johnny Hamilton, Alan Moore, John Hendrie, Alex Forsyth, Jim Duffy, Tony Fitzpatrick, Gordon Chisholm, Paul Kinnaird and Gary McSwegan. It's difficult to track as all the players came through the ranks at Possil YM in completely different generations.

In all I couldn't say who was the best player because they were all wonderful players and some never made it due to one thing or another but they were players of sublime talent and I am a very proud man to have had the honour of being involved with their development in the beautiful game.

All my players were favourites of mine.

Many years ago I compiled a list of players who moved up the ranks to senior and junior level. You can see by the dates how long ago it was.

From Possil YMCA to senior professional.

Neil Leven - Arsenal 1964

George Andrew - West Ham United 1965

John Bustard - Hamilton Academicals 1964

James O'Rourke - Arsenal 1965

David McKnight - St. Mirren 1966

James McGill - Arsenal 1966

Edward Wilkie - Rangers 1966

John Corr - Arsenal 1965

Edward Kelly - Arsenal 1966

John Woodward - Arsenal 1965

Ian Ross - Liverpool 1965

Neil O'Donnell - Norwich City 1966

Norman McCormack - Ayr United 1966

Robert McPherson - Ayr United 1966

James Lindsay - West Ham United 1967

Douglas Eadie - West Ham United 1967

John Wright - Clyde 1966

Derek Robertson - St. Johnstone 1967

Tommy Thomson - Arsenal 1967

Jackie Carmichael - Arsenal 1967

Gerry Walker - Cape Town S. Africa 1967

James Reilly - Arsenal 1968

James Hughes - Arsenal 1968

Robert Archer - Liverpool 1968

Michael Kearney - Aston Villa 1969

From Possil YMCA to junior level.

Gerry Walker - Petershill

Derek Robertson - Petershill

Willie Campbell - Petershill

Norman McKay - Rob Roy

George Irwan - Maryhill Harp

James Hutchison - Maryhill Harp

Stuart Gordon - Kilsyth Rangers

John Donnelly - St. Rochs

William Whyte - Johnstone Burgh

Thomas Young - Vale of Clyde

Jimmy Liddell - Clydebank Juniors

Junior Semple - Pollock

James Campbell - Perthshire

John Currie - Perthshire

Albert Monaghan - Perthshire

Billy Stanton - Baillieston

Joe Collister - St. Rochs

Do you have any funny stories that have happened to you during your football life?
Lots. One that stands out was when I was asked if I could take Bobby Russell – the Rangers legend – to a house in Castlemilk for a surprise meeting for a family member of someone who worked with me at the White Horse. The gentleman was celebrating his 70th birthday and although he wasn´t a Rangers fan as such he just loved to watch Bobby play; he was his favourite player. Bobby Russell (or as I always call him, Robert) kindly obliged so off we went to Castlemilk, up to the family´s house and in we went. After a chat and tea the gentleman asked if it was okay to have a photograph taken; again, Robert was very kind and stood to pose whilst I whipped out my camera. I had to halt the proceedings because in the background – above their heads, was a photo of his Holiness the Pope. It just wasn´t appropriate and would definitely have caused a stir…especially in those days. Anyway, I asked them all to move over to the other side of the room where I could take a picture without fear or consequences and they stood under another picture…just above their heads… this time it was a picture of Sidney Divine.

What about stories that you wish never happened?
One that stands out is when Danny Murray, one of our players, was walking along Saracen Street when a couple of cars screeched beside him and out jumped plain-clothed police officers and pushed Danny against a wall. The police said they were informed that Danny was carrying a gun. Danny was

naturally shocked and what Danny was carrying was actually two bags of dirty football strips from the game that day. Danny was only going along to the local pub for a drink with his assistants – a very common thing to do after a game. He phoned me afterwards and I was stunned to learn of the way he was treated. Here was a man who had given up much of his time to help out with Possil YMCA – now a respected club in various parts of the world – on the receiving end of a very unfortunate and un-necessary incident. I would later call the late Bob Innes, Labour Councillor, and he was outraged! Bob set out to investigate this affair and soon one of the officers involved was not exactly flavour of the month in our area. Bob, great man indeed, went on to become Lord Provost.

What advice would you give to promising young players?
Live right and be honest with yourself.

THE WORKING YEARS

WHEN I WAS THIRTEEN I had this wee job delivering milk and rolls for Granny Malcolm; who ran a local dairy. Granny Malcolm was related to Molly Weir, the great Scottish actress, and the legendary Tom Weir. Her house faced my house at Bardowie Street. Betty O´Donald, who was three years older than me, also delivered the milk and rolls. Religiously at 6.00am each morning Granny Malcolm would leave her house and come across the street to our house where she would holler at Betty´s window: *"Haw, Betty! Haw, Betty!"* Betty would appear at the window to acknowledge her wake-up call. Next it was my turn: *"Haw, Bobby! Haw, Bobby!"* she would shout. I would arrive at the shop at 6.30am, often finishing my shift at around the back of eight. Four shillings and sixpence for my week´s efforts. I would receive my tips at the weekend where I would find under an empty milk bottle a penny or even a silver thruppeny bit; sometimes a sixpence or a wooden thruppeny bit; the luck varied. The biggest tip I received was a whole two shillings and that came from a local bookmaker.

Later in life I would marry Betty Henderson, who´s aunt was married to the bookmaker Johnny Robertson. Betty´s cousin was Betty Roberts who sang with some of the big bands and appeared on radio – which was our great big window to the world: y´see, there was no TV readily available in those days. Betty´s aunt, who married Johnny Robertson moved to a big house in Queen Margaret Drive.

I used to put a line on at the bookies for my dad where bookmaker Johnny Henderson would slip me a sixpence out of his waistcoat pocket. He had many pockets for all the different change he needed but he always knew where the important money was: my sixpence!

After school I would deliver groceries for John Dyar, the corner street grocers at the corner of Carbeth Street and Bardowie Street. Delivering until 6pm, Mon-Sat, earning 4 shillings a week. It was hard work as the groceries outweighed my slim frame. Square wicker baskets were used for transporting the goods and it was most tiring. After dinner I would work in the woodshed next to my close. 6.30 - 9.30pm.

My job was to chop firewood then pile into a bunch where it would be placed into a machine, put the bunch of firewood into it and pulled a lever which brought the wood into a bundle.

We´d bundle the bunch and tie them. Put each bundle into a crate which held thirty-six bundles. We filled four crates which was 144 bundles. 3 shillings was made for me. I would complete any homework that was needed then off to bed a rather tired young man.

Woodshed also made garden gates and fences. After a few years the woodshed closed and the local bookmaker took over.

Soon after the closure I left school at fifteen and got a temp job at the local sawmills. Soon after, my sister Betty got me a start at the White Horse Distillers where I spent a very happy thirty-six years before being made redundant. It was a job I loved very much. I started keeping the bottle hall tidy and getting rid of the rubbish. 32 shillings and sixpence was my weekly wage. I loved the job.

From there I was promoted where I was responsible for setting up machines with the engineers. The machines accommodated all the different types of bottles which was a most interesting job. I must have been doing alright because the managing director approached me and said, "Don´t discuss this with anyone else, Bobby, but I am going to give you an increase of a penny-an-hour." That made me, which in those days was called a five bob man, you got a certain amount of perks because of this.

My call-up to National Service came and went before I was welcomed back to The White Horse by my old boss George Masterton. George was like a father-figure to me. I settled in and a few years later I was promoted to be an assistant to the vat manager in the bottling hall. The vats of course held thousands of gallons of whisky. There were pipes under all the vats that were connected up to all the filling machines; capable of filling 33 bottles per minute. After a few years I was then promoted to assistant manager on the duty store. I was promoted again to manager at the duty page store. Jimmy Mitchell was involved in the duty store for fifty years. I remember Jimmy getting a clock for his forty years´ service. Jimmy was of course proud but after a few months he mentioned to me that the clock didn´t seem to work so he got one of the girls to wrap it up and sent it back to the manufacturer. The manufacturer sent the clock back to Jimmy with a notice: If you put some batteries in the clock it will work. Which caused quite a laugh. Jimmy was a wonderful boss but he was a bit eccentric at times. We´d stay up ´till all times at night taking in all the various football results from various leagues.

I made friends with a lot of the girls who worked at the distillery. Those girls also played a great part in helping to fund our club. I sold the girls Christmas cards and dance tickets for our monthly dance evenings. We all became very close; in fact some might say too close as a lot of the guys dated the girls and some became closer than that by marrying the young madels from the White Horse Distillers; and no! it had nothing to do with the Whisky fumes in the factory. To this day some of those couples still point the blame in my direction for *getting them hooked.*

My wife, Betty and I were recently invited to John Wyles and his wife Rita's ruby wedding anniversary to celebrate their monumental forty years of marital bliss. John played for Possil YMCA U-16s. Norrie McKay and his wife Cathy, Jim Hutchison and wife Violet, Tommy Scoullar and wife Betty, Danny Murray and his good lady Mari were also present on this occasion which, as you can imagine, gave me enormous pleasure to be amongst a great bunch of people who all have known each other for all those decades. I have to say that had I never met Tom Blair and Dougie MacDonald this momentous occasion would probably never have happened.

When I worked in the White Horse Distillers I used to get our workers to bring in jumble sale material that I'd take to the YM to help with our funds.

One particular evening I was on my way home from work with a large parcel full of jumble sale items. It was one of my late nights after working overtime.

The CID officers approached me and said, "Excuse me, sir, can we ask you what you have in the package, and would you mind opening it?" Well, I was a little bit embarrassed because the contents of the parcel consisted of womens' shoes and underwear among other clothing suitable for females: for the club's jumble sale. After some explaining the officers accepted my story and wished me good luck. Apparently there were a spate of break-ins at the local factory and the officers were rightly going around the place with a watchful eye on anything suspicious. Having a football club that organized jumble sale events and some of the jumble items involving clothing actually got me out of what would normally be a very embarrassing moment…thanks, Possil YMCA!

Later in my working life I would find myself working beside many policemen when I was honoured to receive my post as

Head Commissionaire at the Strathclyde Police Headquarters in Glasgow. Those were great years and to this day I am still friends with a large number from the constabulary. Thirteen years in total, executing my duties at Pitt Street and many stories to tell but I´ll leave that to the ones who are either qualified or better than me to write memoirs of the polis days!

Of course, work doesn´t just entail paid employment; it also consists of home duties like DIY – which brings me to the time when young Robert was about two-and-a-half and I was wallpapering the living-room. Betty was out with her friends so I had to keep a watchful eye on Robert as well as hang paper – a mean task or two let me say. I did what all DIY enthusiasts do; I propped the ladder, got the past ready and poured a drink of Irn Bru!

The glass of Irn Bru was at the foot of the ladder and after some thirsty work I would descend from the steps to take a refreshing drink. This would carry on until I had the feeling that I had to fill my glass again. I was sure the last drink I had from the glass would empty it; meaning I´d have to fill it again but the glass was full...maybe the climbing of the ladders, hanging paper and babysitting sort of knocked me off my thinking. Anyway, on this occasion I took a drink and unknown to me the reason the glass was full when I clearly thought it was empty was that young Robert had pee´d into the glass.

Yes, I did take a mouthful which I spat out immediately!

Nowadays I am retired, well, what they call officially retired but I am still active and if I can find a way out of any gardening chores (or any other household chores) you will no doubt find me trawling the various football facilities taking in youth games. That is one job I doubt I will retire from... they´ll probably have to carry me from a fitba pitch!

I have struck up a great rapport and built solid relationships throughout my working years. From my early roll and grocery delivery job to the sawmills; the distillers to the police and in the various football jobs I had in my life has meant I've been very lucky to meet all kinds of people from all walks of life: I wouldn't change it for anything.

Father's under the stairs again
Mother's under the stars again
Sister's floating on mars again
Brother's behind bars again

Cousin's out of luck again
Uncle's out of work again
Auntie's looking at her clock again
...until they all come home again

Grandpa's cheating death again
Grandma's out of breath again
Brother-in-law's smoking meth again
Sister-in-law's watching her health again

Nephews are in trouble again
Nieces are chewing bubble gum again
Step children are playing the double again
Adults are squabbling over scrabble again

A touching moment in Jersey. I´m the one with the longest shorts...or the shortest legs, whichever way you want to look at it. Allan Perris is the other guy, what a player he was.

MY CROWNING GLORY

THE LORD CHAMBERLAIN, commanded by Her Majesty, was to send me and my family an invite to a garden party at the Palace of Holyroodhouse. It was not your normal garden party invitation: it was an investiture held at the Palace in Edinburgh in which my attendance was requested. It was time to fix my smart suit, sharp tie and best shoes; I didn´t hesitate.

I´d only just retired from thirty-six years of working in the White Horse Distillery and thirteen years as Commissionaire with Strathclyde Police so in hindsight (after the initial shock calmed a little) it was a nice retirement brief that our postman delivered to our humble quarters. I received the envelope addressed from none other than No 10 Downing Street. It was a shock to open the letter and to read its contents: I was to be awarded the MBE from Her Majesty. Now, an MBE is something I´d associate with the famous and the people who have truly deserved it, but me? A humble wee boy from the North Glasgow suburbs? Still to this day it´s quite hard to take in. A title attached to my name. Having a first, middle and surname is long enough but now that I have added letters I have to send out my post in long envelopes just to accommodate them.

The date for me and my family to attend this wonderful occasion could not have been more poignant; it was my wife, Betty´s birthday, 1 st July 1998. I chose to receive my honour in Scotland because I am very proud to be Scottish and the people of my community and my country no doubt had a say in this remarkable honour. I´m still the humble boy from the North of Glasgow. I´ve never changed and neither would I want to. Receiving an honour like an MBE and meeting Her Majesty is a very special event and one that no-one could ever forget.

It humbles me more to receive praise or plaudits and a great evening also happened this year in 1998 that will never leave me for as long as I live. Being honoured by Her Majesty is quite astonishing but on a Friday evening, 15th May, I was again commanded to a special honours list that included none other than my dear friends. To be honoured by people you know is quite something else.

The Royal Scottish Automobile Club in Glasgow was the venue. Chairman was my dear friend John McKelvie. My other dear friends who made this night a very special moment for me and my family were John Duncan, who did Grace; Toast, by Laurence Macintyre; Reply, by William McDougall and Auction by Donald McLean. On the testimonial committee were dear friends Les Darling, Ian Cargill, Bob Law and of course, John McKelvie.

This was indeed a momentous moment in my life. Roddy McDonald was there to capture the whole event on camera, beginning with my family and I being picked up at our house by our chauffeur, arranged by Alex Martin. When we arrived at the RAC club we were escorted to the hospitality suite where we met with other dear and great friends before the heartrending moment of being led into the arena by a piper. All very Scottish, all very proud and all very very hard to take in. It was truly a magnificent occasion.

The special guests that evening were prominent figures from their respected environments: John McGuire, well-respected in the automobile industry; Stephen Hendry and Ronnie O'Sullivan, two snooker legends; Bert Paton, Robert Russell and Dixie Deans. It was a blessed honour to be in the company of the Chief Constable, the Deputy Chief Constable, ACC Duncan and all the many people who attended my testimonial dinner.

The video that was made for this occasion has been passed around to family and friends and many have said it was a long time since they laughed so much. The speakers were outstanding…absolutely hilarious. Let's not forget, we auctioned shirts too, which was well-appreciated by all concerned.

There aren't any higher superlatives that I can use to describe my gracious thanks to all who contributed to this tremendous occasion. As I've often said before: to be honoured by higher peers is a remarkable milestone in my life, or anyone's life for that matter, but to be honoured by your great friends – which I call family – is without question the highest honour anyone can hope to receive.

If you are lucky to have friends around you it makes the journey of life that bit special and as much as I am greatly honoured to receive and be a part of these great events it should be me who is honouring them. For all the success Possil YMCA achieved during my tenure I have never measured those great times in terms of cups and medals but the marvellous people I've had the greatest honour to meet – around the world. I am still friends with many from different countries and that is what makes the journey of my life that extra bit special.

The players, the coaches, the managers, the backroom staff, the helpers, the community, the city and beyond have all played a huge part in my life and the fact that I was involved with those great people is for me, my crowning glory.

It's nice to be important but it's more important to be nice.

A momentous occasion for a humble wee boy from Maryhill. Being honoured by Her Majesty the Queen.

NO MEAN CITY

A CHOKING RED DUST explodes, to descend briefly upon the shoulders of hungry youths who scuffle in broken shoes for dominance; swiping aimless kicks at a mere hint of ragged leather. The bending goal posts bore the resemblance of an ancient battle ship´s mast as the scrawny alpha males jostled towards the makeshift six-yard box with their prop for a ball. The area had no isometric shape, just chalked lines drawn out by dragging the best part of the shoe; the penalty spot circled by a twig.

The backdrop of a low sky was reached only by sprawling houses and the occasional passenger airline. Freshly washed clothes would decorate the verandahs; swaying to a kind summer breeze. Howls and screeches of excited play and yells of famous names would bellow out under a red blaes smoke: *"Pele! Puskas! Jairzinho!"*...and the occasional, *"Banks!"* (if the goalie managed to get a touch). The youthful lot kicked their days away without a care in the world with dreams of playing with a real ball on a comfortable playing surface in front of a fanatical crowd.

You could be right in thinking that this is a scene from the favelas (the poverty districts of Rio de Janeiro) and home to popular stars from the Brazilian national teams past and present. If someone told you that this is a short clip from Villa Fiorito (the childhood place of Diego Maradona); one of the world´s most gifted players in his, or any other generation, you wouldn´t feel out of place for believing so.

But this is Glasgow. As equal a football-mad city you´re likely to find anywhere on the planet. The kids may vary in colour, religion or economical backgrounds but the bond is the same.

The feeling for the game of football and the whole package contained in the football-daft youngsters is as passionate, regardless of which side of the equator you are born to.

In pubs all over the city grown men in boys' football clobber gather to debate and criticize in unison; all experts in the field of the beautiful game. They have the answers to the downfall of their teams, they work out the best formation for this coming Saturday's away match and they roar technical instructions toward wide screens. It could be comical if we didn't take it seriously but there is something unbalanced about an unfit man in his fifties hurling a volley of commands to his team's wee left winger, "Get up the park, that's it – back-track noo, get back, get back up there and support the forwards, sling a cross in, ach ye've loast it again, get back, tackle, ye should've given him the baw, come inside, get back oot tae the wing"... I'm knackered just writing this!

It's about passion (and quite rightly so) but we forget that the beautiful game is...well, just a game...or is it? Try booking a five-a-side court in the city on any given evening of the week: "Sorry, fully booked, mate. You'll have to book in advance." "What about thirty-seven weeks, three days and four hours from now?"

"Sorry, mate, Borrusia Mönchengladrags are playing PSV Hideintheoven in the cup. The city hosts many leagues that cater for every group and individual; the love for the game can be seen across the many parks at weekends and under a haze of floodlights; astro and blaes pitches burst at the seams where football-crazy boys and girls participate in training and small-sided games. Most of the talk in and around the city is centred around fitba.

It's a city where a sales knock on your front door in the evening doesn't necessarily mean double-glazing but small boys looking for 'sponsor money' for their local team.

Glasgow boasts two heavyweights in the football world and

the city has often been compared to a large goldfish bowl; a term often heard in relation to the high profile Old Firm players. It's true, Glasgow is a football-crazy city and the beautiful game is more than just a pastime in the eyes of Glaswegians. The city is proud to have its football legends like Sir Alex Ferguson and Kenny Dalglish but Glasgow offers more than just football sons. It is steeped in architectural history and when you talk about the world's greatest you have to mention Charles Rennie Mackintosh in the same breath. In other sports there is no argument as to the greatness of boxer Benny Lynch and the city can proudly brag (and quite rightly so) about the successful musicians, actors and actresses as well as political and business figures. But of all the Glasgow greats this small city has produced we cannot overlook the people of the city. It has been often said that Glasgow is one of the funniest places on earth (or the funniest) and very few could argue. Comedy comes naturally to Glaswegians; it's on the streets that you'll find the funniest joke you've ever heard and the patter from the young and the old can have you in stitches, often begging for more.

A foreigner asked a young Glaswegian what it means to come from the city and what it was like being Scottish. His reply was, "Well, me and my mates go out on the town on a Saturday night. We get dolled up in American jeans, Italian shirts and down German beer. We then head to a Chinese restaurant for something to eat or just get an Indian take away, or sometimes we might fancy a Turkish kebab; then we all go home to our homes and crash out on our Swedish sofas and switch on our Japanese TV sets; sometimes we'll text each other from our Finnish phones and make fun of the night; so in all, it's great to be Scottish. To be a Glaswegian is something we don't think about until someone mentions it I suppose; yes, it is a good place to come from. One person is as funny as the next. There is a stand-up comic in almost all of us." You can say that again, mate.

Way back in the late 70s a small Glaswegian boy, barely into his teens, had the rare opportunity of coming face-to-face with one of the Beatles. He was pushed to the front to get his autograph by excited women, all shy and nervous (the women that is) and the boy, with not a jot in the world, got the autograph, read the signature and handed it over to one of the women who was squeezing her way to the front and said, "Ach, ye can huv it, a thoat it wiz Ian Redford."

Glasgow is famous for the rows of tenements which housed many families. There are many who just have to look at the word 'tenement' and cringe as thoughts of destitution and deprivation flash through their minds but it couldn't be further from the truth. Tenements were buildings where great community bond and spirit grew. They were iconic pieces of architecture; in fact, they still are; they are almost monumental and anyone who had the great pleasure to live in a tenement will verify their true worth.

Residents of these buildings took it in turns to wash the stairs. The windows; very close to your neighbours, were great gateways to the outside world and you didn't need the local news to inform you of what was happening around the area as the women (and sometimes the men) would gab away 'til their hearts were content with the famous Glesga chin-wag gossip.

It was where children felt safe and if either one or both your parents were out on one of the many chores and errands there was always a helpful neighbour that took you in and gave you something to eat. If you lost your key and locked yourself out there was always someone who could 'break in' to your house for you. Yes, the tenements where indeed a place were everyone shared the same way of life. Nobody was better than anyone else and that great community spirit is often not appreciated until you moved away to pastures new: to the great up-and-down stairs world in one of the many overspill towns like East Kilbride or Cumbernauld. Ah! the trauma of emigrating.

The tenements were great for holding our own little concerts and playtime events. All you needed was a blanket, some juice and biscuits, some willing performers and you had a full theatre there with acoustics to boot. What the residents didn't like was the ones who cut through the close. If you didn't belong to that particular building you got an ear-bashing from the lady in the cleaning bib and rollers. There was no graffiti, heaven forbid! Chalking was permitted on the slabs at the front or rear entrance where games of peaver were popular; particularly amongst the girls.

The tenements were great for sending and receiving messages; who needed mobile phones in those days? When the local ice-cream van came round all the kids would run to the foot of the building and yell up for money. The parents would wrap up a coin inside a piece of neatly folded paper (usually the tear-off from a *Mother's Pride* loaf packet) and throw it down to the kids. Some parents would shout a playing kid from the street to run an errand. Bobby's own mum was a victim of one of the 'bad' kids when she hung out a line with a note and money on the end of it. The kid grabbed the note containing the money from the line and of course he vanished, never to be seen again.

In our close, Mrs Russell had put curlers in her hair and assuming she was in no fit state to go outside the house (her words, not mine) she looked out of the window to see if she could find a wean that would run a simple message. My wee sister was four-years-old at this time and was summoned to Mrs Russell's window to receive a Sterling pound note and a verbal command of, "Get me 20 Embassy Regal, and if they don't have Regal you'll just have to bring back something else, I can smoke most brands." Now, my sister obviously just heard the words "if they don't have Regal you'll just have to bring back something else," which she did! The van didn't have Regal and my wee sister was at the van for a long time before returning, struggling with a large cardboard box with a pound note's worth of MB bars, Irn Bru, double nougats, sugary white mice and jelly cola bottles.

The ice-cream van had bolted by this time and Mrs Russell couldn't get the rollers from her hair out in time to catch the driver at his next port of call and as there was so much sweeties and juice she couldn't think of a way to get rid of them other than to invite other weans from the street to get rid of the contents of this huge cardboard box for her. Needless to say a few kids in the street obliged Mrs Russell with her hurried request…without any problems whatsoever!

The tenement is irreplaceable. It has great social and historical value. Sure, we live in what many have described as a more sophisticated environment but in a way we've lost some of the important elements that humans require. It's great we don't have outside toilets and it's marvellous that we can wash and dry our clothes without even leaving the house but we lost something as we gained sophistication and I don't think it will ever come back. Society changed; although I don't know if it became better; we built ourselves outwards and spread across the landscape but as we did; we sort of separated ourselves from each other. Privacy is a great thing but it also arouses curiosity. We now live in a surveillance society where every move is watched by hidden cameras but in the old tenement days everyone knew your business anyway. Well, most people lived the same life in a confined building so you couldn't really have secrets.

The ragman would look foolish nowadays going round the many urban developments in search of textile; I mean, he wouldn't get away with handing out a shrivelled balloon in exchange for a three-quarter length jacket, would he? A neighbour of mine from our tenement days was seen chasing the horse-and-cart down the street because one of his kids gave a way his mother's check coat (which was of material and fashion value) and all the kid got was a plastic trumpet that couldn't even blow a note. The ragman saw the funny side of it, however, and offered the breathless husband – who by now was hanging onto the back of the cart – a better mouthpiece for the instrument.

The backcourts in our street were great for the assortment of games; as Bobby describes in his chapter; and I can remember a great joining moment of togetherness in my back green. I was six-years-old and my neighbour, Fergie Russell, was eight. He dawned his Celtic strip (the full lot including the number on the side of his shorts) and I sported my Rangers strip. We used the clothes poles at the back as goals and played our routine game of headers and kicks…a simple five/eleven´er to start and work our way up to the traditional ten/twenty-one´r. It was half-time and I think Fergie was a head of me in goals and we went back into his house for a juice. Now, improvisation is a word often used growing up in humble environments and we were no different.

The close-mouth at the rear was 'our tunnel' where we would pretend we were running out in front of a massive crowd; actually, there was a crowd; our back greens were formed in a large square and all the neighbours´ back rooms and kitchens all faced the back. A lot of people would watch our games of football and on this particular occasion we had an audience and for a terrific reason. Y´see, at half-time, Fergie and I had this crazy idea to swap strips! I would wear his Celtic strip (which was a bit big for me and as he had thighs like the back-end of a Cortina, he struggled to get into my shorts). We even swapped socks…hygiene? huh, who knew about it at that age? As we emerged from the 'tunnel' we heard a few claps from neighbours and we thought it was because our second-half was about to begin but it turned out the neighbours appreciated the fact that we swapped kit. It was a rare moment indeed and a nice touch I suppose but we didn't have any segregation after school hours. The weekends and anything after 4pm were ours and we didn't care or took part in separation issues; we were just kids having a good time.

Ah! the tenements; somehow the game of chap-door-run-away was never the same running through semi-terraced gardens.

Glasgow boasts a proud industrial history including foreign trade that dates back hundreds of years. Cotton industry (which during its prime employed almost a third of Glasgow's workforce) was a major player in its time and the city was also prominent in glass-making, distilling and fabric printing. The city can also be proud that it was once regarded as one of the richest cities in Europe and the

years prior and up to the First World War the city produced almost one fifth of the ships that sailed on earth's waters. A huge influx of immigrants were instrumental to the economic value of the city.

Glasgow has seen its fair share of change, some for the worst (the war years) and some for the better. It was clear that as industry moved forward into a technical and more service era the city had to eradicate some of the images that for many years had been stereotyped for clearly the wrong reasons. Ever the resourceful city and ever the willing participant for change; Glasgow went about its business of yet again re-inventing itself and today it is one of the most visited cities in Europe.

Maybe that's why Glaswegians are the way they are. Maybe the genes they inherited from their forefathers from those hard labour days gives them their true grit attitude and fighting spirit. In a way the hard working days and fight for survival opened the door to let humour in as a way of escaping the rigours of cold steel and the constant hammering of rivets. Could be why the city has produced many greats in the past, the present and I´m sure there are many still waiting in the wings to carry the flame.

It´s also a place where distance is measured in minutes. "Excuse me, sir, Can you tell me how to get to Queen´s Street Station?"

"Aye, left at the lights then straight on for about two minutes."

The tag that was, for so long, attached to Glasgow: 'no mean city', is gone, replaced by purpose-built buildings, a calmer Clyde and side-street café bars. Cosmopolitan indeed.

Take me hame, wee caur o´ the night
I´m a lang lang way fae the toon
Help me oan tae the platform hen
And help tae sit me doon

I´ve hud a wee dram too many
I´ve left ma sweetheart at the chippy
Could you geez a haun tae haud the pole
And hide me fae the clippie

I am the clippie and less o´ yer cheek
Yer drivin´ me roon the benny
Noo get up the sterrs or aff the bus
if ye huvnae got yer penny

Yer a helluva wummin that few would mess
Yer a tough wee cookie biscuit
I heard you were charged wi assault wan time
for punching a corpy ticket.

To my sister, Betty, who once worked as a conductress before finally reaching tramcar driver status.

FROM THE DRESSING ROOM AND BEYOND

(Part One)

It is impossible not to have known of Bobby Dinnie if you have in any way been involved in Boys´ Club and Youth Football from the mid 50s to 90s.

I had many experiences of Bobby in his time with Possil YM, firstly as a young player with Drumchapel Amateurs and later when I was a young fledgling manager with St. Mirren. Bobby had the wonderful ability to spot young talent and nurture them to greater things and his most famous boy, Kenny Dalglish, was testimony to his ability.

Sir Alex Ferguson CBE

Although he is known to most for his work in football, my Uncle Bobby has been a major influence in my personal life as well as my football life as far back as I can remember.

As a young kid I visited him regularly and was impressed by the amount of various memorabilia on display. To me, these were the ultimate rewards for his endeavour but Bobby assured me that they were simply material tokens and that the true rewards were witnessing the development of all of the young men under his tutelage. This told me a lot about him and made me aspire to be like him and encouraged me to adopt a similar approach.

My first taste of football, like so many from my area, was to play with the local team Possil Park YMCA, which I did, occasionally under Bobby's scrutinous gaze, for a few years before moving onto amateur level. Unfortunately being a member of the family did me no favours in his eyes and it was apparent that coaching and management would be an avenue I could hope to pursue with a greater degree of success and, ultimately, personal satisfaction.

I cut my (assistant) managerial teeth with newly-formed Rosebury Juveniles and then onto top U-21 team Milngavie Wanderers with whom we won all of the titles available during our four year tenure. I had some fantastic times throughout this period but, as Bobby had suggested, I didn't feel as though I was contributing enough to the development and progression of the youth and accepted Bobby's invitation to manage the Possil Park YMCA U-14 team.

This was, if you like, my own prize for a job well done – Bobby always resisted favouritism – and was the start of my own most satisfying period in football. At that age level you need to be a bit of a social worker and child psychologist as well as football manager and it was probably during this time that I leaned on Bobby's experience most of all. He taught me how to handle a variety of situations whilst dealing with fragile young egos and when I should, and should not, include their parents. I also learned that, especially at such a formative age, "If you're going to do something, you have to do it right!" Although we won our fair share of prizes, it was at this time when the progress and advancement of these boys onto a higher grade of football or simply their evolution into manhood became more rewarding than any trophies on offer.

As well as Possil Park YMCA, Bobby is equally associated with Partick Thistle Football Club, to where I was next summoned and helped take the Boys' Club into the Professional Youth set-up where I continued to learn more under his watchful eye.

In summation I would like to thank Bobby for always being around to help and guide me whenever I needed him and for being a great uncle and a wonderful friend. Although I'm not involved in football at the moment I would love to contribute more, if the opportunity arose, and I know that if I could provide a small percentage of what Bobby has done then I'd be offering the game a fantastic service.

Alan Harris

I am personally privileged and honoured to pay tribute to Bobby.

I have know him as a professional scout and as a man of the highest integrity since 1983 when I was Assistant Manager at Rangers FC to the legendary Jock Wallace.

Bobby's ability to identify and nurture young players was outstanding even then and I was delighted that he helped bring young talented players such as Gary McSwegan, John Spencer and Robert Fleck who all went on to star for Rangers and other senior clubs thanks to his scouting wisdom and ability.

Even when I was manager at St. Johnstone, Bobby was always available at the end of a telephone – day or night – to give advice and recommendations about young talented players from across the West of Scotland. The great goal scorer Allan Moore was only one of the many he helped start a new career out with the Glasgow clubs – and go on to great success – and earn a living from the game they loved .

As a person, Bobby was a gentleman in every sense of the word: polite, understanding and always interested and supportive of any young players who came under his wing – and not just the ones who made it to the top levels. Bobby´s interest in young players as individuals wasn´t only if they made it to the big time, but he continued to follow their development as young adults, parents and citizens. Another thing I admired in Bobby that he was always willing to respect the opinion of other people and make sure that what they had to say was given the attention and importance it deserved. A rare quality indeed!

As a professional, Bobby was outstanding: totally

conscientious, dependable, knowledgeable – and a shrewd judge of a young player's potential and character.

This same professional devotion to the game was no less sincere or influential whether he was working with Rangers or in his legendary work with Possil YMCA – in the heart of Glasgow. His support for youngsters in deprived areas and his involvement in Possil YM was as genuine and committed as it was in his dealing with Rangers.

Perhaps one of Bobby's greatest gifts was his genuine honesty when asked about a player. He was only interested in giving a true and professional judgment so that the young player and the club would both benefit from a relationship of mutual respect.

Bobby is understandably respected unreservedly in the world of football and it has been a pleasure for me to have known him, worked with him and now given the chance to pay a tribute to him as a person – and a professional scout and football icon in Scotland.

Alex Totten

Bobby Dinnie gave us all a place and a meaning in our society. He encouraged the young and you could say he kept us away from the streets.

He kept us occupied with the many training nights in Possilpark. Bobby helped my brother, Robert Fleck, during his early football days. Bobby was always there for everyone for advice, support, help and as a guide – if you like – in our lives. He was wonderful for us and even now, thirty years or so later, Bobby Dinnie is still there for us.

Allan Fleck

Bobby was well-known and did a lot for the local community. He gave youngsters the chance to have an organized game of football amidst the rural industrial area where facilities were often short.

Not only did he give belief to players as footballers; he also gave those young men from Possilpark the grounding and belief to become better, as human beings – which many did; not just in the football world but in other environments.

Bertie Auld

It´s difficult to say something about Bobby that hasn´t already been said.

My son, Gary, was the first player from the Ayrshire region to sign for Rangers BC where Bobby was responsible for the club that was connected to Rangers FC. Gary was presented with a blazer and he wouldn´t part with it – not because it was something to do with Rangers – but because Bobby gave it to him. Bobby is addictive, you cannot get enough of him or his company and he is a very fine gentleman.

In the amateur scene (as many will testify) there is a great need to drum up player recruitment business but with Bobby it was the opposite: Players approached him. If there were more Bobby Dinnie´s at the top end of the game or even in government office; we´d all be better off for it.

Billy Robertson

Mister Bobby Dinnie – or as I know him, Mister Possil.

I first met Bobby when I was ten or eleven years of age; introduced by my primary school teacher, Mrs West. Bobby was the head man of Possil YMCA and wanted me to play for them. My father and I had no hesitation in agreeing to this as I liked his warm and friendly approach.

We spent four successful years in a manager and player relationship during which Bobby gained great respect from my father which meant an awful lot to me. This respect must have been mutual as in later years, Bobby named his two sons: Robert and Russell, (after my father).

Bobby was instrumental in my career development as I was soon approached by the then professional club of which Possil were a feeder club to – Sunderland FC. They offered me a two year apprentice professional contract. After a long discussion with my father and Bobby, whose advice I valued, I made my decision to accept their offer. The rest as they say is history…

Many young men have benefited from Bobby's great football experience and knowledge to further their careers.

To finish, I think of Bobby firstly as a great family man – enthusiastic and talented football man with a great ability to spot further talent in which Rangers FC will benefit from.

I am proud and privileged to be regarded as one of Bobby's 'finds' and honoured to count myself as one of his friends.

Robert Russell

Bobby had more faith in me than I had in myself.

On Saturday afternoons he encouraged me to do my best for the team and on Sunday afternoons, because he went to the worship service at the Possil YM hall, I went too and although I didn't realize it at the time, it helped to lay the foundation for my faith in Christ.

Clark Brown

Possil YM was like a family.

When you left your age group (or you left the team for that matter) you always went back to see the up-and-coming younger players. Most of us all took interest in the next generation of Possil players; that tells you about the bond everyone had at the club.

I joined St. Mirren but I couldn´t oust Archie Gemmill; the Scotland legend. He played in my position and was a terrific player. His dedication was incredible so it was difficult for me to get into the team. I was too impatient and I eventually found my way to Australia to play.

To talk about Bobby is quite difficult as it´s probably all been said before, however, if I could say one thing: Bobby was a father to us all, he really looked after us. You couldn´t get away with anything even when he was not around because he always knew what was going on even when he wasn´t exactly present. I remember turning up for a game in a pair of denim flairs; of course that was the style back then, Bobby was having none of it. We had to represent the club as well as ourselves so we were made to put on a smart casual pullover and proper trousers. It was all in the name of discipline and it didn´t do any of us any harm at all; in fact, it did us a power of good, I´m sure the rest of the boys will testify to that.

On a funny note; we had a trip to London to a YMCA hall. A sort of self-service eatery was available for us and Bobby allocated our allowance; this gave us a soup, a dinner and a pudding. Anyway, as we filled our trays up and headed to another part of the hall. We thought there was more seats in the other hall but it turned out there was only one hall: we were looking into a mirror that wasn´t directly in front of us but side-on, which fooled Tommy Young, he crashed into the mirror and we all fell over him. What a sight it must have been.

Going back to the discipline in the group, we even had to look after our boot laces, that was the measure of it but many are grateful for it.

Davie McKnight

When I stepped off the bus in Saracen Street in the early sixties, little did I realize I was about to meet the man who would change my life.

I was in my sixteenth year and having left school some twelve months earlier; with no academic qualifications, I was convinced that my future was extremely bleak and due to my failure in book-learning I would continue my job as a floor sweeper in a print works, forever.

The highlight of my week was turning out at football for King's Park former pupils, on the south side of Glasgow – where you played against experienced thirty-year-olds – who definitely took no prisoners.

I came across a newspaper advert inserted by a YMCA team offering trials to youngsters my age. I immediately put pen to paper to apply for this opportunity but after three weeks and still no reply I decided to grab the bull by the horns and venture north of the city. I found my way via kind directions from the locals and I eventually arrived at the YM hall in Denmark Street where I tracked down my mentor, a Mr Robert Dinnie. From that day my life changed for the better, as had the lives of many other youngsters who were taken under the wing of Mr D.

The kindness and understanding Bobby showed towards me in those days are un-repayable. To him nothing was too much trouble. His drive and personality were an example to all. On a personal basis he gave me the confidence and self belief that I was good enough to become a professional footballer. At a time when I was told to stop living in a dream world of becoming a professional footballer; I made my debut for Celtic reserves at Parkhead in a team that included Davie Hay, Lou Macari, George Connelly and many others. It was Bobby who accompanied me to the match. After the game he was alongside me with the then Celtic manager, Jimmy McGrory. He handed me a pen and I signed forms. I thoroughly enjoyed my spell with the 'Hoops' before a change of management in the mid-sixties. I was told I was 'surplus to requirements'.

Even the man who adopted me years earlier considered I had crossed the 'great divide' and he refused to watch me in a green and white jersey. Only Bobby Dinnie encouraged me.

Departing Celtic devastated me and I wanted to stop playing; something Mr Dinnie refused. I was soon on my way to West Ham where I played in the youth team with Trevor Brooking,

Harry Redknapp and Frank Lampard before making my first-team debut against Spurs. We lot 2-0 and the great Jimmy Greaves and Allan Gilzean both netted.

I was called into the manager's office, the legendary Mr Greenwood's office that is, and I was informed that Bobby was sending down a youngster for a week's trial. It was none other than Kenny Dalglish and he was to share my digs with me. The popular TV programme 'The Untouchables' was all the rage at that time and Kenny was obviously a big fan, particularly of the character played by Robert Stack. If Kenny recited the catchphrase, "Don't mess with Elliott Ness," once, he narrated it ten thousand times. It came to the stage I would lock him out of the room and only allow him back in on the promise he ceased his rendering. Needless to say my plea fell on deaf ears and to this day whenever I hear someone mention 'The Untouchables' or 'Elliott Ness' I look at them in horror. When Kenny announced he wasn't signing I had mixed feelings. I wanted him to stay as he was a smashing wee player and a fellow Scotsman. On the other hand, it meant I'd get a full night's sleep!

As time has passed Bobby's stature in the football world has risen higher and higher, culminating in his well-deserved MBE. A proud moment not only for Bobby but for his charming wife Betty and their sons, Robert and Russell.

Bobby Dinnie MBE
An oasis in Possil.
Douglas Eadie

*Douglas Eadie played for Bournemouth FC and on to North America where he played for Toronto Mets, Rochester Lancers and finally, Fort Lauderdale Strikers, where a certain Gordon Banks was between the sticks. Although Banks had an eye handicap he was still a super shot-stopper.

I have known Bobby since I was five-years-old.

He has been a part of my life ever since I used to play football in the street at my gran's house in Bardowie Street, Possilpark, and was often encouraged by this thirtysomething man and his brother. To me at that time they ran a 'big club' called Possil YM. He has been there at key times of my life – when my grandad died, awards ceremonies, my 16th, 18th and 21st birthdays and most recently my surprise 40th birthday celebrations. At this latter event he said to my sister Tracey that it was his privilege to be there. All my friends who sat with him and our kids listening to his tales of 'Garry as a lad' understood the high regard I feel for him: he is such a gentleman in the truest sense of the word.

That is my Bobby Dinnie – always encouraging us, remembering his players and families, seeking to help improve their lot, where he can – then and now.

He often talked to my grandad as well about my progress over the years and then Bobby came to watch my primary school team, Chirnsyde, for whom I'd only just started playing, aged ten. We had a great team at that time and he signed me after watching only a few games. At that time and for the following three seasons I was a free-scoring centre forward surrounded by superb older players (some of whom I've mentioned below). Bobby and my dad, Greg, and my grandad, Hughie, worked to make me a two-footed footballer. Recently, Bobby reminded me and my ten-year-old son, Craig, about the keepie-uppie tricks with the coins that helped my coordination. In those days I was a bit like Ronaldinho, (if only) i.e. totally right footed. I wonder how many of the guys, who were more gifted footballers than me, that are contributing to this book will recollect and mention the little coaching gems picked up from Bobby that they have passed on.

He and the YM team took me on trips to places around Scotland winning so many trophies, league and cup tournaments. My dad and grandad had to build me a trophy cabinet! Medals were won with: skill, determination, heart, enthusiasm and a real sense of pride instilled by Bobby and his team. He always encouraged us to never be ashamed of our roots but instead be proud of where we came from and set targets for where we wanted to go. I know the pride he still gets from talking to 'his boys' today about the influence that being part of the YM family has had on all of us – and there are thousands of us – and our achievements in all aspects of our lives – sporting and otherwise.

Aside from my family and a few teachers such as Iain Blair and Jack Campbell, no-one has influenced the strong social beliefs I have more than Bobby – he is the inspiration I often recollect to my school kids in my job as a teacher. In my previous career in engineering when things got tough I would often remember his character to colleagues encouraging them to never give up, to work and play hard and have that will to win.

Early invitational tournaments such as Eastercraigs Tournament and Cowal International gave me my first appreciation of the opportunities Bobby afforded myself and numerous team-mates. As we got older, guys like Ross Caven, Joe Dickson, Alan Moore, Laurie Morrison, Robert Fleck, Colin Brodie, John Gregg, John Buchanan, Jim McGill, Ronnie Dunn, Paul Fitzpatrick, Davie and Paul Kinnaird, Jim Leonard, John Thomson, Jim Reid, Grant Reid, Terry McGhee and Raymond McCreath. All, like me, came mostly from areas known as rough and working-class; became successful teammates and winners. Bobby, Jimmy, Norrie McAllister, John Wales and Brian Byrne were nurturing all age groups to be the best they possibly could and not just in footballing terms. Bobby was the kindly father-figure that made him Mr Possil YM. That is not to say he has ever been a soft touch – far from it; I have been at the end of that stare of his a good few times.

Such was, and is, the respect we all have for the man that the few times I've heard him 'lose the rag' and raise his voice we quickly shut up and paid attention or as he'd say, "Pin yer lugs back, son." The few lads who did step out of line were quietly 'transferred' elsewhere.

I played for Bobby's YM right up to my 21st year and enjoyed every game (less the very few we lost) and my chances to play at senior level and nationally for Scottish Universities came as a result of Bobby holding me back for a year at U-14s and converting me firstly to a left-back then right-back. He said, "Garry always had two good feet and was more than fair in the air." His knowledge and contacts within the game set him apart from his peers and meant that we all got the best chances to make the grade as the numerous contributors will verify.

On our trip to Fremont in California we played a number of select teams and one player who stood out for me; (Ross Caven and Brian Byrne, too), was John Doyle; not because he was to go on to play for the USA in FIFA World Cups but because of the initial friendship he and his mates showed us together with the hospitality they and their families afforded us. Oh! and the fact that when we got home to Glasgow and told Bobby about Doyle´s sister, Kelly, being a 'hot' top model he made sure the memories and life changing opportunities of playing in California were never to be forgotten by regaling these tales to parents and grandparents on our behalf.

As I have said earlier, Bobby has been one of the people responsible for the character I have. After a career as a Civil Engineer I am now teaching young people myself. I am now a Secondary School Design and Technology teacher. I am also a Sports Coordinator and I´m only too aware of the numerous people Bobby has helped somewhere along the line. I still meet up with folk who know or know of him.

I have so many stories about him, like: how he would ensure that our fund-raising events to assist 'YM' teams get to far-flung tournaments in California, Holland, New York and the like – used to involve our whole community.

Once, when collecting jumble sale stuff, he managed to return to many a poorer family, "Get a few wee things fur the weans tae wear." Without making them feel like charity cases. He would come along enthusiastically to our fund-raising discos in exotic locations like Milton Community Centre and Possil Point as well as the YM hall; always encouraging those who took part to enjoy and behave themselves.

He was always mindful of the important part our mums played and thanked my mum, Janet, Mrs Caven and Mrs Kinnaird on numerous occasions for the support they gave and often said to us that it was not just your dad who made great lads!

What always amazed me then and even more now Bobby is in his 70's (73, he keeps saying he doesn't feel that young) is how he always gets to places to watch matches – a bit like Santa with no car. Over the years he must have spent a fortune on bus and train tickets – without complaint – that is just his way.

I have come full circle now that Bobby is keeping an eye on my son as a potential player (spookily, aged ten) and will close by wishing my life long friend and one-time mentor continued health and happiness for himself and all his family, thank you so much, Bobby, for times past, the friends I've made and the belief that you shared in us all.

Garry Robertson

Garry, Carole, Craig and Sean Robertson.
Mum Janet, Dad Greig and sister Tracey.

Bobby Dinnie is an asset to Scottish football, and I am delighted that I had the privilege to work alongside a fantastic man.

I worked with Bobby when we were at Partick Thistle FC

together, and everything that people said about this great man is true. He is a perfect gentleman in every sense of the word, never an angry word was ever spoken by Bobby.

Bobby is a credit to himself, his family and all the professional football teams that he has worked with and helped throughout his life.

I am honoured to have known Bobby Dinnie in my life: They broke the mould when they made him.

Gerry Collins

Well, Bobby, we go back a long way. We achieved all we wanted.

You have been one of the best things in football – and still are. All the kids you helped through all the years to help reach their ambition. When we played together I never saw you angry with other players or referees. You were a very good player yourself; with nice touches but most of all you were a team player.

Well, Mr Possilpark, if they don't erect a plaque in your name at Saracen Cross it will be an injustice....

Tommy Scoullar

Easter weekend 1964 and I'm looking to the big board at Central Station to see which platform the train to Birmingham would depart. I felt a tap on the shoulder and I turned around to see Bobby Dinnie.

I was off for a week's trial with West Bromwich Albion.

Bobby had come to wish me luck. He gave me a YMCA scarf as a good luck charm and I still have the scarf to this day. I was back playing for Possil YMCA a week later: West Brom thought I was too good for them!

I was one of the many who played for the YM but didn't make the grade but thanks to Bobby and his backroom staff, I, like loads of other guys, had great times at the YM in

Denmark Street. Yes, even running up the road on a dark, cold, winter's night to train on the black ash in Torr Street.

My time at the YM prepared me for my next step in football, as a committee man at Petershill Juniors and then onto the match committee, reaching the final of the Scottish Cup, twice in the 80s.

Now as match secretary I hope to go one better and win it just like Bobby did with the famous Possil YMCA.

Gordon Spiers

Bobby was entrusted by Rangers FC to take control of their youth system in the early 80s.

Celtic FC youth teams were by far the dominant force and the Ibrox club earmarked Bobby to take control and establish a strong Rangers youth set-up, this alone tells you of the high regard he had for his outstanding work in finding and nurturing talent.

The first impression of Bobby is one of utmost respect for a fantastic gentleman. He came from the old school and was very professional in his approach. Bobby was also a very private person, didn't say a great deal but when he talked – you listened.

Gus MacPherson

Apart from the football, there were other things that brought harmony and friendship to the people of Possilpark.

The YM used to hold dances every month along with jumble sales, raffles and bric-a-bac stalls; which brought in much needed income.

Those were some of my memories from the 1950s.

The sixties was a time for change and came with a pleasant bang! New young boys emerged along with the introduction of some girls. This being the case, the YM went from strength-to-strength and soon we started doing concert parties where we participated in concert events for the older folk of Possilpark.

Now that things had settled down it wasn't long before things started to fade away and some girls starting courting or left to get married; thus leaving us once again with football!

Now that football was once again the integral part of Possil YMCA, people like A. Glassford, D. MacDonald and J. Birkens held the YM together in a football sense until a chap by the name of Bobby Dinnie came in and brought boys from nowhere...and made them into stars.

When I played football it was a privilege to play alongside players such as my cousin John Birkens, my brother John (who became a Grade 1 Referee in Scotland and in England). And there was Bobby Dinnie, and may I say: through those men, I learned a great deal such as respect and courtesy they had towards others.

Ian Birkens

* Ian Birkens gained two Scottish youth caps at U-16 and U-18 level.

Born in 1935 and lovingly 'dragged' up in Possil, but you know what? Possil was a pretty good place to enjoy childhood.

We lived in Killearn Street, a red sandstone block opposite the Schweppes' office building.

Some childhood memories:
Being lifted up onto the back of a Clydesdale horse that pulled the delivery cart for the Caledonian Oat Cakes Company – magic for a wee boy!

Hauled by my mother to the local 'Bobby' to be chastised for being cheeky – it didn't work – I'm still cheeky!

Recollection of my mother in tears because my dad – in his thirties – being called up for the Army to fight the Germans.

Fortunately, six years later – after driving a tank to Normandy and across Europe – returned to us.

Every air-raid I was wrapped in a blanket and carried across the street to Schweppes' basement shelter along with budgies, canaries, cats and dogs and of course…people, to wait on the siren.

Farrell's the bakers in Saracen Street. Straight from the oven, fired to your requirement...*MAGIC WITH BUTTER!* If you had butter! Brilliant rolls.

When I was sixteen-years-old my friend, Angus Howat, suggested I join the Possil YM U-18s football team. At that time I attended a rugby playing school. I must have been reasonably proficient at the footie to command a regular place in the team. Saturday's meant rugby in the morning, football in the afternoon…and multi-cramp at the cinema come the evening.

At that time I didn't fully appreciate that I was about to be a part of probably one of the best U-18s teams of the 50s. I still cherish the medals. A word of praise for our manager, Alex McLaggan. Alex must have required a Radox bath every Saturday evening. On the touchline he kicked and headed every ball, took every free-kick and corner… what a guy!

I moved on to the senior team and met the magical Bobby Dinnie. Bobby was the most entertaining outside-left I ever played alongside – not the best but certainly entertaining. Slip the ball inside the full-back to Bobby, who proceeded to dazzle himself with intricate footwork and the move fell flat again!

After some fifty years I have been re-united with Bobby, Alex Robertson, Gus Howat and Len Miller. We meet for lunch and a pint about every three months. What do we talk about? Possil YM and the fitba.

Bobby, it's been a pleasure: you're a magical guy.

Ian McLean

THE FUNNY THINGS WE SAY

(based on a true rumour)

ISN'T IT FUNNY, some of the things we say; the metaphors, the clichés, the phrases? Are we aware of when we say them? Do we know what they actually mean? I listened in to an open line talk show when I heard the pundit suggesting to the caller that, "he should choose his words carefully" and then I thought to myself, "does the pundit choose his words carefully?" I was later intrigued by the conversations that go on on some of these shows and decided to listen more. I counted the metaphors and the phrases and after so long searching for something a bit different to be included in this book it was there all along and I couldn't see the forest for the... well, you know the rest.

In one sweeping move (I'm sure that's another but we'll leave that on the bench for now) we tuned into radio commentary and watched managers live on TV and compiled our very own Top Twenty of the most commonly used phrases. Yes, they're all there from the obvious "we shot ourselves in the foot" to the ever present "game of two halves".

So why do we use these phrases? Well, it's simple really. Language evolves and most of us are handed down language (vernacular included) but sadly a lot of people don't find it in them to learn those phrases, their origins or their meaning: we just say them out loud and it's perfectly acceptable because everyone says them so we think everyone will know what we mean anyway. Some phrases are passed down from generations but some are quite new. Take "a game of two halves" for instance; this doesn't relate to anything outside of football; it is a direct football saying. The game of football is a game of two halves and no-one is going to argue about that fact but this is a phrase that is slowly dying out because it is clearly over used. I believe if the other phrases become matched to their origins we might see them dwindling too. I personally never liked the phrase "wearing his heart on his sleeve" and probably as I learned its meaning I couldn't use it anymore because it simply does not relate to football at all. The game of two halves is dead but the heart on the sleeve has still to receive its sleeping dart to put us out of our misery.

So who uses these phrases? Just about anyone who can cusp a microphone or a pint tumbler. We say them because we hear them and we automatically believe in them. I became interested in certain phrases after learning another language; I didn't become addicted as such, just curious. It probably started at the beginning of learning another language as we often compare our native words to the new language we are learning but you can't do that. It's a bit like going abroad and buying something; you can't compare each purchased item's value to your own currency; it doesn't work that way. I grew up speaking English but didn't become interested in the history of the language until I started speaking a new language.

Top Twenty run-down of the most popular football phrases:

20. New in at number twenty is the **White Elephant**. I believe it was a nightclub at one point in Glasgow (or probably is in many other places) but the white elephant does exist as a treasured animal. The white elephant is sacred in ancient Thailand and other Asian countries. They were very special and required great attention. Expensive food and other luxuries were provided and they were extremely expensive to take care of. If the leader, the King of Thailand, was unhappy with one of the peasants (or subordinates) he would offer the white elephant as a token. This would probably break the back of the peasant and so often was the case. So, you don´t want a white elephant .

19. Straight in from nowhere is **Schtum.** There´s a rumour going around about a player reportedly ready to sign for another club but neither the media or any members of the two respected clubs are shedding any light on the situation; they are keeping schtum. This is a simple word but unless you know German or have been told of its origin then you probably wouldn´t know that schtum is a yiddish expression from German meaning silent or mute (but spelling is different: its proper spelling is stumm).

18. Jumping (literally) five places to number 18 is the **Cat out of the bag.** Someone, somewhere, has let the cat out of the bag. This phrase stretches back to the old market days where they would substitute a cat for a pig by putting the cat in the bag. If the cat got out of the bag it then blew the trick.

17. A non-mover at number 17 is **Under the cosh,** or better known as a "weighted stick". Simply means under threat. It somehow relates itself to an American phrase "under the gun" so I presume it means you´re definitely in trouble. Cosh is a stick, a length of metal pipe with rubber tubing, used for beatings…yes, you´re definitely in trouble when you come under the cosh.

16. Holding a candle down four places to number 16. Co-commentators (let´s just call them CCs) have purposes for being there, I´m sure. However, they do come up with some of the best lines. I heard one piping in with his tuppence worth (there's another one but we'll get to that later). The CC was comparing a new centre forward to a legend that previously played for one of the teams; he said, "That big fella there couldn't hold a candle to the last legend that wore the number 9." Holding a candle? *Mmmmm,* I wonder where he got that from? Let's see; was our CC referring to a gift-shop? He probably thinks he was but the phrase "holding a candle" dates back to the days before the magical light bulb (that's not a CC phrase, bye-the-way). The apprentices of various trades had a duty in those days and that was to bring more light to the tradesman's work-point. If someone couldn't do that job they were considered not to be able to hold a candle to their journeymen of higher status.

15. Up ten places to number 15. **Argy-Bargy.** During commentary of a game a centre-half may find himself in a small altercation with a bustling centre-forward; resulting in a wee argy-bargy. There's no doubt this is a modification of a Scottish expression argle-bargle which most likely originated from the word argue. This definitely has nothing to do with engaging in a heated argument with an Argentinian.

14. Down three places to number 14. **Hammer and Tongs.** They're going at each other hammer and tongs. Blacksmith's terminology. They would need to work very hard and quick to shape hot metal with time probably against them; hence the connection between the phrase and the speed at which teams or exponents go at for victory.

13. Still at number 13. **Bee's knees.** The team are doing well, the manager's job is safe and the supporters think their club director is the bee's knees. This is a real catchphrase that goes back to the early 1920s and I believe it started in North America. It was at a time where people compared goods of high quality or anything good that happened, to a part of an animal's anatomy. It's just a catchphrase.

12. Up fourteen places to number 12. **A turn up for the books.** A smaller club defeats a big noise from the top division and the phrase "a turn up for the books" is mumbled all around the stadia as the fans depart. Again, this phrase comes from horse-racing and the book refers to the bookmaker's record of placed bets. If a horse won the race unexpectedly, let's say it was an outsider, then it was considered "a turn up for the book." Where the plural comes in no-one really knows. The phrase varies depending on location (book, books).

11. A high-climber in at number 11. **Big girl's blouse.** Two midfielders go in for a tackle in the middle of the park, one doesn't follow through opting to jump out of the tackle prompting roars from the stands, "ya big girl's blouse, ye!" The phrase most likely originates in the north of England. There have been many who say they believe it comes from a UK sitcom in the 1960s but it's debatable as to who started the phrase but we are sure it is a North England idiom; and it's not that old.

10. Another non-mover staying at number 10. **Down to the wire.** The game is even, it's still 2-2 and no-one is dominating the play more than the other; this game could go all the way down to the wire. Football commentators use this very often but it actually doesn't come from football, it was first used in horse-racing. This was back in the days before TV cameras and video evidence. A wire was strung at the finishing line above the race-track, of course, to enable the stewards to identify the winner in a close finish.

9. Down five places to number 9 but still a huge favourite is

Scot free. Phew! The game is over, we won but we were lucky, I think we got off scot free. Contrary to what many believe it has nothing to do with Scotsmen or anything Scottish for that matter. It derives from Scandinavia. Apparently it was some form of tax levy and if you managed to wangle your way out of paying this tax you got off scot free.

8. Up twenty places to number 8 is **Smoke and mirrors.** A team are having a dreadful time of it so far. A lot of talk is coming from the director and high profile members of the board but the fans are having none of it; they want results and they are tired of all the smoke and mirrors. Clearly this states a form of deception and was used by stage magicians to trick the audience. Used more recently and probably due to the commercial involvement in today´s football world.

7. Out of sorts straight in at number 7. The defence fails to clear what looks like an easy ball; they are all out of sorts. Strictly speaking this comes from the print trade. The letter press characters were stored in boxes according to character and size and if any characters were found to be in the wrong box they were considered to be out of sorts.

6. Spill the beans slips down to number 6. Football would not be the same without the amount of rumours and proposed secret signings. Of course, there is always someone who spills the beans. It doesn´t mean they toppled a can of 57 variety but this derives from Greek politics. Beans were positive and negative indicators. White for the positive and black for negative. If someone (the collector) spilled the beans before the votes were complete and a black bean was prominent in view they paused the voting process.

5. Still at 5, the ever popular **Tightening up the purse**

strings. Heard mostly from the financial sectors of clubs and presumably it´s an old wive´s tale but to be honest how many purses do you see today that have strings? It would be better if they said, "we´ve decided to zip up the purse", or, "the club are not going to buy anymore players as we have to button our wallets". Purses in former times were little pouches that could be tightened by strings. Another old saying that doesn´t look like it will go away now or in the near future.

4. Broke his duck rises to number 4. The season is almost half way through its schedule and the big striker has failed to find the net; in fact, he´s still to break his duck. Breaking one´s duck is short because it was actually breaking one´s duck´s egg. Now it is common in most sports but it originates from cricket. The duck´s egg was a zero and it was matched against a player´s name. If the player managed to score he would be able to rise above the zero on the scoreboard; thus breaking his duck´s egg; or as we say today; breaking his duck.

3. Former number 1. **He covered every blade of grass.** Is that right? He covered every blade of grass; you mean, every blade of grass? I´ve seen groundsmen at their work, terrific work they do nevertheless, but even with the best high-tech grass cutting equipment I doubt he´ll be able to cover every blade of grass so what chance does a wee South American number 10 have of achieving this? It´s a clear exaggeration of a player´s work-rate but its origin is relatively unknown.

2. Dropped from number 1 is **A game of two-halves.** Perhaps the most annoying. Managers are now steering clear of this phrase and rightly so. When a manager or a pundit uses this phrase they usually follow up with a sly tongue in the cheek (and that´s one that didn´t make the list). It´s a new one and has been suggested that it actually derives from the beautiful game's commentary and co-commentary although no-one can be certain as to its true origin. Became hugely popular only a couple of decades ago.

1. No surprise at number 1. **We shot ourselves in the foot.** Often said by a team captain after his side gave away all three points or allowed the opposition the chance to get back on level terms. It doesn't necessarily mean he took a revolver out from behind his shin-guards and blew the toes off his Puma Kings. The origin and meaning probably needs no explanation.

Hovering just outside the Top Twenty are two new releases to watch out for. **Heart on his sleeve** and **Tuppence worth.**

Heart on his sleeve. The captain is a great player for the team, he has skill, tenacity and the bit between the teeth (which actually comes from horses that take control of the holders from their rider), In fact, the wee captain wears his heart on his sleeve . This phrase always intrigued me and it's one I personally would never use. It has nothing to do with having the player's aorta outside of his body clinging to the arm of his team's shirt. It is most likely to come from an old Valentine's tradition (French/English). On Valentine's Eve the male group would draw a girl's name from a box and the male would wear that name for a year on his sleeve vowing to protect her for the year's duration. A long long way from a wee hardy midfielder I suppose.

Getting his tuppence worth. Relates back to the open line talk shows and phone-ins. Need I say any more?

You may still get a good night's sleep after reading the assortment of clichés, phrases of colloquial origin (or, as I prefer to say: better said than read) but one thing's for sure: you will listen to commentary and open line talk shows in a different light …and there goes another one…tut!

FROM THE DRESSING ROOM AND BEYOND

(Part Two)

I was born and brought up in Ruchazie in the East End and as a young lad played for a cracking team called Tower Hearts. Our heartland was Garthamlock, Easterhouse and most of the schemes east of Barlinnie.

My first encounter with Bobby was when we played Possil YM at Closeburn Street and I was immediately impressed with way they did things at the YM. Bobby was not a shouter or bawler but when he wanted things done – they got done. I must have had a decent game because I soon joined the YM and spent the next few years winning a bundle of trophies playing alongside some tremendous players. Bobby was always the gentleman but certainly not one to be crossed.

I remember on one occasion when we were playing in an international tournament in New York State and I started thinking I was an better player than I really was.

We were progressing through the rounds against teams from the States, Mexico and everywhere else. I was playing well and scoring a few goals. In the semi-final, things were not going well and I had a spat with one of my fellow YM players. Two minutes later I was hooked and in true temperamental superstar fashion I stormed away to the dressing room – failing to stay and cheer on my mates. Well, the boys fought through to the final and my reward for my cream puff was skelfs on my bottom from sitting on the bench in the final.

Bobby not only taught me a lot about football, but a lot about humility, dignity and how to behave like a man. In days when the word 'legend' is tossed about too freely, Bobby stands out head-and-shoulders. I'm proud to have been associated with him and hope I can call him a friend, guide and mentor. Thanks for everything, Bobby.

Ian Taylor

I first encountered Bobby as an eleven-year-old, when he arrived at my house to sign me for Possil YM.

In the days before child protection legislation, Bobby saw it as important that my parents met and were familiar with the people who would be looking after me, in a football sense. Bobby brought along the two football coaches with whom I would be involved. This was typical Bobby and greatly appreciated by my parents.

The code of discipline Bobby instilled in the Possil YM organization – which included a monetary fine for bad language, not just in games but in training – certainly helped the boys in my team to focus on playing the game. This lesson has stood me in good stead in my adult life and something I have incorporated into my own young football team.

Bobby´s effect on my Possil YM football team maybe best summed up during a game with the now defunct Clydebank 'S' forms. We were losing the game 4-0 at half-time when Bobby turned up to watch the second-half. Such was the effect that Bobby´s presence had: the game finished 4-4. This for me, encapsulated Bobby. You wanted to play for him, and the boys who were previously struggling, redoubled their efforts; such was the esteem that Bobby was held in.

I recently had the pleasure of meeting Bobby, whilst watching my son Andrew play football. Bobby wanted to meet Andrew, whom he did and he told him that his dad had been a great player – although a bit lazy . Thanks, Bobby! Seriously, the fact that Bobby rated me as a footballer still means a lot to me, more so than anyone else´s opinion.

If visitors from outer space were to arrive at our planet and we wanted to create a good first impression we should send Bobby to meet them. His innate decency and humility – allied to his good will and generosity of spirit – would surely win the day.

James McGill

Bobby interviewed me for a managerial/coaching position within the club. It was a strict interview but you can see why as the club were of the highest degree.

We enjoyed tournaments abroad and one year in particular we won everything going, except the Scottish. Still, I enjoyed my time and twenty-one years at the club should tell you that.

Jim Gillespie

I first met Bob Dinnie in 1973, where he and myself both worked at the White Horse Whisky Bond.

I knew all about his involvement in football through my school days and at the Boys' Brigade; a few of my pals played for him at Possil YMCA. I grew up in the Springburn area and Bob was very very well-known. In those days you had to be a very good footballer to get a game with Bob's team, the YM.

I have so many memories of my time knowing Bobby; like when we were working for Rangers Amateurs. A charity evening was arranged for a young boy who unfortunately had cancer. The young lad lived in a small mining village called Longridge. Bob was invited as a guest and he asked a couple of Rangers players to come. They agreed and the young boy was delighted to meet Rangers players as he was a Rangers fan. The weather was bad that night and although we had some idea where we were driving, we would eventually stop and ask for directions. A large building came to our view and we got out to ask someone where our proposed destination spot was; we were actually at a prison...much to our surprise. The prison warden said there were a couple of other men who also stopped before us to ask directions…I think it was a couple of Rangers players!

We headed down the road for a couple of miles where we ended up at a haulage contractors by the name of Patrick Gullhooley. Bob and I were in full Rangers dress of blazers and ties. We knocked on the door and the guy kindly invited us in. The place was full of Celtic paintings and photos and the chap said: "I never thought I´d see the day when two Rangers officials would be in my house." The directions were too difficult to explain verbally so the good man instructed us to follow him in his car where he lead us to the exact spot we initially intended to reach.

Our haulage friend and Celtic fan friend was informed of his good gesture and he received a letter of thanks from Rangers FC.

I am honoured to have been given the chance to work with Bobby and to have formed a friendship that still lasts to this day.

Jim Murphy

I first met Bobby in the early 60s when I joined Possil YMCA U-18s.

I found him to be a very honest man and had a good all-round knowledge of football. I think out best season was1964-65 when we won the Scottish Amateur Cup, the Jubilee Cup and the Williamson Cup. Myself, Ian Ross and Johnny Corr all went on to represent Scotland YMCA in the British YMCA Championship.

Bobby went on for many more years with Possil YMCA but I don't know if he had a better season than the 1964-65 one.

Bobby was always a true gentleman – in victory and defeat – and coming from a place like Possilpark in the early 60s, Bobby is a one-off.

Jimmy McGill

I have had the pleasure of knowing Bobby Dinnie since1985 when he was appointed Head Commissionaire at Strathclyde Police Headquarters where I served as a Chief Inspector.

On speaking with Bobby I immediately recognized that we shared a passion for football. He being a scout for Rangers Football Club and me a failed footballer-cum-amateur referee!

Bobby's humility, respectful attitude and pride in his family shone through, making me look forward to our twice-weekly meetings for coffee in his office. During these meetings we would put the world to right and I would identify to Bobby any player I came across in my refereeing duties whom I thought would be worthy of his expert eye being cast upon them. Bobby being Bobby would report back to me within a week or so giving me his honest opinion of the player, his potential and thanking me for my trouble.

Our meetings would develop from football matters into mutual enquiries regarding our families with Brenda and I being blessed with two sons similar to Bobby and Betty. Bobby was indeed a family man, immensely proud of his immediate family Betty, Robert and Russell and his extended family at Possil YMCA.

Despite our great friendship and mutual respect, Bobby would treat me no different from the other 800 or so employees in Force Headquarters and I would regularly be brought to task by him for not wearing my identity tag within the confines of the building.

On Bobby's retirement in 1998 I was immensely proud and honoured to be asked to chair his testimonial committee comprising of fellow police stalwarts: Les Darling, Bob Law and Ian Cargill. This culminated in a lavish dinner held at the Royal Scottish Automobile Club in Glasgow attended by Bobby, Betty and family where 220 persons from all walks of life: friends, police, football, snooker and politics gathered to pay tribute to a truly great man of the people.

From time to time I still view the video of the evening, proud to have played such a small part in a fine tribute to such a respected man. Seven years further on I still visit Bobby and Betty at their Walnut Road home and keep in touch regularly by phone.

Bobby Dinnie MBE

A caring friend is a treasure, a loving friend is too,

I know that I have both in the friend I have in you

This little chapter is written to say thanks for all you've done

And to say that with friends like you Bobby I am the lucky one.

John McKelvie

I have been involved in football – both youth and professional – for around thirty years. I have met and come across all sorts of people in the game, some nice, others not so nice. I have met a few real gentlemen in the game and I must say: Bobby Dinnie comes into this category. He is a true ambassador for the game, always helpful with a true love of football. Bobby has been in the game a long time, both at youth and senior level – and there are (and have been many people both playing and working) who have a lot to thank Bobby for.

Over the course of a season I would cover lots of games at youth and professional level and at a great deal of these games I would meet Bobby; always the same jovial, friendly, yet very knowledgeable of all the players on the field of play.

Finally what I will say is that what Bobby doesn't know about football is not worth knowing.

Bobby is a top football scout and a real gentleman.
Joe Gaughan

When I was appointed as manager of Rangers Football Club in June 1978 and having been with Rangers as long as I have been, I was well-aware of the need to start a serious youth programme.

To achieve this you need, first and foremost, good scouts to identify young players. Unlike the situation today, there were no youth academies. In those days young players were picked from schoolboy or boys´ club/youth football. To this day, scouts are every bit of important to clubs as they are now and it was very important to have the right kind of person in this job. This is when I first met Bobby Dinnie, who immediately impressed me with, not only his football knowledge, but he was also an outstanding kind of person who we would wish to represent your club when speaking to the parents of young players.

An outstanding example of this was when he asked me if I would take a team of youngsters to play in a public park against Possil YMCA at Possil because he wanted me to watch a striker playing for the opposition. That striker turned out to be Robert Fleck, who played in the Rangers first team on many occasions and then went on to have a successful career with major clubs in England.

Now, some twenty years later, Bobby Dinnie is back scouting for Rangers and is still one of the finest gentlemen you are likely to meet.
John Greig MBE

I have known Bobby Dinnie for more years than I care to remember.

When I started working with Coventry City FC in the early 80s, I approached Bobby and suggested that Possil YM be a nursery team for them. Bobby agreed to this and Coventry City FC manager at the time, Gordon Milne, invited Possil YM down to Coventry for a game at U-16 level. Needless to say, Possil won the game easily, prompting Gordon Milne to ask if he could sign the whole team after the game!

When it was later discovered that Assistant Manager, Ron Wylie, was an ex-Possil lad, a successful partnership was formed.

During this period, Coventry City FC signed John Hendrie – who went on to a very successful career. Others such as John Joyce, Grant Reid and Jim Leonard did not sign for various reasons, nevertheless it was a good partnership where many friendships were formed which have lasted to this day.

Bobby is one of the 'good guys' in football who never had a bad word to say about any of his players. When asked about any of them he would always answer, "Yes, he's a good player!".

John Rice

I went to Possilpark YMCA as a shy thirteen to fourteen-year-old lad; not knowing what to expect! I needn't have worried – Bobby put me at ease immediately with his friendly and welcoming manner and I soon felt part of the club. I progressed through the next couple of years with the help and guidance of Bobby and also playing alongside a terrific group of obviously talented young lads assembled together by Bobby´s excellent judgment and knowledge of football.

Even though I eventually left Possil to sign for Arsenal and have a career as a professional, I have always remembered with fondness my time with Bobby and everyone at Possil and it is a true testament to his dedication that he continues to be involved in football to this day.

That is Bobby Dinnie.

Thanks for everything, Bobby.

John Woodward

I first met Bobby when I was about thirteen-years-old when a friend of mine took me to Possilpark YMCA for a game of football; we played at Perthshire Juniors´ park in a friendly on a Sunday morning.

It was the start of a few really enjoyable years playing football and mixing with a great group of lads who were involved at the YMCA

None of us would have had the opportunity to have enjoyed ourselves if it hadn´t been for the dedication of Bobby Dinnie. People like Bobby are the lifeblood of football and without them the professional game would not be what it is today and many of the lads that made a career out of football that played for Bobby at the YMCA would not have done so without the help of Bobby.

He was an influential figure for many lads who did not make a career out of football and who were also better people for having met and enjoyed the man who is, Bobby Dinnie.

Kenny Dalglish MBE

I have known Bobby since I was ten-years-old. Bobby played for the YMCA Juveniles before moving onto Greenock Juniors as a good left-winger.

This was around 1957. He then started to run the YMCA U-14s – U-18s. He brought in people to help him and things took off from there. They held jumble sales, washing cars et cetera to raise funds and took part in tournaments in Europe and America. Bobby also ran dances about once-a-month which were a great success; and that´s where my older sisters taught me to dance.

In these days we had a Sunday meeting and if you didn´t attend you didn´t play on a Saturday, this changed as time moved on. At these meetings we had different celebrities giving us a talk on football.

Bobby's teams were now on a rollercoaster; there were scouts from Arsenal, Chelsea and Rangers. All came to watch the trial games and the talent on show. I was asked to referee these games which I was delighted to accept with such good players on view. I remember one year in particular when at least seven players from the U-16s had signed for top teams in Scotland and in England. Also, the U-18s team had practically all their players snapped up by junior clubs at the end of the season.

In the sixties, everyone wanted to be a part of Possil YMCA. Bobby started social evenings and many workers from the White Horse Whisky Bond all joined in where we had pantomime at Christmas. The workers took part in Cinderella. We took the Cinderella panto to old folks' homes – they loved it. This was Bobby's way of giving something back to the community. He always wanted to help people and his advice was always good.

I stood at an U-14s game with Bobby and at one stage of the game his number 9 shouted at him to take off another player who allegedly made a bad pass. Bobby took the number 9 off instead. It was his strict discipline that earned respect.

He is so well-respected throughout the football world.

Malcolm MacDonald

As a keen nineteen-year-old playing football for the school team, one of the lads said one day: "Come a get a trial for Possil YM – you'll like it!" That was over thirty-eight years ago, and he was right!

When I was asked to offer some written thoughts as a contribution to a book on the life story of Bobby Dinnie, I was at first taken aback, but quickly felt privileged to do so.

Possil YM has had a great influence on me through the standards of commitment and performance expected of us all who were involved in the club – which over a great number of years has given me lifetime friendships through football as a medium. Bobby Dinnie set those standards.

If you are not familiar with Possilpark and you do not know of Possil YM, it is difficult to explain in a few words the community influence the club has had in the area.

As a player at the YM, you were allowed to go about your business in the area without interruption, such was the respect of the local people for the club and its achievements over the years.

Bobby and his staff of coaches, kit men, physios and general helpers created a competitive environment of high achievement from a wide group of young men, aged fourteen to eighteen, from all over the greater Glasgow area under the banner of Possil YM, and through the successes of the club over a long period of time provided the opportunity for a relatively large number of boys to have professional football careers.

The lads who made it were inspirations to those following in their footsteps and our ambitions were properly channelled by Bobby and his staff to breed a continuous will to win from the teams which the club seemed to produce in an almost production line basis.

When I arrived at the club, the players we were told about were Eddie Kelly, (Arsenal); Jimmy McGill, (Huddersfield); Johnny Hamilton, (Hibs and Rangers); and Tom McAllister, (Sheffield United and West Ham United). these are only a few of a very long line of players who succeeded in the professional ranks.

To be considered good enough to play for 'The YM' brought with it a certain kudos within the area and within youth football circles in the Glasgow area and wider afield. Scouts would regularly attend our matches on the look out for new talent and this high profile made you proud to be associated with the club.

Most of all, Bobby and his colleagues offered us a platform from which to develop as young adults with a sense of self respect through achievement and camaraderie by giving up their time to set the club up in a very professional manner.

Close associations with professional football clubs offered us opportunities to travel to tournaments throughout Scotland and into England, which in its day was a very big deal. At the time I arrived at the club, their relationship with Arsenal was coming to an end – but this was immediately replaced by a new association with Aston Villa which endured during my time there.

Stories of some of the trips away to play at Villa Park (Aston Villa) where Tommy Docherty was manager; Aberdeen for the Scottish YM cup-tie; the Cowal Games Tournament in Dunoon and the day we knocked Fairholme Thistle out of the Scottish Amateur Cup are all stories of legend and great memories. Names of pals at the club then: Gordon Dale, Jimmy McCuskey, Jim Gordon, Harry Curran and Dougie Friedman come easily to mind and the stewardship of Bobby, calmly pacing the touchline with Tommy Young and Johnny Hamilton training us bring a smile to my face on recollection. And as well as all of this, we could play a bit!

The competition for places was tough, but the sense of achievement and the rewards for being selected were high and we always had a great team spirit.

Some of the lads were outstanding players and went on to the professional ranks; the rest of us who could not make that step went on to play with junior clubs, but we all kept playing and that was as a result of the aspirations instilled in us by the influence of our families, friends and 'The YM'.

It is without doubt that the good practices, encouragement and sense of achievement grained through my experiences as a player with Possil YM have positively influenced my life and that Bobby Dinnie, who I consider to be a close personal and family friend, was fundamental in that experience.

Norrie McLeod

Some individuals get the opportunity to positively influence the lives of a few young men.

Very few individuals such as Bobby get the opportunity to positively influence the lives of many. However, with such opportunity comes great responsibility.

Bobby delivered on this responsibility year after year, and he did so in such a low-key manner. I remember the phrase often called out on a cold winter's night training: "Here comes Bobby Dinnie!" and immediately everyone was on their best behaviour. This was not because Bobby was one to raise his voice or chastise, but because he had earned the respect of all who knew him and played at Possil YMCA.

I had five fantastic years at Possil YMCA. Like all Possil teams we were successful and being successful can put a smile on many a young man's face. The core of these teams came from the north east of Glasgow but it was not a necessity. If you wanted to play for Possil then you were given a chance to prove that you were good enough. I played with some great team-mates back then and we stood or fell as one. We all wore the Possil jersey with pride. I'm sure that Bobby will be the first to say that he could not have done it alone, that through the years he was ably supported by a number of individual team managers who also gave their free time to Possil YMCA.

I would like to mention just three other managers that I had the pleasure to represent on the pitch. The first two were the 'dynamic' partnership of Brian Byrne and Jimmy Dinnie. They came from the Bobby Dinnie school of management and the words 'quietly effective' come to mind (although Jimmy was known to tell a referee or two what he thought of them). The third was a completely different character altogether. If you have ever done pre-season training on Benson's Hill then you will never forget wee Jim Pyott.

It is only with the ability to look back that one can properly appreciate what a positive contribution Bobby made to the lives of so many young men. At the time we were just a bunch of young men enjoying our football.

Robert Caven

What does Bobby Dinnie mean to me? A lifelong friend and mentor, a great community youth worker and a gentleman.

Bobby and I have lived in the Possilpark area of Glasgow all our lives. We have love and pride for the people of Possilpark in common and each of us has dedicated our time in making Possilpark a better place to live in.

My brother Danny Murray was the football link with Bobby. He was a player with Possil YMCA and later became one of the team managers. In the late 1970s Bobby had produced a first-class team of managers and up-and-coming football players. Due to their success they were invited to lots of tournaments held abroad in England and Germany and in Scotland such as the Cowal games in Dunoon; not simply one team, but four or five. Money became a problem and football mad men had no time for fund-raising. Bobby gently instructed his managers to find ladies (always the gentleman) who would take over the fund-raising aspect of the club, leaving the men to the production of great football teams. I was roped in to the fund-raising team and this became the start of four decades of community work. And what fun we had.

Bobby manages people by gentle persuasion. He encourages everybody who works with him without prejudice. He makes everything he accomplishes seem easy. Over the last forty years Bobby has mixed with the great and the good but on a local level he still remains Bobby Dinnie: Mr Possil YMCA.

Sadie Gordon

I am most grateful to Bobby Dinnie and Possil YM for giving myself and many other boys from Glasgow the opportunity to join a great institution – one of the top five or six clubs in Glasgow.

Bobby gave us a great education in terms of discipline, dedication, and respect; to respect your team-mates and to respect your opponents but most importantly to respect the adults and team managers who helped run the club.

I was very fortunate to be with the YM from U-14s to the U-21s. Bobby and his brother Jimmy organized the first trip for Possil YM to go to California; funded by the usual discos, raffle

tickets and jumbo sales. What a great experience for a bunch of sixteen-year-olds from the rougher side of town.

I can remember when I first signed. Bobby invited me up to his house in the great room with all the football memorabilia hanging on the walls. I said to myself this man must be important having the football jerseys of famous footballers. Well, he has been to thousands of prospective young players looking to make the grade.

I now live in Australia meeting many Scottish ex-players who all know or have heard about 'the great man'. We often speak about playing against the teams from outside of Glasgow and coming to play at the intimidating Closeburn Street – right in the middle of Possil.

Bobby, thanks for the privilege of knowing and playing for you.

Stephen Marley

I played for the juveniles at Possil YM but to be honest I wasn´t really going to go anywhere. I asked Bobby if I could help out with the running of the U-18s.

This was going back a bit, mind you, to the late 50s. Bobby, George Bloss, and I were responsible for the U-18s´ duties.

Jimmy (Bobby's brother) ran the U-16s with Alex Hosie. It was clear even then that the boys all loved Bobby. I remember a Scottish Cup semi-final involving us and a team up in Broughty Ferry. It was frozen, I still remember it; it was absolutely frozen and to make matters worse our goalkeeper, John Wright – who later went to Clyde – escorted a high ball over the bar, it was a shot or a cross that wasn't putting us in danger but John swung on the crossbar, sort of held onto it as the ball went over and the bar snapped. It took about an hour for a carpenter to come and fix it and we were all waiting around in the freezing cold... torture!

We did make the final where we beat Kilmarnock to lift the Scottish Cup.

On the day Scotland defeated England at Wembley in the famous 3-2 game we were at the match but before that we played Arsenals' youth team at Highbury and beat them. A double for the Scots you could say.

Bobby was a remarkable man, he bought boots for the ones who didn't have the funds for such items. Such was his generosity.

Tommy Douglas

* Tommy emigrated to Canada where he now lives with his wife Ann. He has three children: Colin, Graham and Lorraine.

I joined the YM just after their association with Arsenal had elapsed and the Aston Villa connection had begun.

I have distinct memories of my time at the club, One time in particular, Bobby commanded me to his house and I admit I thought I was in for some sort of ticking-off but to my surprise, Bobby presented me with the full Possil YM kit: the bag, the blazer and the tie. I felt like a million dollars. Most of the guys in our area didn't have two bob to their name but Bobby made us feel we were worth something. This rubbed-off on us on the park because I don't remember us even losing a cup final or many important league games.

A great cup-tie involving us and Kirktonholme – another great team, from East Kilbride – was another of my memories. I normally played on the wing but Bobby wanted me to play right back to mark a tricky and quick winger from their team. It worked, I had a great game and we won the cup.

Another momentous occasion for me was when we headed down to Villa Park to take part in a game against the Villa boys. I think the Aston Villa first team were playing Dunfermline in a pre-season game and we played prior to that match – in front of a large crowd. It was a fantastic experience to play at a top ground in front of that large crowd, so much so because some of the players in our team hadn't ventured as far away before. We were all just young players who grew up in the various housing estates in Glasgow. The Villa boys looked much bigger than us, in fact, they looked huge – but of course – in true Possil YM fashion – we beat them!.

Wes Greer

I was born and brought up in Auchinairn, Bishopbriggs, and knew of Bobby Dinnie in the early days of Possil YM.

Secondary juvenile football was dominated in the early 50s by Campsie Black Watch (Frank Haffey and Bobby Hume era) and then Possil came on the scene. Possil became the team and the star maker was Bobby Dinnie.

In 1986 I was promoted Superintendent and Emergency Planning Officer for Strathclyde Police and for the first time came to work in Police Headquarters. Although I had contact with Bobby through my divisional work at Springburn, Saracen and Maryhill, this is when I developed my friendship with Bobby Dinnie – whom at that time was in charge of all security related matters of visitors to Strathclyde Police Headquarters.

My duties at that time were geared around all emergencies

including Lockerbie. During this time very many important and political figures visited police headquarters and on every occasion Bobby was present to ensure smooth and discreet arrangements in and out of the building.

I have attended meetings in the Home Office and in the Foreign and Commonwealth Office in London where senior civil servants would always ask after him. In fact as late as November 2001 I attended a funeral in Liverpool when the same individuals (now retired) re-counted the memorable visits to Strathclyde Police HQ and of course Bobby was always mentioned.

Bobby Dinnie was very much an integral part of that important time in the development of Strathclyde Police.

I left the police in 1994 in the Rank of Chief Superintendent and was delighted when Bobby and Andy presented me with a personalized shield commemorating my retirement from from the police in 5/8/94.

On 1/9/94 I became the Security Advisor to the Scottish Football Association and after eleven and a bit years retired from looking after the Tartan Army in December 2005 (5/12/05)

I am still involved in the Scottish game as a Scottish Premier League Match Delegate and have responsibilities with UEFA as a member of their Security Panel and also as a UEFA Match Delegate.

My interest and involvement in football has allowed me to continue my friendship with Bobby Dinnie and when his name is mentioned in football circles I am proud to say I know him from football and from Strathclyde Police and that I was honoured to speak at his retirement dinner at the Scottish Automobile Club.

'Great' is an adjective that is used much too frequently and much too lightly of people and events. For Bobby Dinnie, however, nothing less will do. He is a great man who by his

character, personality and above all his human values has contributed so much to the development and careers of young footballers. I am privileged to call him a friend.
Willie McDougall

My association with Bobby goes back many years. I left Clydebank where my position involved working with their youth development scheme. I would join up with Bobby at St. Mirren FC in the late 80s.

I enjoyed my time there working with Bobby. We brought through some great young players: Martin McIntosh, Barry Lavety, John Hillcoat and Martin Baker to name but a few.

Bobby left St. Mirren and we met up again at Partick Thistle FC where again, we blossomed great young players like: Kenny Arthur, Allan Archibald and Martin Lauchlan amongst many others.

Bobby was great for me and he was, and still is to this day, a major help for which I will always be grateful. Bobby was always way ahead of his time with his vision of the game.

On a personal level he has been a truly great friend to myself and my family over many years; a friendship of substantial worth and priceless value.
Alastair MacColl

Bobby has played a huge part in my life; from my very early days as an up-and-coming promising youngster with Rangers; to when I finally turned professional with the Ibrox club. I then went on to enjoy a career with a variety of clubs thereafter.

What struck me most about Bobby: he was more than a football scout. He had this persona and aura about him and his honesty in assessing players really shone. His outlook and professionalism made him stand out amongst many and was so trustworthy in his word.

I left Rangers in 1989 after six years at the club and headed for Southampton. It was then, Bobby was at St. Mirren FC and he showed faith in my ability. I found my way to Love Street at his command and before long I was whisked to a tournament in Holland with the U-19s.

Bobby had faith in me and I believe he rated me as a player of worth. I had great belief and respect for him and I still do today. Bobby Dinnie seemed to float in and out of my life throughout my football career and was as instrumental in my career away from football.

Alex McEwan

I started my footballing career with Possil YMCA at eight-years-old. Mr Bobby Dinnie was good enough to give me a trial and I was signed.

Playing for the Possil YM was fantastic. Everyone who ran the club made you feel welcome and it was like being part of a large extended family.

The teams I played in were always challenging for trophies and we had some great players in Conga, Tosh, Geordie Gray and Tommy McAllister to name but a few.

I remember winning my first five-a-side trophy in the U-12 section, (Bobby Russell, who went on to sign with Glasgow Rangers) played in my team.

The club's youth team were invited to play at Highbury before the Arsenal v Tottenham game. This was amazing! We played in front of a crowd of 50,000 but we were beaten 4-1. I wasn't happy about that, but for a fourteen-year-old from Possilpark it was an experience I would never forget.

I signed for East Stirling when I was fifteen, my first senior club. I played with them for three years and then went on to play with Cambuslang Rangers and a few other junior clubs over the years.

My footballing career even took me to Australia for a few

years. I had just got married and the opportunity came to go, it seemed too good a chance to miss. We went to Melbourne. I played in two cup finals in the Olympic Stadium. I played with some fantastic players like former Manchester United player Tony Young – who had played alongside Bestie – my hero. Some of the other lads were former England Internationalist Martin Peters and Scotland's Eamonn Bannon.

When we came home I ended my playing days with Ashfield Juniors. Funnily enough, just along the road from where I started and under the management of a former Possil YM manager, Junior Semple – a lovely guy.

Apart from my dad – who came to all my games – the biggest influence in my career was Bobby Dinnie. He taught me a great deal about discipline on and off the field and I have a lot to be grateful to him for. Thanks to him giving me my chance I had some fantastic times playing the beautiful game that I am passionate about.

Alex Tulloch

When I started playing football for the local Church team, St Monica's, in Milton, it was always my ambition to play for Possil YMCA, run by Bobby Dinnie.

The 'YM' were held in such high regard because Bobby looked after everyone in all the teams; as they were all his own sons.

I remember how in awe I was of him whenever he came to games – he was the man: the 'Jock Stein of amateur football'. I remember a certain player by the name of Pat McGonigal, who played with me in my school team, used to talk about how well the Possil teams were ran, I was so jealous. Fortunately for me I was eventually picked for them (I think it was the lack of height that kept me back). I was so proud to run out in my Possil YM strip at Closeburn Street, 'The Fortress', as we called it.

Bobby was always on hand for a piece of advice if he saw something in your play that could be improved. He brought through so many good players that you always listened to what he had to say. The good thing about the YM was we were always in cup finals because you were playing with all the best players that Bobby had spotted and managed to persuade to come to the YM from the other local teams. Through Bobby's guidance, myself, Robert Fleck and Gary Robertson were selected for the Scottish Amateur select team that played against Ireland, which we won 1-0. I still have my cap to prove it.

I remember the good times at the YM; like when they took us to America for three weeks. My mum and dad were very proud that I played for the YM and organized a Ladies' and Gents' match at Cowlairs to raise money for the trip. My Uncle Ian won't forget that in a hurry: my Aunt Betty tackled him and broke his leg!

Saturday afternoons couldn't come quick enough for me. I was so proud to catch a bus down to Possil; carrying my Possil YM hold-all with my boots in it. About four or five of us would meet up and travel together and we all became friends, although we all lived in different areas. That was the beauty of it all: playing for Possil YM.

I got my first move to Dumbarton whilst playing for the U-21s. I thought my chance had passed by this age but Bobby always told me to have faith in my ability. Something I preach to my players to this day. Bobby laid the foundation of a decent career with the advice I received from him when I was young. He installed discipline, respect, manners and most of all hard work and honesty for which I will always be grateful. My career has taken me to many clubs including Hearts, St. Johnstone, Dunfermline, Livingston, Airdrie, Partick Thistle, Queen of the South and Morton. I've tried to remember the advice Bobby gave me all those years ago and to hopefully pass it on. Now, the manager of Stirling Albion, I realize how much an influence a manager can have on young players trying to make it in football and I will be eternally grateful that I learned at a young age from one of the best.

Allan Moore

I've known Bobby for over thirty years. My son, Ian, played for the famous Possil YMCA from the age of twelve right through the various age groups until he was seventeen.

During his playing days I attended a number of games involving the various teams. I became friendly with Bobby, the general manager, and have remained friends ever since. Bobby is a true gentleman in every sense and all those who know him look up to him as a true sportsman. His philosophy on life is obviously "always play the game". Ian learned a lot from Bobby which obviously stood him in good stead during his life and as a Principal Physical Education Teacher.

The dressing room before games – where you had about fourteen boys all on a high – all talking at the one time – laughing and joking. Enter Bobby, who would stand, not utter a word and silence would descend on the room. All the time I've known Bobby I've never heard him raise his voice.

After his entrance he would inspect all the players and make sure their football shirts were tucked into their shorts and socks properly pulled up. Boots were given a thorough inspection, no excuses given. Dirty boots, with an explanation from the offending player, had been playing for the school team that morning and had no time to clean them made no difference to Bobby. "You will find boot cleaner in the kit bag and I'll be back in five minutes time and your boots will be clean." The player's boots were properly cleaned on Bobby's return.

An incident I will always remember: the team was about to

leave the dressing room ready for the game when one of the players shouted: "Let´s get into this mob!" The player was taken aside and told in no uncertain manner that no team will be referred to as a 'mob'.

That was Bobby´s respectful attitude he had for any opponents of Possil YMCA.

A very respectful gentleman.

Bill McMurray

IN CONVERSATION

In conversation with Alex Forsyth

MY MEMORIES OF POSSIL YM go way back to around 1966-67 when I played for a school team in Baillieston. Bobby and other Possil YM members obviously heard about me and invited me for training at Possil YM. Of course, I wanted to better myself outside of school team football. A couple of nights per week training (I believe it was a Monday and Thursday evening) with Possil YM were great for me, the training was superb, we were trained properly and we were respected.

It was a good time for my career because my father wanted me to go into football and Possil, along with Bobby, gave me this great incentive to gain and if I did have ability it would allow me to go on and prove myself. I will always remember the people at the club. The training was first-class and everyone at the club was superb. We even had a doctor at the club to look after you. The kit was spot on and you had to behave yourself; I always did anyway. The club even gave my wee mate Willie a trial. Willie was a wee outside-right for the school team. It was a long way for me to travel and Willie was good company for me on these travels to the club. He was also a nice wee player.

I left my house at around 6.00pm on training evenings to get to the club for 7.30pm. It was what I wanted to do, to prove myself. I wanted to be there and to see if if I was good enough to become a player. The enthusiasm was there and I thoroughly enjoyed it.

I was paid half-a-crown for my expenses. That was enough for my travel and a fish supper at Buchanan Street Station; sometimes I'd manage to throw in a Mars bar as well if the doctor of the club gave us a lift and that saved money. My parents encouraged me too and they thought the world of Bobby. They were always at me to behave, look after myself and always made a point to see how my football was progressing; they showed great interest.

After a year or two at Possil I had the chance to go to Arsenal for training. I remember going down there with Possil as a team where we played the Arsenal youth team at Highbury in front of 40,000. They had a lot of good Scottish boys playing for the first-team at that time like George Graham, Ian Ure, Frank McLintock, Joe Baker and of course our own boys like Eddie Kelly, Jack Carmichael, John Corr, Jim McGill and John Woodward. A lot of the first-team players at Arsenal were good to us too like Pat Rice and Bob Wilson. George Graham came from my hometown and he'd always ask how I was getting on.

Little did I know I would be invited to Arsenal to play for the youth team. Eventually I would find my way to Partick Thistle where Scott Symon was the manager. I had a trial down at Dumbarton and Mr Symon instructed me to come in the next day where I signed. That would be 1967-68 season. I played for a few years at Thistle then I signed for Man United in 1972. I enjoyed almost seven years at Old Trafford before heading up north again to Ibrox then had spells with Motherwell, Accies and a couple of years at junior level.

The important thing in my career would always go back to Possil YMCA. The stability, the professionalism, the enthusiasm, the discipline and the people involved at the club were absolutely fantastic. They looked after you. You had to do what you were told; you really had to toe-the-line otherwise you wouldn't be there for too long. The people who ran the club always looked out for you. I'll never ever forget those people and the club and we always used to say that Mr Bobby Dinnie was Mr Possil YM.

Possil had players all over the place. Everywhere you went; whether it was Dundee United, Partick Thistle, wherever, you only had to look at the books to see where the players came from. The name of Possil cropped up everywhere. That tells you what the YM was and it started the careers of many players. I would say that every footballer that started at the YM has done well and have the greatest respect for the club, for Bobby and for the family.

Of course, I had a great start myself at the club. It was run properly, I never had any problems; even travelling into Possil; which was a tough area. I never encountered one ounce of bother with anyone. Everybody had respect for anyone who worked with Possil YM and they were one of the best amateur teams in Scotland; if not the best; and it all boils down to Bobby Dinnie.

It has been a pleasure to have known Bobby, he started my off my football career and I´ll never forget Mr Possil, Bobby Dinnie.

Alex Forsyth

* Alex Forsyth enjoyed a great career north and south of the border. He was a terrific player and servant to the many clubs he represented and another one of Possil YM´s greatest sons. His dedication and attitude to the professional game would no doubt be a superb asset for any youngster hoping to carve out a career in football today. Alex kindly gave his interview without any notes or preparation; such is the man´s honesty. He is also an icon and another of the city´s legends.

The Scout: *The Bobby Dinnie Story*

In conversation with Bob Smith

IT'S STRANGE WHEN your son or daughter asks you, "Were you any good as a player when you were young, daddy?" And then a laugh comes on to your face as you remember some funny things that roll into your mind; sadly, not football skills but more the many pranks and incidents that you were part of, or the instigator of.

It gives me great delight to be able to recount some of the stories associated with Possil YM and the man behind the very significant impact – not just in a football sense – but in the shaping and directing of so many young lives of boys who listened and learned from the perfect gent, Bobby Dinnie.

It was a strange introduction for me to the team, playing for them in one hand but also being in a unique situation where I was working in the local rent office. Now, in this area of Possilpark – often tagged with hardship – there was a certain respect, maybe even fear, that you had a somewhat even small influence in working in the local housing office, albeit in a lowly role and maybe aware of some of the issues facing some of my team-mates´ parents.

Relating to this working life I recount a few stories which emanated from this involvement and how two paths of work met and maybe, just maybe, would change my life and make me become a professional footballer---Oh God! If that could only have happened.

Story 1.

My first position within the housing department was as a repairs clerk and my role was to take a list of repairs from the tenants – once they paid their rent. One particular incident comes to mind when Bobby informed all the teams that the YM were fund-raising and the best way to do this was to hold a jumble sale. This meant all the boys were to muck in with their support. However, I came up with a novel idea that when tenants were asking me to sort out their repairs I could, at the same time, enquire if they had any spare jumble in their house and we would pick it up.

This idea snowballed somewhat as Bobby and his other team managers could not cope with the demand I had engendered with this slick way of getting jumble in by merging my day job with my football life. It worked a treat and my recollection is that the monies raised by the YM was the highest ever recorded through the cheek and some would say enterprise of a young Mr Smith, aged 16-years-old.

Story 2.

Working coincidentally with me in the housing department was a gentleman called Doug MacDonald, who was secretary of the Glasgow YMCA and who unfortunately had MS as a muscle wasting illness. Dougie had to get around the office using a walking stick or a zimmer but showed great perseverance to fight against this disability and was a great football supporter, both in the work he done in supporting young lads but also in his interest in following Glasgow Rangers FC.

To assist Dougie with his disability he was fortunate to own a three-wheeler car which was specially for individuals like him that were physically disabled. One evening Rangers were playing at Firhill against Partick Thistle just along the road from our office, where we were working late one night. I had picked up from Dougie that he was intending to go to the game and enquired if I could go with him in his wee special three-wheeler, which at best was only equipped to transport him alone, never mind a strapping 16-year-old boy. Once the boss had popped off he shouted to me, "Are you ready?"

Quickly, and without a second thought, I jumped in, squeezing Dougie ever so tightly and presuming all was well in terms of the door was securely closed for safety reasons – my own!

No sooner had the invalid car – to give its proper name, turned round the first corner, yours truly duly fell out of the car and started to roll down the hill. Poor Dougie didn´t know whether to laugh or cry as I was soaked to the skin, my clothes were torn and my hands were bleeding as I attempted to save myself and my blushes.

But that incident was only the start of things for poor Dougie as he learned that the young Mr Smith was indeed quite a handful. The game itself was neither here nor there but dotted along the track at any big game in the 60s you saw a procession of light blue invalid cars like Dougie´s. Now, for the laugh of a lifetime (Dougie´s words, not mine), I was sitting on a small three-legged chair beside Dougie and was deemed to be a helper but generally there should only have been Dougie there himself.

Anyway, the ball went out for a throw-in and got stuck under Dougie´s car. Making a quick headway to us was wee Willie Henderson, a brilliant winger with Rangers, who was desperate to retrieve the ball and get on with the game. But, young Smith, the cheeky upstart, got there first, lifted the ball to his hands and started to do a keepy-uppy display that any Rangers player would be proud of. Wee Willie wasn´t pleased – he was keen to get on with the game but the crowd were howling and in stitches at this cheeky but funny action of the helper to the invalid motor passenger.

The story wasn´t quite yet finished as I was spoken to by the stewards in front of all the crowd and given a tongue-lashing with fingers being pointed. Needless to say, this was the red flag to the bull as the crowd turned on the steward and began to sing at the top of their voices, *"Oh! Spot the looney!"* I never attended another football game with Dougie and that was the nearest I ever got to being a team-mate of a Rangers player.

Story 3.

Still, my involvement with working in the housing department refused to go away and again, maybe, just maybe, could help to influence my football career. One day, out of the blue, I received a phone-call from Bobby asking me to turn up early at our annual venue, the Glasgow Pavilion, when we had an away game. Looking at my football career maybe had I known, I should have been better going inside the theatre and letting real players get on with their game. However, I received this call from Bobby and it sounded rather urgent. He wanted me to meet with him and wait for it---Joe Hill, the mighty Arsenal scout, who had so much clout in wooing young hopefuls down to England and as you will read in other chapters, becoming mighty successful footballers.

At last my prayers were being answered, this was me on the way to becoming a legend: Robert Smith of Arsenal, yes it sounded rather good. I never slept the night before, heading balls, scoring important goals and dreaming of becoming famous. Next morning I was up at the shot-of-dawn and quickly focused on my life-changing meeting. I met with Bobby and Joe and it got even better when Joe asked Bobby to leave the two of us. My heart was pounding as Joe asked how I was keeping and was I enjoying my football? Any time now he would reveal the next move about Arsenal, surely. The hammer-blow of hammer-blows. Joe said, "Son, I know from Bobby that you work in the housing department. Any chance you could speak on my sister´s behalf to your boss to see if she could get a bigger house in the area?" My face dropped and so did my heart---yes, that was the closest I probably got to signing for the almighty Gunners.

But how, that at that time, the insignificant job I had with the local housing department, little did I realize the role it would play in a strange and humorous part in my life and also that of Possil YM´s Bobby Dinnie.

Story 4.

Playing for Possil YM provided me with the chance of going down to England on tour to play against other English youth sides. We were housed in the local London YMCA where young Smith encountered a bit of fun---or challenge.

One morning, going for breakfast and standing at the self-service part of the catering suite, I looked at the man standing beside me and the more I stared the more inquisitive I became. I said (rather loud) to my team-mate that I am sure I know the man standing next to me and that he was also famous. Just at that, he turned round and smiled and spoke in his own imitable way. I was standing next to the famous comedian, Frankie Howard, who spanned the next two decades and here was I, a wee boy from Maryhill, mixing with the famous. Frankie spoke at length with me, kidding and joking; even asking me my name. That evening he shouted my name in the foyer and asked me about the game that afternoon. I was fair chuffed that a famous personality knew me personally and again next morning in the catering suite he joked with me ten-to-the-penny.

These stories were a great and favourite part of my life and only when I look back and ponder on the impact and the influence played in it by Bobby did you really appreciate the role he has played for so many in shaping young men to follow Christian virtues but also contributing greatly to building their self-esteem and confidence.

I am always eternally grateful to 'Mr Possil' for his wonderful blessing and interest and now working in a local authority – heading a sports team – out gigging in pubs and clubs, playing music and comedy spots, then clearly his early promptings have worked out brilliantly for me.

Once a showman, always. I strayed into working as a commentator for radio and television, covering all the major football games...and guess who's one of our avid listeners?

Yes, the wee boy from Maryhill has done not too bad for himself, due in no small way to the man with the MBE gong and I share great pride on his well-deserved achievements.

Bob Smith

* Bob Smith is an all-rounder in the entertainment circles. Famous for his distinctive commentary voice and frequent on Radio Clyde. He was also Commercial Manager for two professional clubs: Partick Thistle and Morton respectively.

In conversation with Norrie McKay

I BUMPED INTO a good friend of mine, Johnny Wyles, in Saracen Street. He asked me what I was doing with myself. He asked me to go down to the YM and I was pleased to see so many faces that I knew when I arrived at the YM. This was going back a bit; decades.

I wanted to be a part of the club right away and I was met by Bobby Dinnie, who came over to introduce himself to me. After that I was determined to have a go. I attended training, where Bobby was always present, taking the training himself. I enjoyed it, the training was great; strict but great. I played on the Saturday after my first initial training sessions and I never looked back after that.

My highlight playing for the YM was winning the cups that we won, winning the league three years running and being selected for Scotland U-18s v Ireland. Soon after there were a number of teams interested in me but I made my way to Arsenal for trials. I put up a good show and I was told there was a good chance I was going to sign. Neil Leven was there at Highbury. I came home and signed for Rob Roy and at the same time Chelsea showed interest. Bobby Dinnie gave me a right telling off and I do regret it. I should have listened to the people who knew. I was by this time in pain with a knee injury.

I played for fun and I found the game to be easy; well, the way I played anyway. I was comfortable on both my right and left side. Bobby said I had talent, a unique player he would say and he told me that I personally didn´t think how good a player I was; I just played the game as I felt.

What the YM did for me was gave me discipline. I left the YM with more discipline than what I had when I first went there. I made a good life for myself thanks to the YM. The YM held concerts that were great for the people and of course brought in much needed cash to run the club and the hall to a standard that was required for a club like the YM. I sang but not with music; music put me off; I sang on my own and didn´t need any backing at all. 'Moon River' and 'When I fall in love' were the titles I sang. It was great, all the people like Rita and Nan who did great work in keeping the hall clean including the one-and-only sink we had.

I´d love to go back forty-odd years and start all over again. I loved walking down to Bardowie Street where Bobby´s dad would be hanging out the window and we´d have a great natter with each other. It was like a family concern. He was also an incredible guy and he´d invite me up and we´d sit at his fireplace where he would offer me great advice; where I was going wrong but just as importantly what I was doing right. Bobby´s brother Jimmy often said to me, "Norrie, I don´t think you realize how good you actually are." I didn´t because I had so many great players around me.

One time we were due to play a game but the referee was threatening to call the game off due to the mist. The game was on and Bobby instructed me to play outside-left. I couldn´t believe it but I didn´t answer back, I just got on with it and I scored six goals that day.

I have a couple of years to go before my retirement and I´m looking forward to spending time with my wife.

To sum it all up I would like to say a big thank you to Bobby and the good people I met in the club.

Norrie McKay

FROM THE DRESSING ROOM AND BEYOND

(Part Three)

In the mid 60s every young boy in Possilpark wanted to play football and the only team to play for was the YM. As well as being an extremely successful team, many of the players went on to play football at the very highest level in Scotland, England and abroad. Obviously they had the talent and ability but just as important was the help and guidance they got from Bobby Dinnie.

Billy Whyte

I can remember as though it was yesterday, the first game I ever refereed after passing my referee's examination way back in 1961. Possilpark YMCA v Sandyhills YMCA at U-16 level in St Augustine's school in the North of Glasgow. In charge of the Possilpark team was Bobby Dinnie and playing for Possil was one Kenny Dalglish. Possilpark were one of the very top teams at this level and as I progressed in the YMCA league our paths crossed many times. Just after I was promoted to class 1, I was asked to go with Possilpark to an international tournament in Oneonta – just outside New York. It was a brilliant competition in all aspects; the standard of play was superb and each competing team had to have a referee in their party. Possilpark reached and won the final in a wonderful match against St Louis. This began a long friendship with Bobby and his family which continues to this day.

As our paths continue to cross (although our roles in the game have changed somewhat), it has been a privilege to know him for some forty-five years in a sport where total dedication and integrity are not always easy to find.

Brian McGinlay

I first met Bobby after he phoned me to say that he was interested in bringing my son, Justin, into the Rangers coaching set-up.

What followed has been a truly enjoyable and rewarding relationship. Bobby is the complete gentleman. He has an incredibly self-effacing personality and never brags about all he has achieved in the game. To discover (after much probing) that he had been so intimately involved in the nurturing of the young Kenny Dalglish among others was a typically significant fact that he chose not to volunteer. That he was wounded in action during the Korean War was another.

Bobby has an over-riding belief that football ability is only one part of the equation when developing the complete young footballer. Just as important to him are manners, education and personality. He takes a very special interest in the progress of those he discovers. Apart from during a period of ill-health, Bobby attended every one of Justin's training sessions, even in the most appalling weather. I cannot thank him enough for this and the total faith he displayed in my son's potential.

He once described Justin as possessing natural ability he had not seen in a boy for many years. From a man of Bobby Dinnie's stature, that really is a compliment to treasure.

Danny McBryan

Bobby is a man of dignity and integrity who is always available to help at anytime. I am now a scout at Celtic Football Club but I have to confess that Bobby helped me along my path by passing on his knowledge.

Even as far back as the Possil YMCA days he was a person I always admired and respected and could approach for advice. Kenny Dalglish was only one of the many individuals Bobby

nurtured and helped. Not only does he have an eye for spotting talent but his leadership is superb.
Eddie McCulloch

Bobby Dinnie is the main reason Possil YMCA is known and respected countrywide.

He has done so much for football and his community that he fully deserves any recognition he receives. He is also a true gentleman.
Gary McSwegan

Having left behind the successful years at Possil YMCA to play in both South Africa and Australia, I have made a point of keeping in touch with Bobby and to this day remain indebted for the direction in my life that he installed in me as a teenager.
Gerry Walker

Whenever I think of Bobby Dinnie I always smile.

I don´t wish to speak about Bobby´s vast length of time in football as there will be far more and better qualified people than me who will be able to do that in abundance, I would like to talk about 'The Man´, his kindness, sense of humour, humility, dignity, loyalty, and professionalism.

I first met Bobby many years ago whilst coaching at Partick Thistle FC; although his reputation had preceded him long before that. I was totally in awe of him during our first meeting, however, his interpersonal skills shone through and he made me feel so comfortable and at ease. I personally learned so much from him by watching, listening and just being in his company. Bobby has the wonderful knack of remembering faces and names and is blessed with a great memory which is just as well because the amount of people who would approach him to say, "I played with Possil YMCA forty years ago," and Bobby could tell them what position and their team-mates: frightening.

I have never in all the time I have known him ever heard him say a bad word about anyone or heard anyone speak badly of him. I am honoured to be asked to contribute to Bobby's book and more importantly to be regarded as a friend.

Graham Diamond

Vivid memories flood back to me when I think of my time as a player with the great Possil YMCA.

I was very fortunate to play at a great club and under the great Bobby Dinnie. It was there I inwardly inherited the nickname 'Toshack' at the club; which was surrounded by quality players and great characters so nick-names were bound to be ten-a-penny.

There was another player in the team that was famous in our community: Laddie, my dog, who would dawn Possil team gear and was actually not a bad player.

Bobby had this unique way of talking to his players and in particular he always managed to rope myself into collecting jumble sale material for our fund-raising events. He had this sort of sliver tongue, if you like, and an uncanny way of talking players round – even the most brazen members of the club, like myself.

Discipline was a major factor at the club and it was normal that Bobby would visit or contact our households just to verify we were in bed early before match-days. It wasn't punishment, it was a code of conduct we had to adhere to as young players and when you look at the success of the club you can see that sort of discipline played a big part in it.

Bobby's brother, Jimmy, was also a big influence in and around the club and all the players and the community had total respect for both of them. They were father-figures within the club and that didn't end when the football stopped; they took their spirited methods outside the game and injected great belief into the heart of the community.

I recall when we were due to play in a cup-tie, a couple of us were refused half-fair on the bus because the conductor didn´t believe we were travelling juveniles – under the age that qualified us for adult fair exemption. Probably rightly so as we had facial growth – even at such a young age. The team we were due to play against also protested as they didn´t believe we were the right age for participation.

It goes without saying that I have the greatest respect for Bobby Dinnie. He was my mentor and I would put him in the same lines as my own father.

Harry Curran

In the current climate of professional sport it is quite unusual to come across a true gentleman.

Bobby Dinnie is one of that rare breed. He is a man whose word is his bond. He is a man who has a rare talent for spotting top quality potential in his sport of football. I have known Bobby for a number of years and in my time in sport never have I come across a man who quietly and professionally gets on with the job. As I understand he took a young man to Rangers; who turned him down…!

Chief Scout Jimmy Smith – ex-centre-forward for Rangers; after promising he would take Kenny, came to Bobby and said he´d decided not to take Kenny on as he was slightly 'hippy' around the waist and won´t become any faster.

Rangers´ loss was Celtic´s gain – the man Kenny Dalglish went on of course to become one of Scotland´s greatest ever players and of course he went on to be a Liverpool legend. Kenny may well have made it under his own steam but my experience of sport has shown talent disappearing because they were not in the right place at the right time and perhaps more important they did not have a believer. Bob Dinnie was a believer. If I were chairman of a football club I would want

him on my scouting staff...lang may his lum reek!.
Ian Doyle

Our boys' club team in Anderston was connected to St Johnstone – who were then managed by Alex Totten. Bobby joined us together and it turned out to be a very fruitful partnership.

Bobby gave young players the chance to step up in the game. A real good opportunity awaited the ones who were good players and many of them would not have made it if it wasn't for him.
Ian Ramsay

I have a long association with Bobby – going back many years. Bobby Dinnie and Gerry Marley were two men who often brought young players through their respected youth systems.

Bobby indeed has made an outstanding contribution to the game and he has always been a gentleman, in and out of football.
Jack Steedman

* Jack Steedman was a former Possil YMCA player and later made a substantial contribution to the Scottish game.

I joined Possil YM U-16s with my mate, Kenny Dalglish.

Our team included myself, Kenny, Johnny Hamilton, Eddie Kelly and Gerry O'Brien to name but a few. These young boys from ordinary working class backgrounds went on to make a name for themselves in the game. Most probably because of their exceptional talent, their obvious love for football and maybe the fact that they played for arguably the best team in Glasgow, run by Mr Bobby Dinnie.

No need to tell you what Kenny achieved in the game. As for myself, I was a professional for fifteen years representing the following clubs: Queen of the South, Alloa, Arbroath, Brechin, and Dumbarton. I would probably never have achieved this had I not had the good grounding that Bobby and Possil YM gave me.

Everyone in those days loved to train and play for the YM. Even our parents were proud that we were Possil YM players and I remember my dad and Kenny´s dad bringing oranges and bovril to matches for the players. Speaking of generations of players and fathers, my own son, Barry, now plays for Forfar Athletic and Kenny´s boy, Paul, recently enjoyed spells with Livingston and Hibernian.

Bobby Dinnie was Possil YM, it has to be said. He ran the club with great passion and passed on his knowledge, expertise and generated enthusiasm. On behalf of all the boys I hope none of us ever let you down, Bobby, because you certainly didn´t let us down…that´s for sure.

Jim Donald

I first met Bobby when I played a few years for the senior YMCA team following recovery from a bad knee injury.

At that particular time there were a number of teams at Possil YM run by various people but generally overseen by Bobby – but in a manner you still felt the 'boss'. The social activities were excellent – dances, concerts, pantomimes and visits to the elderly, with Christmas visits to hospitals. It was at one of those dances that I met my wife and we´ve been happily married for forty-five years.

The year we got married we had a second honeymoon in Jersey together – with 75% of my team – plus Bobby. It was typical of the spirit within Possil. It was during that holiday that Bobby asked me to run his senior team (on a short term basis). I did sign on a 'short term basis' – and enjoyed ten very successful years.

As a team we were very successful, winning trophies every

one of those years. We also played a number of friendlies from amateur teams in Sheffield and a Luton youth select; enjoying success on each occasion. A number of my players over the years had the opportunity to step up to junior and even senior level. Some did, but quite a few were happy to stay at Possil YM. It was a measure of the esteem we all had in Bobby. He was never demanding, never arrogant but always helpful when needed.

It came to a point when I had to make a difficult decision. I was also a very keen golfer and by 1970 I was on the threshold of being selected to play for Scotland. I missed out on that occasion but I decided to put 100% into representing my country the following year. I spoke to Bobby and as usual he was very understanding. I advised that I had two former players who would be willing to take over the running of the team. The change over was very smooth and Possil YM continued on its winning ways.

It is a part of my life I hold very dearly, knowing Bobby and being associated with Possil YM was a wonderful experience and being a friend of Bobby Dinnie MBE is part of our family.

Bobby Dinnie *is* Possil.

I did get to represent my country at golf when I was capped for Scotland in 1972.

Jim Hay

I first met Bobby in 1969 as a young boy who wanted to play for the best team in Glasgow.

After a trial game, Bobby asked me to sign on – not knowing that this relationship was to last and develop to the present day.

Some of my memories about Bobby and the individuals I met whilst at the Possil YMCA are funny and some not so funny.

Soon after signing for Possil YM we were due to play a team

from Ayr, in the Scottish Cup – away from home. The team travelled by mini-bus and a coach was hired for supporters – mainly family members of our team. This was exciting for me, I asked my father and uncle if they would like to travel to see me play for my new team, I was so excited because they said yes. On the day of the game we were to meet at the YMCA hall in Denmark Street, Possilpark. My father and uncle went for a small dram in the local ale-house before travelling. It was nearly time for the buses to leave when I noticed my father and uncle had not arrived. I ran round the corner, into the pub, to tell them the bus was leaving and they had to hurry or they would miss the bus and the chance to see me playing for the Possil YM. I was so proud. When we arrived at Ayr something was telling me that all was not right. The players were told to go out and inspect the park I was told, "Jim, you stay here." The management wanted a word with me. It came as a shock to me to be told I was to be dropped from the team, as someone told Bobby they had seen me leaving the pub and I must have been drinking before the game. I had some explaining to do about trying to get my father and uncle out of the pub so they could see me play. Fortunately my explanation was accepted but I was told under no circumstances was I to go near a public house again; if I wanted to continue my career as a player with Possil YM

During my time with Possil YM U-18s, which I loved every minute of, we were to play our U-16s in a friendly. This was always a competitive game and the U-16s were always up for it – to beat their elders and peers. There was a young boy playing who had signed for Glasgow Rangers. Bobby Russell was his name, the stories were circulating that this small slim boy was something special. Scouts were always at Possil YM games and this was no exception, even though it was a friendly, the talent spotters were out. Guess what, I was against this special kid, Robert Russell, and there was no way I was going to allow him to make a fool of me on the park. Twenty minutes into the game and you could see he was a player and a crunching tackle from yours truly was to follow to let him know I don't play friendlies. Minutes later I was substituted, the reason given was to give some of the fringe players a game.

Bobby Russell went on to have a successful career with Rangers and Bobby Dinnie's sons were to be named Robert and Russell.

After playing semi-professional in the junior grade for a few years, due to injury, I started coaching with Possil´s youth club, who were a successful U-21 team; which my brother was involved in running. Bobby asked if I could run an U-21s for Possil YMCA. This I did, as I loved the YM and had so much respect for Bobby.

When I was manager of the U-21s, Bobby asked if I would like to take the team to Germany and compete in a European tournament. Yes! was the answer. We fund-raised for around a year. Bobby told us the transport was arranged, and would leave Possil YMCA at 9.00pm on the departure date. This was exciting times for me, my players and our U-18s; who were also travelling with us, to play in a tournament for their age group. The Press were there to see the group leave. The players with their Possil ties and Possil football bags. This is what life is all about, was my opinion. Bobby said to me, "Jim, you´re in charge, all the best, and come back with the European Cup. Keep up the good name of Possil YMCA." were his last words. The bus left Denmark Street, we had around a twenty hour journey in front of us, to reach Frankfurt in the then West Germany. The bus driver took a wrong turning at George´s Road, into a new housing estate, which was a dead end. A shout from the players was, "We´re not even out of Possil and the driver has got us lost." I tried to explain it was just a small mistake and we should still reach our destination on time, not to worry. Thirty-six hours later we were still on the road – although nearly at our destination point. The driver had got 'lost in France', and we were refused access at three border fronts, to proceed into Belgium. Despite all this the U-21s won the tournament and also beat professional side Rot Weiss in a friendly game afterwards.

I can´t thank Bobby enough for guiding me through life. He has always been a father-figure to myself and thousands of other young hopefuls who wanted to have a career in football. Bobby was always there, willing to listen and give good advice to all. During my time managing Possil YM – which lasted approximately ten years, I was asked if I would be interested in running my local youth club in Balornock, (Brunswick Youth Club). This was a new challenge for me, which I did not think I could do, as it involved working with all age groups; toddlers through to senior citizens of the local community. I was to be employed full time as a Project Coordinator running a voluntary organization community centre; this was all new to me. Twenty-three years later and I am still involved at the Brunswick Centre and have been employed by Glasgow City Council for seventeen years as a Community Education Worker.

I will always be grateful for the sound advice and encouragement Bobby gave me then, to take the opportunity, as in his opinion, I would make a good community leader.

My wife, Anne organized a surprise 50th birthday party for me four years ago in the Brunswick Centre. Guess who I met there? Bobby Dinnie and his wife, Betty.

Thanks for everything Bobby.

Jim Pyott

I first met Bobby Dinnie around 1953-54 when I was a young boy playing for Possil YMCA youth team.

Bobby was playing for the senior team then – a very highly respected player, and with his great communication skills, can remember just how welcoming he made everyone feel during our training nights in Denmark Street hall.

Through Bobby Dinnie, Possil YMCA has become renowned throughout the UK for producing players; having developed them from a very young age.

Speaking from a personal point-of-view, through Possil YMCA, I went on to play professional football with Partick Thistle and Ayr United, playing also in America, Germany and Canada.

Possil YMCA and Bobby Dinnie not only produced footballers, but had a great effect on character building and Christian values within the club.

I am very proud to be a friend of Bobby and his dear wife Betty – two wonderful people.

Jimmy Ross

Bobby Dinnie? What a cracking guy!

What he did for the people of Possilpark is incredible. The team he developed, Possil YMCA, had some terrific players of outstanding quality. Everyone knew the likes of Kenny Dalglish and Johnny Hamilton but there were a number of top-class players under Bobby's wing that made a name for themselves in the game.

Bobby was something else, a one-off, unique. I didn't think I was good enough but Bobby pushed me with an enormous amount of positive encouragement; I think he favoured the underdog, if you ask me.

I was in and out of the team and I never really felt I was good enough to merit a place among all the other class players but Bobby reassured me I would get a chance if I just hung in there. He was right. There is a famous photo taken by the media titled 'The Golden Boys of Possilpark' and Bobby insisted that I be in the picture with the other lads.

John McColligan

* John McColligan is acclaimed for scoring against the famous Lisbon Lions during his spell with Clyde FC.

From growing up in the sticks in Kirkintilloch and playing for Lennoxtown Boys´ Club, the name of Possil YM always had a certain aura about it.

As a result, I jumped at the opportunity of having a trial match at fourteen-years-old. However, there was a slight problem; I was on holiday with my parents in Arisaig, but this was a chance not to be missed. As it turned out, the monster rail round-trip turned out to be one of the most important journeys in my career.

Before long I realized Bobby was 'Mr Possil'. Respected like no other, by players, parents, coaches, officials, opposing teams and of course football scouts. Bobby´s YM set many a player onto bigger and better things. I'm sure my nineteen years as a pro, south of the border, wouldn't have been achieved without my grounding at Possil.

Within months I was on trial at Coventry. Bobby´s vision created the link to the Sky Blues. I enjoyed my football immensely at Possil and stayed until I signed apprentice for Coventry.

Bobby, Eric Walker – a special man to me, often said: "Bobby´s a gent and one in a million."

You certainly are, and after everything you have put into the game, you deserve all the plaudits. Thanks, Bobby.

John Hendrie

I was ten-years-old when Bobby invited me to Possil YMCA.

Bobby actually took the time to come to my house and meet my parents to invite me to join his club. Obviously I felt honoured and I admit I was a little bit nervous having the 'great' Mr Dinnie sitting there talking to me and my parents and making it clear he wanted me in his team. It was an honour and a moment I will never forget.

It was his way of doing things. He was so respectful and it made you feel you were worth a place in his plans and it was a great feeling; especially being so young, to be asked to play for a great team under a great man.

You didn´t just join a football team when you signed for Possil YMCA – you were invited to Mr Dinnie´s house where he and his wife Betty always made you feel very welcome and it really felt that you were a part of a family and not only a member of a football club.

Of course, it was a tough neighbourhood and I shudder to think if it wasn´t for Mr Dinnie: goodness knows where I would have ended up – it was that sort of environment – I could have struggled. But, once Mr Dinnie got a hold of you, you were safe, very safe and on the right road. If it wasn´t for him I would never have been able to visit places like the United States and Germany. I mean, how many young boys from our area could say they got the chance to see those countries at such a young age and under football circumstances? It was all down to Mr Dinnie. He did so much for the community.

He was such a fatherly-figure and when you walked down the street with him you felt secure: he commanded so much respect from the community and beyond.

I never heard him raise his voice and although he installed discipline in all of us it wasn´t by rule or fear, it wasn´t ruthless either; it was pure honesty and he had this aura about him that you couldn´t help but respond to.

Mr Dinnie´s favourite line was: "Right, boys, YM hall, boots polished!" This was his match-day meeting call. Incidentally, I did an impersonation of him in front of my team-mates; unknown to me he was standing behind me.

I couldn´t praise Mr Dinnie highly enough. All I can say is: if there were more Bobby Dinnies in the community the world would be a better place, that´s for sure.

John Thomson

Where to start?

I have known 'our' Bobby since I was about fifteen or sixteen-years-old and believe I am the better for knowing him.

I had the privilege of playing for the first team Bobby managed. I remember talking to Bobby outside his close in Bardowie Street, trying to talk him into taking over the team as Dougie MacDonald said he was the man for the job; the rest as they say, is history.

I am personally thankful to Bobby and the Possil YM for steering me in the right direction, but for them in those days, who knows?

We had great teams in the first two or three years, winning trophies for the first time in some years. I´m glad to say that after my time, they just got better and better.

I met my wife, Rita, in the YM. We have been happily married for forty years. We had Bobby and some of the 'old boys': Hutchie, Norrie, Danny, Bobby and the wives out to Linwood for our anniversary in August 2005: we had a blast!

Bobby: he´s the greatest and deserves every accolade he has been given.

John Wyles

I first met Bobby some forty-five years ago when I took up refereeing and he was a leading light with Possilpark YMCA.

Although the team were very successful, Bobby was never to the fore blowing his trumpet, but very much in the background pointing these young men in the right direction both on and off the park and I'm sure that the respect you gave me early in my career no doubt assisted me to what I achieved in refereeing.

Bobby, I wish you every success in the future and many thanks for the memories.

Kenny Hope

I suppose no book about Bobby Dinnie would be complete without reference to Possil YMCA and my father, Douglas MacDonald.

From my perspective the YM was my dad and Bobby: two peas from the same pod. They lived and breathed football. Bobby still does of course and his contribution to football and the positive effect he has had on so many lives is beyond comparison. Great players have been guided by them, even world-class players have a lot to thank the YM for. Kenny Dalglish and Bobby Russell to name but two.

My father's involvement in the YMCA began as a player when he joined the YMCA in Sauchiehall Street. He later moved to Possil when Possilpark YMCA was formed in 1934. He played then managed and later became secretary of Possilpark YMCA. He also was the secretary of the Glasgow YMCA. This involved running the leagues, indeed Saturday evening in our house was a case of manning the phones, getting the results in as quickly as possible and phoning them into the Evening Times newspaper.

My dad was also involved with the Scottish YM and his contribution to football was recognized with a Civic Reception in Glasgow on 16th September 1981. A special plaque, in tribute to my father, was unveiled by Kenny Dalglish at the opening of Possil Point, the new Youth Centre in 1995. Bobby of course was honoured with a MBE, which was certainly no more than what he deserves, for a life dedicated to the game.

As my father's condition of multiple sclerosis became more debilitating much of the clerical side of things was taken on by my mother, who throughout his life supported him. The success my father had is also due to the support my mother gave him and she also deserves recognition and credit for her part in the success of the YMCA.

The YMCA in Possil was more than a breeding ground for talented footballers. My father and Bobby Dinnie gave hundreds of ordinary boys like myself the chance to live for their dream. That was their real gift. Their time, encouragement and endless effort gave us ordinary boys a goal, a challenge and a sense of belonging. Possil YMCA was not just a youth club: it was a way of life for many boys growing up in and around Possil, myself included and without the drive and enthusiasm of the 'two peas' then I am sure Possilpark YMCA would not have had the success it had.

The YMCA served the community not only via football. There were games nights, table tennis, snooker, badminton, judo, concerts and Sunday Bible class. At the heart of all this activity, my dad and Bobby.

As a young boy I can remember going with my dad to watch Possil play. I used to play on the side of the park with the black ash of Cowlairs. As I became older I actually watched the games and so became hooked on football. Of course I later played on the Cowlairs pitches many times and have the scars to prove it! I can also remember as a young child being mesmerized by all the activity going on in the YM hall and the smell of Winter Green on match-days. Another memory which sticks in my mind came from the back room where some of the girls were meeting and the front hall was entertained with a chorus of: *"I want to be Bobby's Girl"*. It wasn't just the players that wanted to catch Bobby's eye.

As a player, I became aware of Bobby around the age of thirteen. I was desperate to play football and I was lucky enough to play with some gifted players. Bobby instilled in us a sense of respect. Respect for ourselves, our fellow players and a pride in our team. We were representatives. I remember him telling us that our socks had to be pulled up properly, our jerseys tucked into our shorts and our boots spotlessly clean. They were inspected before we left the changing rooms and if we were not up to scratch we didn't get on the pitch to play. He told us that when we went out onto the park we would look like footballers, look like a team and play like one. Seems simple enough but the psychology certainly had its effects. Possil YMCA was respected wherever the team played. It even made a mediocre player like me feel like a footballer.

Training nights were terrific, too. As youngsters we could on occasion train with the older players, the U-18s and U-21s. The hall would be alive with activity. We were worked hard but it gave us a real sense of achievement.

On special nights we had our sessions taken by professionals. Possil YMCA were linked to the Gunners and as a result of this I remember Frank McLintock, of Arsenal coming up to take a training night. Having him there helped encourage us and give us the belief that one day perhaps we could emulate him. I can still hear his voice booming round the hall! The relationship also meant that the team played in Arsenal colours. I can remember pulling on an Arsenal top and travelling in the Arsenal mini-bus to our league matches. What a feeling! A real team bus. Real footballers. I'm sure it had the opposition worried before we set foot on the pitch.

However, there was also disappointment as there is at all levels of football. Being part of the YM helped build my character, although I did not realize it at the time. Disappointment is a hard thing to accept and when I was told that I was not in the team it was a terrible feeling. We travelled to play at Queenieburn and I was told that I was not chosen to play. I felt dreadful. I cannot think of anything, even today, that has been more disappointing than being dropped. Queenieburn were short of players and a few of us were asked to turn out for them. I couldn't. I could not play against Possil. It just did not feel right. That was a long day and although we won it seemed a very long journey home.

Another occasion when I was seriously disappointed was

when the squad was selected to travel to London to visit and play at Highbury. I didn't make the squad. I was shattered. There was great excitement around the club but I was so disappointed. The best players were of course chosen and that was and is how it should be. There were no favours, not even for Dougie's boy. Honesty and integrity throughout. A club run as it should be. Now looking back I can see it helped me deal with situations as I have gone through life, but it was a bitter pill to take at the time.

Later on around the age of nineteen or twenty I played with Possil as an over age player with one of the youth teams and it was a privilege to be invited back by Bobby to help work with the team. Although I was only there a relatively short time, I have great memories and like to think I helped in carrying on the Dinnie philosophy: respect and friendship.

Indeed as a school teacher taking my own teams I have tried to instill in them the good habits I grew up with in Possil YMCA. Though I grew up and moved away the spirit of Possil YMCA has always been with me. I have much to thank Bobby Dinnie and my father for, not only for encouraging and developing the little football talent I had but for their parts in making me who I am today. That is the true legacy of the YM and the men who made it so.

Murray MacDonald

I am proud to say I was the first young Possil player that Arsenal signed.

Joe Hill was the man who picked me up and I was later to be followed by other Possil greats like Eddie Kelly. In fact, Possil YM had a long list of great players; namely Norrie McKay, George Andrews and Dougie Eadie. London was the other side of the world for us youngsters. I took the trip myself at the very young age of thirteen and was met at King's Cross. Arsenal was a terrific club and both Arsenal and Possil YM complimented each other. The competition for places at Highbury was fierce, nevertheless. In the youth and reserve teams there were youngsters from all over.

On Bobby; he was a gentleman. He was more than a manager, he was the overlord and looked over everything with fine detail. He always seemed to get the best out of youngsters and I wish there were more like Bobby in the football world.

Neil Leven

In a glittering career, Raymond Stewart won ten Scotland caps, an FA Cup winners' medal, a Milk Cup winners' medal – both with West Ham, and he never lost at Wembley on the five occasions he played there.

His Wembley love affair began when he captained the Scotland U-15 schoolboys' team to victory against England and he later played in the full Scotland side that beat England 1-0 in 1981.

Then, of course, there were his two magic Wembley moments with West Ham plus a Charity Shield win.

But in a career which also encompassed playing spells at Dundee United and St. Johnstone; coaching spells whilst on Saints' and Stirling Albion's books, and manager's jobs at Livingstone, Stirling Albion and Forfar, Raymond came to know an awful lot of football people.

One of those was Bobby Dinnie. And, such is the respect Raymond has for Bobby that, to this day, he refers to him not as 'Bobby' but as 'Mr Dinnie'.

"I first met Bobby when I was with St. Johnstone," Raymond recalled.

"I was the club's reserve and youth coach and Bobby was Chief Scout – and a very good one at that. We became good friends and trusted each other – and we still do. At that time, Bobby worked at Strathclyde Police HQ and he introduced me to a lot of his friends there. When I took over as Stirling team boss, he scouted for me but the club then decided to axe him due to finance. And asking Bobby to step down was the hardest football decision I've had to make. I knew Bobby wouldn't be out the game for long and he got back into it at Partick. And I still respect and value his opinion. I speak to him all the time. He's always there for me. And there is no doubt in my mind that football needs more people like Bobby Dinnie."

Raymond Stewart

There is so much to say about the man's warmth and kindness, the tributes would be long and loud.

Bobby has been a friend of mine now for some fifteen years. I first met him as a work colleague when I moved to an office where he was already based. As a new boy in that environment I felt a bit like a fish out of water, but it was Bobby who made me feel welcome offering advice and assistance, making my move easy.

This is the stamp of the man, from that day on I was able to learn a great deal about Bobby. I spoke to him for long periods about his life and times, his family, his work and obviously his football. Through it all it was obvious he was a devoted family man who served his community with distinction.

Football-wise I have nothing but admiration for his work at Possil YM. It goes without saying that he is responsible for shaping the lives of a number of young men, some made it big, such as the one and only Kenny Dalglish, others' lives have been suitably shaped and steered in a proper manner thanks to Bobby's guidance and dedication. Bobby Dinnie, A true gentleman, a true friend.

Robert Morris

My first recollection of Bobby was as a young kid playing for Eastercraigs some twenty-five years ago. Bobby had the persona of a scout standing at the touchline...immaculately dressed; and not forgetting the hat.

I later joined Rangers as a schoolboy signing where my father gained great respect and trust for Bobby.

It wasn´t until I joined Partick Thistle eighteen years ago and again ten years later on – a second stint as player/coach – when the club was going through some extreme challenges to remain in existence, that I meet up with Bobby again.

It seemed Bobby never aged from the first time I saw him. I took the reserves and Bobby would support the games, providing me with encouragement to bring on the youths that he had brought to the club; their development into the senior squad was paramount to the survival of the club.

This was the time that I realized his 100% commitment in the young players, always an ear, highly encouraging of them to express their talents and could tell me about any player in any league if talented as well as their background.

If only more football-minded folk could demonstrate the values that Bobby upheld then the Scottish game would be some much further forward. I will always have total respect for Bobby Dinnie.

Sammy Johnston

In life you find there are no coincidences. People come into your life and they can make such an impact on yours. This takes me to the first time I met Mr Dinnie (Bobby, to me); I was thirteen-years-old and was invited to play for the 'mighty' Possil YM.

I heard such glowing reports and I was almost too scared to go for my first game. It was there that I met Bobby Dinnie. He approached me, shook my hand, introducing himself to me. He made me feel so welcome and reassured that I knew I had come to play for the right club. From a very early age I regarded Mr Dinnie as a father figure and a very close friend.

I have so many good memories of my playing days at Possil YMCA.

I have fantastic memories of playing at the Cowal Tournament at U-16 level.

The bonding of the players driving to and from Dunoon for the tournament was unique but not only our team, we bonded with the other teams taking part in the tournament.

Yes, Possil YMCA had become my family and I grew up, the guidance I had from Bobby has helped me immensely.

Playing for Possil gave me maturity and discipline at a very early age and I loved my time there.

I played a game on a Saturday and received an injury which would rule me out for the cup final match against Clydebank Strollers on the following Wednesday. I had to have four stitches to the wound but I was so desperate to play I took the stitches out myself. That's how much I loved playing for the club. Being a part of Possil YMCA made winners out of us, in football and in life. Mr Dinnie's guidance helped me and when I finally hung up my boots I got involved in youth team football; mainly to give back the great times I had as a youth player myself at the YM. I'm sure many other players who played under Bobby's guidance did the same.

I met up with Bobby again when I was coaching my youth team. Bobby was scouting for Partick Thistle at this time. He came to a lot of our games offering encouragement and it gave me so much belief that I took my own boys to a final at Hampden Park. A couple of years later I found myself at Partick Thistle's pro youth and I'm sure Mr Dinnie had something to do with that.

Possil YMCA have created not only fine footballers but fine men, too, who are always going to be great ambassadors for the YM. In summary: playing for Possil YMCA meant playing for your family, your family name and the pride of Possil YMCA.

To me, Bobby Dinnie is the 'Jock Stein of youth football'. I met Jock Stein and both Bobby and Jock made the hairs on the back of my neck stand up. Football needs that kind of leader of quality or football would surely die.

I am very proud that I met Bobby and his family. He must have the most patient wife, but then again, that would make for another book. Thank you, Mr Dinnie, for being a part of my life.

Steven Scott

One of Bobby's most famous lines: "Get some cherry blossom on those boots," was testimony to the discipline he installed in all who had the privilege to play or be a part of Possil YMCA. Most of us were just boys from Possilpark and surrounding sprawling housing estates but he managed to get the best out of everyone with the way he treated us. We all looked our best in sharp blazers that made us proud to represent the club.

Bobby got right down to the grassroots of the game with us. He turned us into fit players.

He took us to the United States and to be honest it was quite a world Bobby showed us. Here was I, a wee boy from Glasgow's East End – who shared a bedroom with two sisters, and before I knew it, I was given this great opportunity to visit the other side of the world…and, to play football… incredible.

Gerry Marley was another great influence in my early football career. Bobby and Gerry were synonymous for their outstanding work to the game at youth level.

Possil YMCA emulated the great Real Madrid: we beat Entracht Frankfurt 2-0. On our trip to Germany we beat the German giants' youth team and here's me, the wee humble boy from the East End, on the scoring sheet with both goals.

Tommy Gormley

* Possil YMCA emulating the great Real Madrid is of course tongue-in-cheek reference to Real Madrid´s 7-3 thrashing of Entracht Frankfurt. Arguably the greatest European Cup final ever staged. Hampden park, Glasgow in 1960.

My relationship with Bobby goes back to 1969 when my father (Findlay Blain) worked with Bobby in the White Horse Distillers.

I had just finished playing for my BB team and was on the look out for a new club. My father asked Bobby if I could come along for a trial and this started a playing career with Possil YM of six years and a friendship now lasting some thirty-seven years!

To sum up Bobby in a few words is impossible, but he is indeed a true gentleman and someone – who through his passion for football – helped shape my life and the lives of hundreds of other young footballers. He impressed me with his honesty, integrity and the respect he showed to everyone taught me tremendous lessons, which I have carried through my life.

William Blain

I am happy to take this opportunity to congratulate Bob Dinnie on his splendid work and achievements over many years as Chairman of Possilpark YMCA.

Well-known as an integral part of YMCA Glasgow over several decades, Possil YM as it is popularly known, has presented generations of young people with boundless opportunities for skills training and personal achievement. High standards were set, respect for all was de rigueur, and for so many young people often coming from the most deprived areas of Glasgow, dreams really did come true.

The achievements of members who subsequently became household names particularly in the world of association football are well-documented and represented in this book. For them and for all the others who were part of the great Possil YM family over the years one man stood out in the team of excellent leaders and coaches. That gentleman was Bob Dinnie and it is truly fitting that in recent times Bob's contribution to the local as well as the wider community has achieved the public recognition which it deserves.

As a true lifetime volunteer leader of YMCA Glasgow, Bob has constantly demonstrated that dignity and respect for others which we now have the opportunity to return in full measure. And, by the way, Bob is moving Possil YM forward once again for another generation of young people including some of Scotland's new citizens who have found refuge in Glasgow from many troubled parts of the world. We salute you, Bob.

William Harte

Anyway, were do I start about a guy who is the only person I know who could sit down with you and talk about football; particularly the Scottish game?

I owe Bobby a great debt for his advice and always being there for me in my career. I was a good but average player but when I went into coaching; firstly with Ashfield then with Petershill, but most successfully with Pollok. That is were my coaching took off, winning not only Pollok´s first Scottish Cup but placing Pollok to be one of the best junior teams in Scotland and by winning the best non-league team of Great Britain award. This was a great honour not only for me but down to the teaching of how to run a football team from the apprenticeship that I learned from Bobby Dinnie.

I moved on to concentrate on my two sons who have done well in their football careers but eventually had some bad luck with injuries. My oldest son, Scott, has won every honour with Glentoran in Northern Ireland but was unfortunate to sustain three broken legs (the same leg) and this year has had to retire.

My other son, David, was five years at Rangers but he also fell to the injury bogey but has done well in America playing for Willmington Hammerheads in North Carolina.

So, you can see that football is in the family all through a wonderful guy called Bobby Dinnie MBE...a joke, they should have given him a Knighthood.

Tommy Young

Having known Bobby for several years, and more recently working alongside him with Rangers FC, without doubt he is one of the most respected gentleman in Scottish football, a true and genuine friend.

Stewart Graham

I had the great fortune to have spent many years at Possil YMCA, beginning as a twelve-year-old youngster. I had the honour of playing for the club and later to be given a coaching role; all during the times when the club were connected to two English league giants: Arsenal FC and Aston Villa respectively.

I knew then, that I was involved in a great thing with Possil YMCA. We were very aware we were playing and working under a true legend in Bobby Dinnie; not only in the football sense but also as a man. It was clear that Bobby gave his life to football, the community, Possil YMCA and to all the people around him. It didn´t matter what age group you played under or who you were, Bobby treated everyone the same. Mr Dinnie taught us dignity, manners, honour and how to apply ourselves on and off the park. He had this uncanny ability to shape boys into fine young men. Many made the grade in the game and of course many didn´t but collectively I´m sure they all took a bit of Possil YMCA and Bobby Dinnie with them through their lives.

In a way I always wondered if he dedicated too much time to football when it was clear he had a family away from the game but Bobby said, "We are all his family." And that is just one of the reasons what makes Bobby Dinnie MBE such an icon.

It was a pleasure and a privilege to have met him, to have worked under him and it is an honour to still know him. I couldn´t speak more highly of him.

Sammy Smith

It is always a privilege to be asked by someone to contribute a few lines for a forthcoming publication. When that someone is a true and trusted friend; in this case: the incomparable Bobby Dinnie, it becomes a more enticing prospect.

The first thing to say is that Bobby is a real gentleman in every sense of the word. I have known him primarily in the context of that great Glasgow institution: Partick Thistle Football Club. I am very passionate about 'The Jags', for whom Bobby´s nephew, Allan, played 189 first-team games and I appreciate perhaps more than most the valuable contribution Bobby made to the Firhill cause during his time there; working in the important field of youth development.

All of those who know Bobby will know he is modest and unassuming, but could be firm with his charges when necessary; whilst always remaining scrupulously fair. The young players under his wing always had the utmost respect for him at all times, and that tells you its own story. Bobby always had a shrewd eye for football talent and he played a big part in the football education of many young hopefuls.

When Bobby ran the Thistle youth team I always looked forward, eagerly, to my Sunday afternoons watching the young lads strutting their stuff. It was a refreshing experience and very rewarding. He was always therapeutic if the big team hadn´t done too well the day before.

We travelled as far away as Dingwall where we defeated Ross County 1-0, thanks to a goal from Chris Edwards, but the venue would often be the much more accessible, Petershill

Park (alas, now departed from the scene). Alex Robertson and Niall MacTaggart would be there; we all got on very well together. Those were really happy days, now gone, never to return.

Some years ago we travelled to Holland, the scene of a fairly prestigious youth tournament in which Thistle participated. Bobby is really a bit of a 'home bird' but he enjoyed the experience along with Brown McMaster, Bob McConley, Billy McPhie, Alex Robertson, myself and other Thistle personnel. Incidentally, the young 'Jags' performed very well.

Bobby is well-known for his tireless efforts on behalf of Possil YM, where his record, spanning many years, is second to none. His unstinting devotion knew no bounds. This selflessness was typical of the man when he became the recipient of the MBE, which could not have been awarded to anyone more deserving.

Bobby is a real family man, fiercely proud of his sons, Russell and Robert. The icing on the cake comes in the shape of the recent arrival of his first grandson, Joe – a real treasure. I speak from experience: in his younger days, Bobby was no mean footballer himself, possessor of a really 'wicked' left foot. Maybe now there´s a another 'wicked' left foot in the offing.

I have appreciated the opportunity to pay this small tribute to Bobby: one of life´s good guys.

Robert W. Reid

I have known Bobby Dinnie for about thirty years. I first met Bobby when I went for trials for Possil YMCA. Bobby was there along with Jimmy Dinnie (Bobby´s brother).

I played well but not good enough for me to sign for Possil. I will always remember Jimmy saying to me, "If you want to play for Possil you have to dress like a footballer, put your jersey inside your shorts and always make sure your boots are polished and socks are up." I had a bad leg and was not good enough anyway, so that was the end of my playing days with Possil YMCA.

It was a few years later before I was to join Possil YMCA as a manager. I was working beside Bobby in the White Horse Whisky Bond, when a friend of mine asked me if I would like to go to a fund-raising night for Possil. At the night out the place was full of ex-players who had played with Possil before they went on to become pro; players with teams like Rangers, Celtic, Liverpool, Arsenal, et cetera. Near the end of the night, Bobby was thanking everyone who had helped make the night a success. Bobby also said that Possil were always looking for people to help run their teams. I had a talk with him and told him I was already running a small local team called Allander United BC. Bobby told me to meet him on Tuesday night at a place called Closeburn Park in Possilpark.

I met Bobby and the first thing he asked me was why I wanted to join Possil. I must have passed my interview because I started to work with the U-13s, under Robert Dingwell, and at the end of the season Bobby asked me if I would like to take the new U-13s for the coming season. Right away I said yes. Bobby then told me he had entered us for a tournament in Ayr with teams from all over the world. Our team had only been together for about two months before we played our first game, but full credit to the players we had at that time we went on to win the cup. Every night I would phone Bobby to let him know how we got on. Bobby would tell me scouts from all over Scotland and England had already been on the phone to him telling him how the team had played, but not one of them said Possil would win the cup. Bobby said, "Listen, there is only one way to shut them up and that is to win it." We did! The team winning that cup was for the faith that Bobby had showed in putting us in the tournament in the first place.

When Possil and everyone starts talking about Bobby, everybody knows him. Not just in Scotland but also in

England, teams like Arsenal, Liverpool, Man United, Aston Villa, QPR and many more. Bobby Dinnie has one thing that even all the top managers in Scotland and England don't have and that is the respect of everyone that knows him.

I remember one night Bobby and myself were at an U-13s game; one of the parents came round and asked Bobby if he remembered him. He played with Possil fifteen years ago. Bobby said yes and asked about his older brother, who had also played with Possil. The parent said he was great and was round the other side of the ground and it was him who had noticed Bobby. The parent continued to say that his brother had sent him round to see if it was okay if he smoked whilst coming over to speak to Bobby. This was someone who was about thirty-eight asking if he could smoke; that's the respect for you.

Bobby's wife Betty used to tell me that when they were going out it would take them about an hour or more to go to the shops which were only five minutes away. Everyone would stop and talk to Bobby.

I would also like to thank Bobby for getting James 'Chico' Reilly and myself to Partick Thistle as scouts, to later become kit men.

I was going to finish with something like Bobby was just an ordinary man but he isn't.

He is Bobby Dinnie MBE. Possil YMCA.

Thanks Bobby for all the good times. One thing for sure is that there is no-one that could ever say a bad word about Bobby. I have never heard Bobby saying a bad word about anyone and like myself, Bobby has a very understanding wife, Betty, who is behind him. Betty has only one rule and that is: "Don't call when Coronation Street is on."

Ricky Roughan

I first encountered Bob in the summer of 1993 and that

meeting could be said to have changed my life...well, the weekends and a few evenings a week at least, as over the next seven or eight years I would find myself trailing across the country watching youth team matches from Dumbarton to Dingwall, Kirkintilloch to Kirkaldy, and Larkhall to Livingston!

You see, I'm a Partick Thistle fan, I freely admit it, as is my good friend Alex Robertson, but as well as being a Jags fan Alex was a member of the Partick Thistle Youth Committee of the time and was the person instrumental in bringing Bob Dinnie to Firhill.

Alex's association with Bob went way back to the 1950s when he played for Bob´s Possil YM side; so when he was approached by the Thistle Chairman Brown McMaster with regards to suggesting a suitable candidate to take on the role of chief scout for the club there was only ever going to be one name in the running.

I well remember the phone call from Alex explaining that he was now going to be involved with the scouting and day-to-day running of the youth set-up at Firhill and that he would be working alongside the newly appointed Chief Scout Bob Dinnie. As he ran through Bob´s C.V. I realized that Thistle had finally got it right, I was still trying to come to terms with all of this when almost as an afterthought he added, "Oh! and did you know that it was also Bob who discovered Kenny Dalglish?"

It was shortly after this that I finally met Bob, standing outside the main entrance to Firhill, dressed in his uniform of hat, coat, collar and tie, and of course the mandatory shiny shoes. He turned out to be a charming, knowledgeable man that was always prepared to listen to your point of view (regardless of how daft it was). It was always an education attending a match with Bob, his suggestions as to how things could be improved tactically and his analysis of certain player´s strengths and weaknesses, what position they would be best playing in and most importantly his ability to spot talent were a real eye opener to someone like me who knew considerably less about football than he thought he did. To this day if I am at a youth game with Bob I still feel rather pleased with myself if I manage to pick out the player Bob has his eye on.

Bob now set about the task of revamping the youth set-up at Firhill and to that end brought in a succession of coaches who would make a difference. Obviously you don't implement a whole new infrastructure overnight but steady progress was being made with each passing season and by the time 1997 came along things were starting to look good. The first notable success for Bob came at U-16s level where coaches Drew Todd and Fraser Gilchrist were put in charge of a very promising group of youngsters. All the hard work of the previous four years was about to pay dividends as the young Jags lifted the U-16s Scottish Cup.

On a May evening at Petershill Park, Thistle triumphed over West Park by seven goals to nil. It was one of the most devastating displays of football I have ever seen at any level, and what's more it came against a team that had already beaten the Jags on league business earlier in the season. Through all this excitement Bob stood watching serenely with a contented look on his face as opposed to Alex and I who were rather more animated.

Bob repeated the U-16s´ success the following season with the U-15s. Coached by, soon to be Glasgow City Councillor, Allan Stewart, Thistle again won the national trophy this time defeating Netherdale Community by 3-1.

Success at youth team level is not only gauged by silverware obtained but also by how many youngsters make it through the ranks to the first-team. Eventually, between the U-15s and U-16s teams no fewer than seven youngsters would feature at some point in the full Jags side.

Other achievements during this period included:

- 1997 Glasgow Cup finalists

- 1996/97 U-16 Amateur League runners-up

- 1998/99 U-16 Amateur League runners-up

- 1998/99 Professional U-18 Youth League 3rd place

- 1999/00 Professional U-18 Youth League runners-up

- 1999/00 U-13 SYCA League Champions

- 1999/00 U-12 Morecombe and Lancaster Cup winners

By the 1999/00 season things were going really well, Bob had supplied the Jags with a steady stream of first-team regulars including Kenny Arthur (now in his testimonial year), Martin Lauchlan, Jamie McKenzie, Robert Dunn, Alan Archibald, Kevin McCann, Willie Howie, Andy Gibson and Derek Lyle. We also had some excellent prospects in our various youth teams and Bob had great plans for the club including a Thistle youth academy. A trip was even made down to Newcastle Uniteds´ academy to see how they ran things. Little did we know that the plug was about to be pulled on Bob´s tenure at Firhill and all the great work of the last seven years utterly wasted.

In hindsight I think the main problem was that Partick Thistle had been relegated to the Second Division in season 97/98 and had failed to get back up at the first time of asking. Cue the return of Jags´ hero, John Lambie, however even the Maryhill Messiah found things tough going the following season as promotion again proved to be elusive. These failures and there financial implications were ultimately to work against Bob. It would appear that when money is tight at a football club the youth set-up is the first thing to suffer, with all available resources being channelled towards the first-team, and Firhill proved to be no different to anywhere else in this respect. Bob´s time with the Jags was over and with it went any direction or purpose for what remained of our youth policy.

Was the club right to do what it did? Well, history will show that Partick Thistle FC were crowned Second Division champions in 2000/01 winning the league by an incredible eighteen point margin but on the flip side we were left with a youth set-up which was a shadow of it´s former self.

After leaving Firhill Bob had a brief spell with Stirling Albion before once again moving on. I remember Bob and Alex attending a game at Firhill shortly thereafter, Bob had just advised me that he had acquired a new job and I knew I had the difficult task of telling my then, eight-year-old son the details. You see, Niall Jnr just loves Bob (might be something to do with the £1 bung Bob slips him every time they meet?) so I decided the news had to be broken gently: "Niall, Bob´s got a new job," I said.

"Is he coming back here?" he replied with enthusiasm.

"No, he's going to Rangers."

The look of shock and horror on his face was hilarious. Once it was explained that even Bob needed to earn a living he seemed to accept it but regardless of whatever team he works for; to us, Bob will always be a Firhill legend.

Alex and I often reminisce about the good old days during Bob´s time and I know for a fact that we both miss it. For me Alex summed it up perfectly just recently when he said, "They were great times for all of us privileged to be part of his team." Says it all really.

Niall MacTaggart

After match-days on a Saturday, Douglas would come home with two full bags of football kit to be washed. I would spend ages in front of the sink – and I mean sink – there was no washing machine. I'd be washing and rinsing before the whole lot would hang in the back green to dry. I did match reports and team-sheets for the club as well as looking after the kit. It was not something I thought about, we just did those things because it was a part of our lives and we got on with it with pleasure.

The members of Possil YMCA would often have club meetings in the YM hall before congregating in our house afterwards in Bardowie Street for tea and toast (often burned, which some preferred).

The club were great at organizing fund-raising functions which often included dances which were most enjoyable. The club as a whole was great for meeting people and for sharing a unique community spirit.

Douglas and Bobby were very close indeed and Bobby has been wonderful for the whole area. If you want to know what it was like being a 'footballer's wife' I think Betty – Bobby's wife – would be better suited to answer that one.

Katie MacDonald

I was at Possil YMCA from the age of sixteen to twenty. I loved the job there as I was surrounded by great people and our club was famous for nurturing great players like Kenny Dalglish and Robert Fleck, amongst many others.

I was given duties which I carried out willingly as it was an honour to be part of a club that had so many connections to professional clubs. Some terrific players played for us like John Hendrie, Grant Reid, Joe Dickson, Paul Kelly, John O'Brien, Sean Bainbridge, Chris Robertson and Billy Ritchie. Possil YM had a vast amount of players who eventually played at senior level.

With 'The Boss', Bobby, it was great to work alongside him and Norrie McAllister. The late Jimmy Steele was another great YM man. He joined in the early 80s in a coaching role and managed the U-15 and U-18s – winning various trophies. Jimmy was a wonderful man and loved by players and staff alike. I still miss the Possil YM, it was my life.

John McCartney

In 1956 I started playing for Possil YMCA juvenile teams. We were very successful and enjoyed many league and cup ties on the red blaes park at Chirnsyde school.

In 1959 I was called up for National Service. On coming out of the Army I returned to the YM and played for the second team, who played in the Glasgow YMCA League. After a few years, John Birkens – who ran the team, retired – and I took over. I worked together with Alister Rutherford. The team won many cups and on one occasion we drove down to the Midlands in England overnight to buy the trophies for the team.

When Alister left to work in England I took the team into the West of Scotland League. We started in Division Seven and won promotion in consecutive occasions to Division One. We enjoyed many great times at the YM from running fund-raising jumble sales assisted by my wife, Cathie – who washed and ironed the team´s strips – as did the players´ wives and girlfriends. We also ran many fund-raising dances in the hall. Christmas parties for the local children were always fun.

I stopped running the team in 1999.

John Clarkson

Bobby and I met up for the first time fifty years ago when we faced each other as opponents in a Glasgow YMCA League match.

He was playing for his beloved Possilpark YMCA and I was

with local rivals Somerville Church. Many a good tussle we had on the field of play. Bobby was a very good left-winger at that time. He was a skilful player and he was a credit to others by his sportsmanship on and off the field of play. He was a credit to his club and to the game of football.

When we meet nowadays we still have a good laugh when we speak about the time he played for the Glasgow YMCA representative team in a challenge match at Dundee against their counterparts from that city. One of my own team, Charlie Morson, had also been selected to play in the game and midway through the second-half Bobby made an effort to back-head a throw in – unfortunately Charlie was immediately behind him as both jumped for the same ball, Charlie was struck on the bridge of the nose by the head of Bobby.

It is the only occasion that I can remember seeing a player ending up with two gorgeous black eyes coming off a park at the end of a match and having to make the journey home to Glasgow having great difficulty in seeing anything in front of his face.

After moving up to the junior ranks for a while, Bobby returned to Possilpark YMCA to manage a team at the club. He became a very successful manager. Bobby and I both became members of the League Management Committee and we served together on that committee for many years and commenced a friendship which has lasted for more than forty years.

He is a most helpful person and on a number of occasions during our time running a club he was kind enough to loan me sets of jerseys for my own team when we had colour clashes against other clubs and only had one set of jerseys at our disposal.

We still run into each other occasionally and always have a good blether about the 'old days'. It is indeed a pleasure and privilege to know Bobby.

Jimmy Smith

He made a point of personally meeting and introducing himself to get to know each boy and his family.

He always encouraged and nurtured his players no matter what talent you had – you were always the same in his eyes and there was no time for prima donnas.

He was respected by all: players, families and the people of Possilpark.

As far as I am concerned he was and still is Possil YMCA.

Bobby, you are a legend.

Jim McCluskey

I was young when I met Bobby and later I would become a member of the club where I carried out varied tasks and duties. There was always something going on at the club like table tennis, snooker, badminton et cetera as well as concert parties where we´d take the show to the pensioners in the area. It was there that I met Bobby Dinnie.

Anything that was done at the club was through Bobby. He orchestrated everything from fund-raising, kit, trips et cetera. He really was the man that made everything tick. I am pleased to say that our friendship has lasted some forty-six years.

Alex Hosie

It was my pleasure to be associated with Possil YM at U-18 level during the late 1970s.

Bobby Dinnie had already established Possil as one of the best and most disciplined youth teams in Glasgow. In an era and area troubled by hardship, Bobby Dinnie gave young guys like myself and many more like me a fantastic opportunity to develop as a young footballer and did it with tremendous enthusiasm and dedication.

I´m sure Bobby will receive many accolades and he deserves

every one. I will always be grateful for all the help Bobby and his brother, Jimmy and Brian Byrne gave me during my time with Possil. Their advice and football knowledge were hugely instrumental in helping me become a professional footballer.

Jim Duffy

I was one of the many fortunate ones to play football for Possil YM before turning out for a senior club, Clyde.

In our area we had really great young players who furthered their careers like Jimmy Mann, who played for Sunderland. It was a different era we played in: no substitutes in those days, no trying to influence the referee and you could certainly tackle during my time in football. I was called up for National Service and even in the midst of our operations we still managed to get a game of football. I played on the same pitch as Bobby Charlton, Eric Smith and Dave McKay; all football legends.

On Bobby: he was a really good friend of mine, I knew him very well and I have fond memories of the football in those times.

I emigrated to Canada in 1964 where I have lived ever since. I am married to Jean and we have five children: Steven, James Jnr, Karen, Janette and Wendy.

James Fisher

* James is the grandson of the former Hibs player James Fisher.

Bobby has made a big contribution to my life.

In my early career I enjoyed a fair amount of success with Possil YMCA. We won almost everything back then and I have fond memories of our Scottish Cup win which meant we were the first ever YM organization to win the penultimate trophy.

To put down in words why we were so successful is mostly down to the way Bobby organized a group of boys from the hard-working industrial area. He had discipline and never needed to raise his voice. It certainly did me in good stead.

I had offers to go abroad and play but Bobby told me to hang on, I will get a club, and a club that would be right for me. How right he was. I did hang on and eventually I found my way to Liverpool where I enjoyed playing under the late great Bill Shankly.

Bobby looked after everyone on and off the park and all his players were his favourites.

I am privileged and honoured to have played for Possil YMCA.

They gave me my first chance in football.

Ian Ross

Bobby is a man who has contributed more to the Scottish game than most, and is highly respected in the youth game.

He is always greeted at many venues, with great enthusiasm by former players of Possil YM, of whom there are a considerable number. Both my father and myself have known Bobby down through the years, while he was at Possil and then as a scout – through to our involvement in running Rossvale Boys´ Club. He is a scout of the old school and believes that there is a proper way to do things, which is the reason he is so well-respected.

A true gentleman.

Ian Grey

I played for Possil YM in the early 70s. Bobby was the man who asked to play for the club and I thoroughly enjoyed my time there. You could always see that he was the man who was in charge and who also had 100% respect from all the players and coaches.

He was a hard man, but a very fair man to play for. Even at training you could tell when Bobby had arrived as the full hall/gym would go quiet. Bobby, on his many scouting missions, (I wouldn't like to think of how many matches he has watched) unearthed a lot of football talent, many of who became big names in the football world, not just in Scotland, but I am sure people elsewhere in the book will have mentioned this numerous times.

I can´t pay Bobby enough respect.

Harry Robertson

Throughout life´s journey some of us are blessed with a healthy fulsome life and for a variety of reasons we have to be thankful for the life we have lived.

For those of us who have had the honour and pleasure of meeting and getting to know Bobby Dinnie, our lives surely have been enriched and for the twenty-one years I´ve known him, I feel able to comment on the life of a wonderful man I can genuinely call a friend.

If you consult a dictionary; the definition of the word 'gentleman' reads: A man of the highest honour, courtesy and morality: in effect, a wholesome definition of Bobby Dinnie.

Bobby is a man who is extremely proud of his family – and rightly so; a family who are extremely proud of him.

Bobby Dinnie cannot be described in one sentence or paragraph, however, suffice to say I am honoured and privileged to know him as a colleague and friend; a friendship I hope will last for for many years to come. For those of us privileged enough to know him we have a very great deal to be thankful of. Bobby Dinnie MBE, a true gentleman.

Graham Smillie

I started a boys' football team around 1968 called Cowlairs Hearts – named after Cowlairs football pitches which were situated on the border of Springburn and Possilpark.

At that time the pitches were made of black ash which came

from coal-fired power stations: there's many a fifty, sixty and seventy-year-old walking around Glasgow today with the black ash still in their old football wounds.

At that time most young boys spent every spare minute kicking a ball, so it was quite easy to start an organized team.

I first came into contact with Bobby Dinnie when he phoned me and asked our U-16 team to play Possil YM in a friendly match at Maryhill Juniors' Lochburn Park. We had a very good young winger, John Pelosi, who in the space of two years had progressed from an average player to a very good footballer. Bobby knew about this lad and obviously realized he had the potential to go further in the game. I remember Bobby Russell played for Possil YM that day and although he was two years younger than most of the others on the park, he was the best player on show: something special.

After the match at Lochburn, Bobby invited me to bring John Pelosi and one other player of my choice to play a trial in Newcastle being organized for Aston Villa. As a result of this game John Pelosi signed for Aston Villa as an apprentice professional. John continued his football career in Scotland with Motherwell and St. Johnstone. Bobby Dinnie had given John the opportunity to join one of the biggest clubs in England and make a career in football. The boost this gave our wee club was tremendous, we attracted better players and all our teams benefited greatly.

Cowlairs Hearts played in a different league from Possil YM. Bobby was often in contact with me to arrange friendly matches and trials. One such match sticks out in my memory; it was in the early 1970s when we played Possil YM at Closeburn Park, in Possilpark. I thought we had a very good team and we would give the YM a good run for their money. However, I was in for a rude awakening: Possil YM ran over the top of us. No wonder, they had two outstanding players on show that day: Tony Fitzpatrick and Jimmy McCluskey. They banged in eight goals, these two players never let up from the kick-off to the final whistle, they were professional footballers in the making. Tony Fitzpatrick had a successful career in football. I always admired his commitment to football. Bobby Dinnie had unearthed another success. I learned a valuable lesson that day: Bobby Dinnie's teams don't play friendly matches.

In 1970 I had started my teaching career in Barrhead High school. I eventually moved away from Springburn and went to live in Barrhead, at this time I lost contact with Bobby, however, in a few years time we were to meet up again through football.

From the mid-seventies to the mid-eighties I was the General Secretary of the Paisley and District Youth Football League. I had started another boys' team in Barrhead along with some local football enthusiasts.

At that time we were not among the elite youth leagues in Scotland, however, that was to change – thanks to Bobby Dinnie and others.

We had a good league with some well-established Renfrewshire boys' football teams such as: Clarkston Ams, Gleniffer Thistle, Barrhead BC, Johnstone United and the two Linwood teams, St. Convals and Linwood Rangers.

Bobby phoned me and said he wanted to put a couple of teams in the Paisley League. Good as his word, Possil YM joined our league and other teams were not long in following this trend including Goodyear BC, from Drumchapel; Shamrock BC, from Port Glasgow/Greenock; and many others.

Teams from the Paisley League were now winning the Scottish Cup at every age group, we were now competing with the best. The league select teams at U-15 and U-16s level won the national inter-league trophies on many occasions; more than holding their own with the Scottish Amateur YFL,

Lanarkshire YMCA and Ayrshire Amateur Youth League.

Bobby's decision to join the league was a master stroke, the league was transformed and all the clubs benefited. Some of the outstanding Possil YM players who played at that time were Robert Fleck, John Hendrie and Ross Caven. All three had successful careers in football. I had great pleasure over the years following the careers of the above mentioned players in the senior game and they were a credit to their mentor.

I personally would like to pay tribute to Bobby Dinnie for his support, advice and encouragement at that particular time when I was General Secretary. He has a great understanding and a wide vision of what is involved in youth football. He has integrity and when you ask him for advice you know you can rely on it implicitly.

In the past fifty years, Bobby has been part of special group of football activists working in youth football who have made significant contributions to their communities and at the same have helped talented young footballers to progress to the senior game and make their careers in football. Don't forget, there were no blueprints to guide people like Bobby. Here was a new situation where professional clubs from all over Britain were taking on boys straight from school. As a schoolteacher I am fully aware of the importance of looking after the welfare and helping young people to make their way in the world. I was trained to do this and it was part of my job. In Bobby's case he was self-taught and what a good job he made of it. It is easy to understand the universal appeal of an organization such as the YMCA when you look at the calibre of its leaders like Bobby.

For all his great qualities and the sterling work he has done, Bobby Dinnie was and still is a straightforward, approachable, sincere and helpful person; one of life's great gentlemen. In my opinion, one of his greatest legacies is the number of people involved today at all levels in football who have been influenced and encouraged by Bobby to make their mark – no matter how big or small – on the great game.

Finally, I would like to offer my kindest regards and best wishes to the whole Dinnie family and long may they prosper.

Gilbert Baird

Bobby Dinnie has been instrumental in helping so many kids experience their dream of playing senior football.

He showed those at Possil YMCA how to believe in themselves as individuals and as players and his commitment and enthusiasm was second to none. He has been a great influence in my own career and is one of the most approachable people in the game.

George Adams

Oh Lord,

Please help to guide my words

Let them be soft and tender

Because tomorrow, I may have to eat them

Father Francis

In those days we made our own light entertainment. Of course, we had no TV back then so we made do with what we could and football was an entertainment that didn´t cost a lot and almost anyone could join in.

We had a wee league amongst ourselves and our team was Bardowie Rovers. It was very humble because we didn´t have proper playing facilities as such. Games were more notably played on black ash pitches. St Theresa's had some good footballers and so did the Boys' Brigade. There was a lot of football going on and we also had indoor activities like darts and such like. The young people of the community had somewhere to go; between our Churches, their halls and the simple games of football we had in the street where we would use defunct air-raid shelters as goals. In all, it was quite a time.

I devoted my life to my Church, my faith and my work in spreading good in the world and you can say the same about Bobby because he was so wrapped up in his football where he saw the great need for giving the young ones a perspective and if that meant through a simple game of football then that was the way it was to be. The world has a lot to thank Bobby for. He has so much to look forward to and he has such a lot to look back on, too.

Father Francis *Frank* **Meagher**

The pure professionalism of how the club was run in its day was a true credit to Bobby and all his staff.

Thinking back to my time, which was thirty-seven years ago, we had managers, trainers and kit staff who looked after the kit; we were like professionals. We had physiotherapists who treated your injuries and on top of this we were paid expenses to play for a top club. At no time in my career at the club was I asked to pay for anything.

The club was always being invited to play in friendlies and competitions throughout the UK and in my time I travelled the length and breadth of the country, doing so for the club. This was terrific for team-spirit and the friendships that were forged on these outings galvanized us into such a formidable team and club. Many of the guys I played with back then are still friends and we like nothing better than to reminisce when we get together. We always set out to win any game but we always wanted to leave an impression on our opponents that we were indeed a first-class team. Sometimes the opposition could not handle the football we played and resorted to some rough stuff but like all good teams we were capable of handling ourselves in this department.

I remember one such trip when we were invited down to Aston Villa to take part in a tournament, which included their youth team and a few other professional clubs in the area. Before we headed down to the tournament it was stressed to us how difficult a tournament it would be and we had to be at our best just to put up a good show. On arrival to Villa´s training ground and viewing the facilities they had was for us, a massive incentive to do well. We knew we were all good footballers but here was a chance to prove we could play on the biggest pitches we´d ever came across and to play against the best professional youngsters that the English clubs had in that area. To be honest, I don´t think many people gave us any real chance of winning a game never mind going on to win the tournament itself. The prize for winning the tournament was a pair of ADIDAS boots for each player from the winning team: To this day I´m still waiting on Aston Villa sending me my boots!

What Bobby achieved at the club in a football sense was unbelievable and the amount of boys who went on to taste professional football was incredible. I personally went on from the club to sign professional forms with Preston North End.

Possil YM were drawn against a top team from outside of Glasgow in the Scottish Cup. This team were tipped by many to go on an win the competition. They played on a big grass surface and could play passing football – or so they said, anyway. On the day of the match the team turned up at Closeburn school in Possil, which was a major shock to them. They asked where the pitch was and we informed them it was up the road at Torr Street – which was a tight black ash pitch. On returning from inspecting the pitch the match officials from their team said it was not a football pitch but a waste ground; and tried to get the game called off. The referee refused but did instruct Bobby to organize corner flags and make the lines on the pitch more visible.

We were busy warming up on the pitch, thinking how Bobby was going to get corner flags and line the pitch. Next thing, a few of our local Possil supporters turned up with boxes of soap powder and proceeded to line the pitch. Another couple of fans ripped pailings off a garden fence and nailed handkerchiefs to the pailing to improvise as corner flags. You should have seen the look on the faces of the other team…it was priceless. We beat the team and I think it was my best game in a Possil YM.

Donny Chisholm

It didn´t matter if you were one of the top players in Bobby´s club, you had to show other qualities as well and one of the things that Bobby insisted on was that all his players attended service on a Sunday afternoon. Back then we were all just typical Glasgow kids playing a simple game of fitba with our wee street team 'The Mansion Middens', at our favourite haunt: the famous black ash pitch at Torr Street.

We´d finish our big 'side-up' and race to get to the service on time. There we were, standing at the back with only our black ash faces on show. We were just happy that no-one saw what we were wearing: denims tucked into football socks and the clinking of our screw-in studs must have sounded like a marching army.

In earnest it wasn´t such a bad thing to have discipline. Bobby not only taught us the meaning of being a part of a great club and community but he brought to us the meaning of life and its importance of being a good human being. The respect for Bobby is immense, from all sorts of people and from all walks of life.

Danny Murray

I've known Bobby for many years; mostly through football. He was responsible for organizing all Possil YMCA training and lets for games. All Bobby's players were well-treated – not just the stars. I am sure many will remember the happy days playing for Possil YMCA.

I helped to run St. Theresa's Boys' Guild football team for a number of years and although we were in different leagues, we met in cup ties and it was all very friendly rivalry and most of the boys in both teams came from Possilpark. All the years Bobby was with the YMCA, meant being on the touchline every Saturday and sometimes weekdays in all kinds of weather during the season, which shows 100% commitment and dedication.

I wish Bobby all the best for the future and I'm sure everyone who has known Bobby Dinnie have found him to be a true gentleman.

Charlie McKenna

* Charlie McKenna and Eddie Brady were both awarded the Bene Merenti by His Holiness the Pope for their outstanding services to St Theresa's youth. Charlie had originally given six weeks of his time to St Theresa's but his stay stretched to forty-two years. Charlie enjoyed a fruitful football career dawning the shirts of St. Rochs, Shettleston Juniors, Springburn United, Ashfield, Forest Mechanics, Peebles Rovers and Hamilton Accies in the 1950s. He played alongside the three Dunn brothers and Tommy Ring. All four played for Clyde FC.

I first met Bobby in the early 50s when I was a schoolboy playing for Glasgow and I was asked if I would like to play for Possil YMCA on Saturday afternoons.

Often gaining youth honours I progressed through to the YM U-21s, which was run by Archie McKay and Bob Lowe.

In 1957 Archie McKay moved away from Glasgow and David Morrison took over. David had three sons who played for the juveniles at different times: Joe, Jim and young David. At this time I decided to stop playing on the advice of a consultant. David asked me to help him with the team. David would do the secretarial duties and I would take care of the training on Monday and Wednesday evenings.

This worked very well and gradually we became a force within Glasgow and many boys from all over wanted to play for us; quite a coup in those days as there weren't so many motor cars on the road.

Sadly, in 1962 David Morrison suffered a massive heart attack one Saturday afternoon at Queen's Park recreational park and passed away that evening.

I was then asked to take over as secretary and I immediately asked Thomas Hamilton to help out as he was good at bringing in young talent. His own son, John 'Dingy' Hamilton, eventually played for Hibs before transferring to Rangers.

There were more great players who moved up to senior level: Jimmy Ross, (Ayr United and Partick Thistle); Walter Gerrard, (Clydebank and Hong Kong Rangers); Walter Glen, (Arbroath); Billy Clarke, (Motherwell); Jim Johnstone, (Rangers); Allan Cooper, (Adelaide, Australia). We also had the greatest goalkeeper in Bobby Clarke who is famous for playing for Scotland. He played for Queen's Park FC and Aberdeen. It's worth pointing out that Bobby played for our U-21 juvenile team when he was much younger than his team-mates. I think he must have been fifteen or sixteen and playing at U-21 level.

In my opinion our greatest ever day was the 1965-66 season when we beat Bathgate Thistle 1-0 at the Meadowbank stadium, to lift the Scottish Juvenile Cup. In a twist of fate, the secretary of Bathgate Thistle was none other than our own Jimmy Mann, another of Bobby's boys, who played for Possil YM before finding his way to Sunderland.

Bill Shedden

It was in the early 1990s while I was running a boys' football team in the south side of Glasgow – namely, Victoria Cross Boys' Club – who played at the old Scottish First Division team Third Lanark's ground, Cathkin Park. I was introduced to a football scout called Bobby Dinnie, who I can now say is a life long friend.

Most football managers and coaches involved in youth football knew Bobby and the major impact he played in Scottish youth football over the years, especially in Glasgow where he established Possil YM in the north of Glasgow – where many of the boys made it to the professional game. Bobby was instrumental in requesting that my own boys' team Victoria Cross change their name to Partick Thistle FC U-14/15s, as Bobby was now a prominent football official with Partick Thistle FC. This was a great move for myself and the boys' club, who would get the opportunity to train with a Scottish First Division club. Working with Bobby was a great experience for the boys and almost every game we played as Partick Thistle FC, Bobby was there to check on the progress of the young players.

In 1996 Partick Thistle U-16s won the Scottish Amateur Cup, which was a great achievement for Bobby and Partick Thistle FC, but a much better achievement was to follow the following year, in 1997 when teaming up with Tommy Reid and Bobby; Partick Thistle went on to win the Scottish Amateur Cup again...two years in a row.

I can say this much in conclusion: it had been a great honour for me, through the years, to have worked and enjoyed the company of someone like Bobby Dinnie, his wife Betty and his two sons, Robert and Russell; we have enjoyed many a social chat over a cup of tea.

I understand Bobby is now with Glasgow Rangers as a scout and is still attending football games throughout Scotland.

Good luck and good health in the future – to you, Bobby Dinnie MBE.

Allan Stewart

Possil YMCA always had a good reputation for football so my father had taken my older brother there when he was fifteen. When I turned fifteen – four years later in 1959 – I was taken to the YM hall in Denmark Street to play for the boys' team.

My dad introduced me to Bobby when he was still playing football for Greenock Juniors. Bobby was a bit of a hero to us younger lads as he was well-known as a 'good wee winger'.

When I joined the youths in 1960 Bobby took over the team after he retired early with an injury and led us to my first medal in 1961. I still remember the night. We were presented with our medals at a dinner in the centre of Glasgow and Jimmy Hutchison, one of our players, had to go to hospital with a fish bone stuck in his throat.

In the summer of 1962, Bobby and three of our players, George Fisher, Vic Revie and myself went to Jersey on holiday. This was several firsts for us lads as we had never flown and never travelled out of Scotland. We had a fabulous time with wonderful weather and great beaches, the only problem being Bobby having to have a bad tooth removed and then getting a really painful abscess. For four or five days Bobby never moved too far from his bottle of Anadins.

At the end of the summer of 1962 the core of our youth team decided we did not want to join the juveniles – who we thought were becoming elitist – (or maybe because they did not want us), so we decided to form our own team and entered the senior league as Possilpark YMCA 'B'. This was done after discussion with Bobby and was led by four factors.

- The Juvenile League was full

- The Senior League had a vacancy

- The current Possil seniors at the time seemed quite old to us and they became Possilpark YMCA 'A'.

- Bobby agreed to help get us started during that first season by helping with strips and training et cetera... and finding us a decent manager.

We struggled during that first season with a different manager every other week and finished the season in the lower reaches of the league.

Bobby, George Fisher and I went to Jersey again in the summer of 1963 and on the second night Bobby announced that he had finally found the perfect man to be our manager and all we had to do now was convince him of that. One of Bobby's friends and a colleague, Nan, who had just got married to a guy called Jimmy Hay – who had played football for Possil YM and Rhu Amateurs but had now retired early. They were on their honeymoon in St. Helier, Jersey. As all Bobby had was a street name for the hotel, tracking them down was slightly tricky, involving shouting up at windows, but we eventually found them and surprisingly Jimmy agreed to take the job.

Within one season we had won the league and over the next twenty years had an unprecedented run of success in the senior league winning almost 30 trophies.

Although by the early 1970s I was running the team after a bad knee injury I could still call on Bobby to help when we were fundraising. He had a coterie of past 'mothers' who could make more money at a tombola stall than you could believe and they would help any friend of Bobby.

I had a wonderful family but even then Bobby Dinnie helped to keep me on the straight and narrow and when I remember the family circumstances of some of my team-mates and literally thousands of boys since then, the true worth of Bobby Dinnie may never really be appreciated.

Bobby Dinnie is a living legend in Possil but is still a lovely man with an amazing memory for 'his boys' and their families.

Alister Rutherford

Everything about Bobby was extremely professional.

He executed his work with fine detail. When Possil YMCA were connected to Arsenal we wore their kit and on match-days the dressing room was set and kitted out like a proper professional club; it was Bobby's way, always immaculate and although we played our games at the humble Closeburn Street we felt like we were playing at Highbury; such was the way we felt in our professionally sponsored strips.

Jimmy Dinnie was our kit man back then and he made sure all the shirts were properly hanging on pegs and the shorts and socks neatly folded on the bench. Bobby would come in and he knew if anything was out of place, he didn't need to inspect all the strips he knew instinctively if someone had moved anything.

His professional touch worked wonders for the whole generations of players who were lucky enough to wear the Possil YMCA colours.

Alex McMillan

I played in the 1960s and 70s for Possil YMCA It was an outstanding team way back then with the likes of Eddie Kelly, Kenny Dalglish, Ian Ross and Eugene MacDonald...who could header a brick wall, let me tell you.

I don't think at any time did the YM have any weaknesses in their side. We were famous for our Arsenal connection.

It was Tommy Young who took me to the YM and I'm glad he did. Bobby Dinnie was the master, he knew the right things to say at the right time and to the right people. You could hear a pin drop when he entered a room; such was the respect all the people had for him. After all those years he still commands that same respect. I still feel like that wee boy who played decades ago whenever I meet Bobby.

I was a young kid who wasn't easily embarrassed (if you know what I mean?) but Bobby sort of tamed me. He had this way and no matter who you were, you responded. Everything was done in an orderly fashion from dress sense to even coming off the bus at away games the correct way. No shouting or bawling, just a nice order with mature behaviour.

What can I say about Bobby Dinnie? I have the greatest respect for the man for so many things, simple as that.

Albert Monaghan

It is a privilege to pay tribute by means of a contribution to this book to Bobby Dinnie.

Bobby is without question one of the most generous and talented individuals that Scottish football has ever known.

His enormous contribution to our national game and the success achieved by many clubs and individuals alike cannot be overstated. His unselfish devotion to scouting in youth football is respected by all who have known him and in particular those who have benefited from Bobby being a part of their lives.

Bobby's respect for those who work in the voluntary sector within youth football is what made me look upon him as a mentor in the mid-to-late sixties when I first started Hillwood Boys' Club. Bobby ran the very successful Possil YM and despite our clubs being great rivals, Bobby was as he is today, very approachable and it was this that made me determined that my club would achieve great success if I listened and learned from people like Bobby Dinnie.

Scouting greats like Bobby Dinnie and the late Bobby Calder (Aberdeen FC) can be differentiated from others without being disrespectful by saying that, they did not consider that they were doing a job, it was, and is, simply their way of life.

I recently heard of a suggestion that it was perhaps time for Bobby to get his slippers on and retire. The void could never be filled if Bobby retired. Anyway, Bobby's scouting network has taken him to Europe recently so I doubt he will be retiring from the game just yet.

Directors, players and associates of many of our top clubs throughout British football regard Bobby as a legend and that description is well-deserved.

William Smith

I always wanted to play for the YM since I was ten-years-old.

My first club was Dundas Vale before moving on to Dykemuir Star. Dundas Vale was the team my dad ran. A pal from school called Peter O'Hara went with me to Bobby Dinnie's house at 192 Bardowie Street in Possilpark and I stood all nervous whilst Peter chapped the door. The door swung open and there stood the most loved man in the whole community. With his face smiling down upon us he asked, "Can I help you, son?" I managed to summon up enough courage to ask if I could have a trial for the Possil YM team. Bobby said, "Come away on in, lads." Peter and I went into Bobby's impressive room which was filled with trophies and photographs of famous people like Kenny Dalglish and Ian Ross et cetera. Whilst Peter and I took in all that surrounded us, Bobby said that we should meet him at Torr Street; a black ash football ground in Possil.

I arrived at Torr Street the following Sunday to find there were a lot of players already there. Bobby put me on about half-an-hour before the end of the game. When the game finished I was sure I had no chance of getting to join the YM but he did ask me to come to training at the primary school the following Tuesday.

I turned up to train on the Tuesday night. This was where I was first introduced to Tam Young, who was the coach. This was my first time at real training and it seemed to be professionally done. The players and his training methods were superb. At the end of that first training session I really knew and felt I was a part of the very special Possil YM family.

This is also where I met Jimmy Dinnie (Bobby's brother), Archie and Hector. These men played a major role in my own personal development and also, that of the rest of the lads in the team.

Throughout my early time in Possil YM I went on to meet great and many fantastic players in: Bobby Russell, (Rangers); John Kennoway, (one of the finest midfield players I've ever seen); Ian Taylor, Jimmy McCluskey, Harry Curran, Wes Greer and George Gray – played in the older team but became close friends.

From my very first training session at the school that Tuesday night, Bobby became like a second father to me. He was always there when you were down, always ready to offer fair but good discipline, he was a caring and very special man.

Few people have impressed me in my lifetime; football or otherwise, and Bobby Dinnie was one of them. Bobby had a great aura but real humbleness and was truly a great man. I feel so privileged to say I played for the great Possil YM.

Tony Fitzpatrick

I recall that my first meeting with Bobby Dinnie was in the summer of 1979 when I was sixteen.

I had just finished a season of U-18 football with another boys' club and had been offered a trial with Possil YM.

During the trial game I was aware that Bobby had appeared at the side of the park to cast his eye over proceedings. His presence had the same impact as that of a headmaster taking up his position at the back of the class to monitor your performance. Our group awaited his verdict and my fate was along the lines that I just lacked a bit of strength to play for the U-18 team at that time. Bobby suggested, in the nicest possible way, that I try dropping back down to play for the U-17 team. Like any other sixteen-year-old I wasn't too impressed with Mr Dinnie's view – what did he know?

The answer was – he just knew.

He was proved to be 100% correct. In my first U-17 game I banged in a goal from all of a yard and my time at Possil YM was off and running. Within a couple of seasons I had winners' medals in the League, West of Scotland Cup and Scottish Cup, had trials with First Division Clydebank FC and had played in football tournaments in California, USA and Frankfurt, Germany. Bobby even managed to persuade me to play against the travelling show people while they were based at the Kelvin Hall between Christmas and New Year!

At sixteen, Bobby's assessment wasn't what I had wanted to hear but it was an honest and constructive assessment and opened the door to some wonderful times and experiences.

Looking back – Bobby Dinnie was like the 'Chairman' or 'Chief Executive' who oversaw all that happened at Possil YM. As well as being able to quickly identify quality players he instinctively knew what was best in each situation. He thereby ensured that his teams at all age levels were well-managed and successful. Bobby had a presence; a quite calming presence. In all the years I played under Bobby, or was in his company, I never saw him interfere with the decisions of his team managers – I never saw him angry, raise his voice or speak in anything other than a dignified manner.

In many ways Bobby was also ahead of his time. Today,

football stars make money from running football academies while charitable organizations seek ways to achieve social inclusion. All those years ago there was no profit motive, Bobby saw a need within Possilpark and had the desire to do what was required to give youngsters – regardless of their background - the opportunity to enjoy themselves through football with Possil YM – football academy and social inclusion rolled into one.

I met with Bobby recently after a gap of many years. We talked and enjoyed one another´s company for sometime and I was very much aware that the conversation didn't revolve around Bobby Dinnie, his MBE or his role with Rangers; what struck me instead was that he had a wonderfully close relationship with his wife, was a proud father telling of the progress of his sons Robert and Russell and that he revelled in stories of the past as well as taking a keen interest in the progress of our family.

Football is what Bobby Dinnie is known for and rightly so, for he was, and is, an extremely shrewd judge when it comes to footballing talent. He is, however, much more than that and a précis of experiences over the years at Possil YM could never do him justice.

Put simply, he is a gentleman: a gentleman in the purest sense of the word.

Stuart Girvan

My earliest memories of the YM stem from my brother´s involvement with the club. Robert was a small but pacey striker who spent all of his youth football years at Possil and ultimately plated U-21 football with the club.

I attended Robert´s matches with my father (also Robert). Following this early contact with the club I was keen to follow in his footsteps.

I began to play football at primary school – Miltonbank. It

was one of four primary schools in the Milton area; the others being St Ambrose, St Augustine and Chirnside. This early involvement was to introduce me to many of the team mates that would join me at Possil in the years to follow. After joining the YM at U-13 it quickly became clear that the club had attracted the cream of the talent from Milton, Springburn and Possilpark, with one or two additions from elsewhere.

Highlights of my time at Possil include participation at the Cowal Games and travelling with the club to California. I had watched my brother play at the Cowal Games and was very keen to get involved in this international football event. I was fortunate to get my wish – at U-15 level I believe, and also win the tournament. However, the highlight was the trip to California. It was my first overseas holiday without my parents and was an amazing experience. To be given the opportunity to travel to the US and to play football was a great privilege.

In my second year at U-16 I was provided the opportunity to train and play with Queen's Park Rangers. Terry Venables was manager at that time and George Graham youth team coach. Whilst I was not good enough to secure a professional contract the experience was a great insight into professional football.

U-16 was my last year at Possil. The following season I signed for Queen's Park Football Club where I remained for twenty years as a player and continue to be involved as a director of the club. During that period I won both a Reserve League Cup runners-up medal and a Third Division championship medal.

Much of my success in football was down to the encouragement, support and experience of my formative years at Possil YM. I am hugely indebted to Bobby for the time and effort that he devoted to managing and organizing the club to provide myself and many, many others the opportunity to enjoy our national sport. It is my privilege to contribute this brief piece to his story.

Ross Caven

We practiced almost every night with the band before we started doing little charity gigs with the shows taking part in the Ashfield at that time. We often took the stage at the breaks to entertain the crowd before the main band came back on.

We were probably too young to play in the pub and club circuit as we were all aged around seventeen and eighteen.

Bobby arranged, with his staff, some shows at Christmas and New Year. It was great entertainment and experience; we even had a following in the area who would turn up at our gigs and events.

The band were together for about seven or eight years before we went our separate ways. We did manage to get back playing again some time later in our lives.

The drink took over me. From then on in it was a long haul through the AA meetings that I attended almost every night. Thanks to my meetings and the AA I would be back with my family and my life has taken great shape.

In the early years Bobby took us off the streets. At that time the city was renowned for its gang culture so the streets were not a safe place for youngsters to hang around. Bobby gave the young ones a purpose and somewhere to go and he was always there for them in any time or circumstance of need. He was a pinnacle figure and a wonderful guardian for the young people of Possilpark.

What Bobby Dinnie has done for Possilpark is incredible…he´s irreplaceable.

Robert Carrenduff

A chance remark in 1976 to a footballing friend of mine led to me meeting Bobby Dinnie.

It also led to a close friendship that has lasted thirty years. I played amateur football for Possilpark YMCA senior team for twelve years and decided I would like to give something back to the YMCA for all the good times I had enjoyed with them and I liked the idea of running a kids' team.

About a month later my friend said Bobby Dinnie would like to meet me with a view to looking after the U-13s at Possilpark YMCA. Now, I knew of Bobby, and to say hello, but to have a conversation lasting more than a few minutes was all I had ever had with him. Now, here I was having an interview to see if I was suitable to look after a team. It was daunting to say the least but after a few minutes he put me at ease and later offered me the task of looking after the boys' team.

Bobby liked to keep his eye on all the teams, to watch individuals and was always on hand with advice but did not interfere if it was not needed. It was a full-time job looking after seven teams; some played on Saturdays, the rest on Sundays. It was quite remarkable at times how he managed to do it, considering he did not drive. There was also funds to be raised to subsidize the teams for new strips and for trips and tournaments so this meant jumble sales and dances to arrange in the YMCA hall in Denmark Street, Possilpark.

A big thanks must go to the committee Bobby selected and the parents of the boys who kindly donated jumble or helped out on the day or night of the fundraiser.

We won the Cowal Tournament for the U-13s in 1977. The presentation was held on a Sunday night and such was the stature Bobby held that we were late for the last ferry back to Glasgow but a message was relayed to the captain and needless to say we made it on board – albeit fifteen minutes late.

Six years on Bobby asked me if I would like to assist him in scouting players for St. Mirren then St. Johnstone and then help him to run the Rangers Amateurs – who were at that time Glasgow Rangers' youth team. Thanks to Bobby I rubbed shoulders with many famous people who I would normally see only on television; too many to name but a few were: John

Greig, Jock Wallace, Bobby Shearer, Tony Fitzpatrick, Frank McGarvey, Alex Totten, Bruce Rioch, Colin Todd and lastly – the great Jock Stein.

On our scouting trips I was always amazed how Bobby could remember the names of kids that played for one of the YMCA teams and years later they were parents themselves; yet he recognized not only the face but the full name

No matter where we went Bobby always met someone he knew connected with football: Aberdeen, Inverness, and Dumfries. We went to Notts County´s ground in Nottingham; at last I thought surely no one here would know him. I was wrong! We were outside the ground passing time when this gentleman came towards us and said, "Bobby Dinnie, I haven't seen you for years how are you?" So I think in every corner of Britain there is probably someone who knows Bobby Dinnie.

We watched the player who was being touted as the next best thing. He scored three goals and his team won that day. I asked Bobby what he thought and he said to me, "Is he better than what we have?" I had to agree that he wasn't so therefore we didn't sign him, as a footnote his big transfer never transpired.

One honour I had with Bobby was to sit with him in the maternity when his wife Betty gave birth to Russell, his youngest son. We were watching a game and as Bobby didn't drive I had to take him to the hospital when he got a call to say his wife had gone into labour.

To think my journey with Bobby all started with a chance remark in a pub and I know my friendship will last for many years to come.

Norman McAllister

My two boys Billy and Drew played for Possil YMCA. I have fond memories of the fund-raising work we did and of course the fund-raising nights that took place at the hall.

We organized dances where we even took our own booze –

it was such a laugh – and here we were all doing the can-can. Those were great nights and the people involved were just marvellous.

On the football side of things it was such a pleasure to see the young boys enjoying themselves. They were so happy and very much at home playing football and for Possil YMCA. My late husband Eric and I enjoyed every minute of being a part of the team. I remember trips to places like Dunoon where they held the Cowall Tournament.

Bobby Dinnie is highly thought of in the community. Eric was especially fond of him, he thought the world of Bobby.

Mae Walker

It was my mother, Nelly McLeod, (who of course became a McMillan) that introduced me into the YM.

My husband, David, two sons, David Jnr and Stuart played a part in the YM as did my daughter Elizabeth McMillan (now McNeil).

We had great and wonderful times with our jumble sale and dance nights that ultimately resulted in raising funds for the club. It also gave the young members of the local community something to get involved in and it certainly had positive effects. Disco evenings held on a weekly basis gave the youngsters a place to go and let themselves loose. In a good way it got kids off the streets. Christmas time was especially good because the YM hall was back-to-back with Saracen Police Office and the weans would fire snowballs at them and then run into the hall for protection. A small moment of mischief and if that was the only tearaway problem we had to face today it wouldn´t be at all that bad a world to live in.

The Cowal Tournament in Dunoon was a wonderful occasion for us and the whole team. Some of the boys slept in the Church hall. A great adventure for them and some had taken their own sleeping bags. Sadie Gordon and I never saw much of the games as we were too busy preparing and cooking meals for the lads. You could tell if they won a game or not by the look on their faces as they walked in the hall but Possil rarely lost so it was uncommon when they did get beat.

What would I change in today´s environment? A good community centre open more than one night per week, in fact, five nights would be better.

Kay McMillan

* Kay McMillan is involved with Good-As-New. A Church charity that works coherently with the local community. They receive good condition unwanted or no longer required goods from community members and in return they are taken in and resold to the members of the community who would benefit from those goods. Good-As-New offer clothes for children and adults, curtains, baby ware like prams et cetera and many more items that all find their way back into the community. Indeed an uplifting and spirited organization.

The first time I met Bobby was about 1977 at a Paisley and District
Amateur Football League meeting in the Saint Margaret´s hall, Paisley.

We were introduced to each other by Gibby Baird who was the president of the league. We formed a lasting friendship, Bobby had a great ability to make people feel at ease In his company

One of the reasons Bobby stood out at all football grounds was his trademark deerstalker hat.

When he arrived at the Cowan Park with one or more of his teams to play against Barrhead Boys´ Club, he always had a chat with our team coaches, some of them would ask me who Bobby Dinnie was as he never had any airs and graces. They could not believe he was the President of Possil YM – he just went about his business very quietly and efficiently.

In all the time I have known him I have never seen him lose his temper at the side of the park. Sometimes he would be very upset about something that occurred on the football park but would never show his anger in public: a true professional and sportsman.

When Possil YM came to Barrhead and there were problems on the football park, I would always phone Bobby after the game and discuss any incident regarding his club. He would either say he knew all about the problem or listen to what I had to say about the incident, he would always thank me and say he would deal with the problem. In my heart I knew that would happen.

Bobby invited Barrhead Boys´ Club to the Possil gala day – football tournament, there was a small lad playing in the U-13s for Saint Mary´s Boys´ Guild of Possil. I went over to Bobby and asked the lad´s name as I felt he could make a name for himself. About seven years later I was at Firhill watching Partick Thistle reserves play against St. Mirren reserves. As I watched this young lad running I thought I had seen him playing somewhere before; so I phoned Bobby when I arrived home. As I described the player he started to laugh and said his name was Chic Charnley. That proved to me that he followed all the youngsters in his area. After I got to know and trust Bobby I would phone and ask him for advice he never once said he was too busy to listen to me and Barrhead Boys´ Clubs´ problems. After our conversation he would always say, "Phone me anytime."

Bobby Dinnie had total respect from all committee and players of Possil YM – considering the tough area in Glasgow, where his club was based – he certainly helped to keep hundreds of young lads out of trouble. This must be his greatest achievement in his sporting life. In Summary the best

way for me to sum up Bobby Dinnie is simply: a true gent a good friend and a great ambassador for youth football. Or, in other words 'a legend in his own time'.
John Willock

In the changing rooms you can imagine the banter; the loud vocals before each game. Players would naturally be tense, apprehensive and eager to get out and play.

Bobby would appear out of nowhere and the whole room would fall silent; out of respect. Bobby´s look was enough. He didn´t have to say anything; in fact he said so much without uttering a word. It wasn´t out of fear, it was complete respect and he was respected by everyone.

As soon as Bobby vacated the vicinity there would be a long pause before we got back to being our buoyant and vocal self. You can say the decibel level rose after that.

Bobby approached me years later after a game I was involved in. Bobby said, "I´m glad you succeeded, John. Of all the players, you were always the one player I should have pushed to go senior." I was embarrassed that such a great man could say such a touching thing.
John Conlin

* No young player wants to miss a game of football and in particular no-one wanted to miss playing for Possil YMCA. They were successful, there were medals up for grabs and cups to hold aloft so it was always important to be ready to rise to such challenges.

John Conlin is famous for an incident that occurred prior to an important cup-tie. John broke his left arm and was in plaster. He was so desperate to play and he knew Bobby Dinnie – or anyone else at the club – would not permit him to play with a 'stooky'. John, in typical Glaswegian spirit, opted to play doctor on himself. He found his way into a public toilet in the city centre of Glasgow, ran his left arm under the tap to soak the plaster and proceeded to hack off the stooky with what can only be described as an unhygienic instrument. All this just to play a simple game of fitba. *Marvellous.*

Bobby and I go way back, perhaps further than I care to imagine.

We were together in Korea and Hong Kong where we did our National Service together. So young we were and of course the inevitable happened where life takes over; you go your own ways but before you know it we found ourselves re-united again after fifty years. I must say, however, that during all that time that I didn´t see Bobby I always spoke about him, I always thought about him, and it was a magical moment when we met up again. It was as if we were never apart.

Bobby was and still is a truly wonderful man. He is the same now as when he was a young man doing his service overseas. He didn´t change much, he was always a sincere, honest and genuine man. He didn´t have any of the 'expected' habits that most young men accumulate like smoking, cursing and I don´t recall him being a drinker of any capacity. Neither did he complain about anything and of all the good qualities he had at sport and as a person he never bragged about them; he just seemed to have this unique personality. His outlook on life was tremendous.

I learned that he received the MBE from Her Majesty and to be honest it couldn´t have happened to a nicer guy.

One of life´s greatest pleasures was meeting Bobby, being in his company and to be considered a friend of him.

A lovely man, a great guy and a wonderful friend.
Jock Rodden

I joined the YM football club around 1965 when I was asked

by my brother Bobby to help out for a few weeks. Little did I know that I was still there twenty years later.

However, I must say, I enjoyed it all the same. I was very fortunate to have four trips to America with the club (one to up state New York and three to California). The trips to California were organized by three Scots: Bobby Clarke, Hughie Kinnear and Gordon Ritchie. Gordon was a Paisley buddy and Hughie Kinnear played for Yoker Athletic. Sadly, those three men have all passed away.

Hughie Kinnear's son, Dominic, is at this moment the manager of San Jose Earthquakes.

I personally would like to thank the wonderful people who looked after me in New York: the Morgan family, whom the father was Chief Electrician at the New York Port Authority. Frank Morgan's office was on the 66th floor off the ill-fated twin towers and it was an experience looking out of his office to see the Statue of Liberty: unforgettable!

I would also like to mention the people of Fremont, California, who took the boys into their homes, especially Arthur and Lily Gormley, Gordon and Margaret Ritchie (who were both Scots) and who I stayed with. Also at Half Moon Bay, my hosts Tom and Lovella Barry; who I am still friends with.

Mark Pierce, who also hosted the boys and in fact, some of the men had Mark speaking in a Glaswegian accent!

I would also like to mention a lady whom we met in Half Moon Bay, who originally came from 202 Saracen Street, Possilpark and treated all the boys to Disneyland. Her own name was Helen Harley, who, when in her younger days went to America and met her Danish husband. They both went into business and became millionaires.

Before all the trips to America I had a caravan at Prestwick, Ayrshire. I heard about Jock Wallace training Rangers players in the sand dunes so we used to take the players down on a

Sunday for a session.

I have memories of our annual Easter trip to Bradford, to the Liberal Club that was organized by a gentleman called Jim Geraghty – who is still my friend to this day. Jim has mentioned the scenario where the digs that were previously arranged for our boys didn´t work out and Jim and his great wife, Margaret, put the boys up…cramming as many bodies as possible resulted in one of the boys sleeping in the bath!

It has been a great pleasure meeting up with the boys I was associated with during my time at Possil YMCA. Some of them made the grade in football and others I hear have done well for themselves in business and all other areas of life.

Jimmy Dinnie

Bobby has been rightly named the 'star spotter' within the youth football scene, in Glasgow, for the past forty years.

I first came upon Bobby in the mid-sixties when I played for Eastercraigs; when we played Bobby´s Possil YM. This was the start of his unleashing a conveyor belt of talent – which has gone on relentlessly since. Many players have reached the very highest level, and Bobby has had a major influence in their development.

More recently, I have had the pleasure of working with Bobby at Rangers FC. In his scouting role, he, as always, is the perfect ambassador, and provides an unrivalled wealth of experience and enthusiasm.

Lastly, he is a perfect gentleman, and a good friend.

Jim Mullin

Back in the late 80s, I took over Cross Lane Associated Football Club. There were a lot of talented young football players but a lot of work had to be done to get new strips, balls, nets and most important of all; a place, a ground. After one season in a lower league we finished mid-table.

The Scout: *The Bobby Dinnie Story*

As the years went by we built up a gifted team with players such as Jimmy Lawler and the Williams brothers, alongside many others. But in years to come, conversation will repeatedly turn to Possilpark, time and time again.

Possil YM's visit to Bradford was met by a former player, Bob McCann, who organized the trip, welcomed by my late wife, Margaret, and myself. As the boys settled in, the afternoon game approached and I think Possil just won. Saturday evening and the lads had a great night, they really enjoyed themselves but Sunday morning in the dressing room was different; the mood changed. I remember Bobby coming in and he said, "Don't get changed, you're not playing." he told the boys. And with a smile he looked at me and said, "I'll tell you later." At half-time I set about finding out what was going on. "Jim, I caught them kissing some girls last night." (tongue-in-cheek, if you excuse the pun.) "What if they had been drinking?" I asked Bobby. No answer.

Possil's next visit was something we thought would never happen. On the Friday before the team arrived I found that things were not up to standard, so had to book Bobby and Jimmy into a hotel for bed and breakfast. That night I asked Margaret what do we do now and she said, "Well, there's only one thing we can do, we'll put them up, they can stop here." Sunday morning and there were bodies all over; even the bathroom! Good fun, until…"breakfast's up!" "Oh my God!" I heard Margaret say, as she realized how many mouths she had to feed, and sixteen breakfasts she did manage.

Twelve months later we came to Glasgow and what a reception we got. One of my players, Brian Williams, and myself stopped with Bobby and his good wife, Betty – who made us feel very welcome; as did the people at the club we visited on Saturday evening; where they laid out food and drink. Some of the boys I see now still talk about that weekend, but many are now married with children and no longer play football.

Our last visit from Possil was very enjoyable, with our club members going in to make sure the boys were being looked after. A surprise for Bobby, Jimmy and the players came at half-time when the City of Bradford Pipe Band provided entertainment, and again back at the club before the boys left for the long journey back to Glasgow.

Bobby, Jimmy and everyone at Possil YMCA, may I, on behalf of all your friends in Bradford, congratulate you for all the hard work you have done and the success you encountered. And to Bobby, from myself, I hope the people of Glasgow will reward him for his service and loyalty to the club.

Jim Geraghty

I joined the YM when I was thirteen-years-old. I was there for about four years until I was seventeen. During that time I participated in most sports and activities there. The most important being football, as I went from playing for Possil YM to playing junior/senior football for fourteen years.

During my time at Possil YMCA, Bobby Dinnie was a great inspiration to me in his knowledge and coaching abilities of the game. My time along with Bobby, and the team who ran the club, were to be a big part in my life growing up. It was there I met most of my friends and I went there at every opportunity. I also met my wife, Violet, there – who also went to the club – and we´ve been together for forty years and have two great kids, Derek and Louise.

Bobby was a great leader and deserves every praise.

It was through Bobby´s endeavour and ability that I went on to play football at senior and junior level; playing alongside players like Danny McGrain, Paul Wilson, Tony Green, Henry Hall and many others.

I would like to thank Bobby – who was a big part of my life – and my wife´s, too.

I would never have met her had it not been for Bobby and the YMCA.

James Hutchison

When my brother Colin and I began scouting for players in the Glasgow area for our family club, Clydebank, we met a small band of people we grew to trust and respect. Bobby belonged to that group. (Bobby´s telephone number was one memorized by constant use). In the years that followed that initial feeling was only strengthened.

Even when Bobby was directly working with a particular team his focus was always on the futures of all the kids; not simply the stand-outs. No-one had a bad word for Bobby and his brother Jimmy. In these times when the professional game has taken on youth development I cannot think of anyone who has facilitated kids working their way up in soccer better than Bobby did with the YM.

Memory 1.

Bobby giving his own kids money for ice cream at a game...so he could concentrate on the game.

Memory 2.

Telling me of a young player, Robert Fleck: we went to see him, the opposition did not turn up, we left. They then turned up an hour late. Fleckie scored six and signed for Rangers!

Memory 3.

Telling me of Gary McSwegan: went to watch him, team played into a gale, 0-0 at half-time. We had to leave. Second half, 10-0. Gary scored nine. Signed for Rangers.

Memory 4.

Always asking after players we signed for Clydebank from the YM.

It is easy to talk of legends. To hundreds of soccer people that have met Bobby he has achieved that accolade. He is part of a soccer social history in Glasgow.
Ian Steedman

Bobby did a tremendous amount for Possil as a team and for the community of Possilpark.

It didn´t matter where you came from, who you were, or your background, all were equal as far as Bobby was concerned.

His teachings of equality are evident when we were presented with our kit and blazers; which were Royal blue. I took stick from some of my friends including my father for wearing blue but Bobby asked, "Do you feel comfortable in the blazer, son?" I did feel comfortable and I did answer Bobby with an honest yes. Bobby said, "Well, that´s all that matters, as long as you feel comfortable in the blazer, that´s all that counts."

From that moment on I realized how important his words were. Bobby taught us tolerance and acceptance of others, which I use to this very day.
Hugh McColligan

It was in the late 70s, when I was about fourteen-years-old, when I started playing with Possilpark YMCA Football Club.

At that time, Possil YM, or, The YM as it was better known, had teams ranging from U-13s through to over 21s and over all in charge was Bobby Dinnie, known as Mr Possil.

During this period – and indeed at the time of writing – Possilpark, Glasgow was a socially deprived area with an unhealthy crime rate, however, Bobby was not only respected by team managers and players alike but also the local community.

I recall being sent by the YM to Coventry... (that's the city of Coventry) for a trial. My fellow team-mate at that time was John Hendrie, who signed for the sky blues and continued a very successful professional football career, travelling to many English football clubs.

Meantime, I came back to Glasgow and with Bobby's connections with Glasgow Rangers FC, it wouldn't be long before I was on trial with Rangers' youth team and completing pre-season training at the infamous Gullane Sands with the then new manager, John Grieg and his team, including the legendary Davie Cooper.

I wasn't signed by Rangers but Bob being Bob, persisted and arranged for me to be sent to Norwich City FC where I was to start my professional football career.

Eventually, I would leave Norwich and do the circuit of clubs back in Scotland.

I lost contact with Bobby for a number of years during this period but we were soon to meet up again when I finished my professional career in 1991 to join Strathclyde Police. Little did I know that Bobby was the Head of Commissionaires at Strathclyde Police Headquarters, in Glasgow city centre.

When I met Bobby for the first time in years, he could quickly rhyme off all the clubs I had played with over the years. Bobby's interest didn't just stop at the YM, he was the type of man who knew who had gone where and what they were doing. Bobby had that genuine and natural curiosity on how people were doing.

From then on, I was to meet Bobby on a regular basis, whether through the work environment or at youth football matches, standing in the howling wind and pouring rain, while Bobby scouted for the next Kenny Dalglish.

To sum up Bobby's influence on me; I was about fourteen-years-old and had paid my £50 deposit for my High School Spanish holiday trip, however, I was soon to learn that this trip coincided with the Cowal football tournament in Dunoon, where the YM were normally well-represented at all age groups. I cancelled my Spanish holiday, received my £50 deposit and instead travelled to nearby Dunoon. The contrast in holidays were: one week residing in a Church hall, sleeping on a mattress on the floor and one week sunning yourself in a 3 star Spanish hotel.

There are many everlasting happy memories of my childhood at the YM which would not have been possible without Mr Possil – alias Bobby Dinnie. The highest accolade I could give Bobby is that there have been a number of people involved in the success of my football career but only two people have had a major influence; my father, Angus, being number one and Bobby coming a close second.

I certainly didn't reach the heights of the Kenny Dalglishs of this world but I can say without any shadow of doubt: Bobby Dinnie gave me the opportunity to enjoy the 'great game', probably just as much as the great Kenny Dalglish, and for that I am eternally grateful.

Thanks, Bobby.

Grant Reid

Bobby´s appetite and enthusiasm for football is insatiable.

He has great experience, wisdom and a very knowledgeable eye; as streams of successful players have progressed under him, into senior football will testify.

Rewards for Bobby came in the shape of satisfaction and pride watching that progression.

The time spent training, taking teams and watching matches, will only ever be truly recognized by those who know him.

I and many other players are indebted to one of the most respected men in the game, for all of the guidance given to them over the years.

Bobby, many thanks.

Gordon Chisholm

Everyone has stories and memories of their life. I would – and I am honoured, privileged; call it whatever – like to say a little word about *Sir* Bobby Dinnie.

I joined Possil YMCA around April 1967 as an U-14 player. Myself and my friend, Jamie Hughes, would travel from Garthamlock to Glasgow city centre, then catch the bus to Possilpark; I think it was the No 47 or 28 bus we took. Two or three evenings in the week we would make this trip; and on most nights you can imagine the weather.

We would finish school at 4pm and head home to collect our kit, catch the bus at 4.45pm into the centre of Glasgow. We´d arrive at Buchanan Street Station, walk to the King´s theatre, to Hope Street and catch the bus which would take us to Possil where we´d arrive after six. We would all be in or around the YM hall, each team had one hour or so to train. If the weather was really bad we would train in the hall, if it was not too bad; say, thunderstorms or a hurricane, we´d train outside. "Boys, got to be tough if you want to play here." This was when I first came across Tam Young. I´m sure before Tam was born he was in the army or somewhere regimental. Yes, this man would take training and did he love to see you sweating! He was a fitness fanatic.

When I look back, well, if you want to be a player then you have to work hard. When Tommy Young was finished with you you´d have thought you just completed a shift down a coal mine, (aye, with a bag of coal on your back).

I was at the YM for about two weeks when Bobby Dinnie summoned me to the YM room, in the hall. This was where we had our office and physio room. I met our club doctor/physio, Hector. I played two trial games and trained five or six nights.

He said, "Son, you are a good wee player and you are hard, we are going to sign you." Well, here we are talking about the Possil YM; you would have thought it was Real Madrid. If I remember to this day, when I walked out the physio room all the boys were there waiting on me, all shaking my hand and introducing me to everyone. When I signed, Bobby said to me, "George, make sure you don´t let this club down, I am fair but we don´t stand for fools, so, just get on with it, and most of all, enjoy yourself." The following week I was kitted out in grey trousers, blazers, collar and tie and the YM bag – in maroon and yellow. This was a dream. Possil, in those days was a place were, if you didn´t come from Possil, it was dangerous to go into, but if you had the YM bag, the local gang members would shout, *"C´mon the YM!"* This made us feel great.

We were one of the best clubs in Scotland. Amongst others there were Harmony Row, Eastercraigs, Drumchapel Amateurs, Glasgow United, Glasgow Amateurs, Mosspark and loads of other top drawer teams. To me, we were the No1. I was Possil, through-and-through. We won cups, titles, trips to Highbury, tours and day outings. We held jumble sales and everything to fill the mind and heart; this was all organized by Bobby and his staff. I remember Junior Semple, Hector, wee Archie, and Jimmy and George (Bobby´s brothers). Jimmy was close to all the boys and would join in with the jokes and banter. Great times, Jimmy, love you, wee man.

I was chosen to play for Scotland YMCA 16s. I suppose that was the highlight of my career. I had trials for Arsenal, Aston Villa and I believe a few other clubs were looking at me. If I´m honest now, if I had been more dedicated, who knows?...But no tears from me.

I keep in touch with Bobby and I must say he hasn´t changed one single bit, he´s a gentleman.

Bobby, I say this on behalf of all the players: honest, we all loved the YM, 'great times'. Let me also say a big big thank you to Betty (Bobby's wife) for all the lovely clean strips. Betty, you must have gone through so much hard work and not forgetting the queues of kids at your door for a plate of hot soup or mince-and-tatties: Aye, Betty, they can't tell me about tea ladies, you were in front of them all.

I had the pleasure of meeting and becoming a friend of George Best; through another great friend, Bill McMurdo. I had George up on many occasions in Glasgow and on one occasion I asked him if he'd come to my pub and smash open a bottle that was full of coins and money, for a charity. I said, "George, it's for an old boys' club I played for when I was a kid."

"No problem, wee man, who's the club?" was George's reply.

I told him it was Possil YM, the club Kenny Dalglish played for.

George replied, "Oh! Bobby Dinnie's club? I've never met him but I hear he is a gentleman."

George Best came up and smashed open the charity bottle, he never let Possil YM down although he may have with other top clubs and managers. He knew Bobby was a gentleman but possibly, George Best thought he couldn't let the wee man down – I may never get another chance at Possil YM.

George Gray

I can remember as far back when I was five-years-old, living in Sloy Street, and watching the YM players training. Myself and a lot of other kids in the area would all join in, running behind players as they warmed up or were being put through their paces.

Normally a coach, a manager, or even an adult, would not allow such a thing to happen; you would expect anyone for that matter to chase the kids as a 'nuisance' but this wasn't the case with Bobby Dinnie and his YM club. Ten to twenty children would all run behind the players and no-one took offence to this; it was part of the tight bond and good spirit within the community that everyone (including weans) were allowed to take part in YM activity.

I joined the YM at the age of seven where I would further enjoy more years playing through the ranks of the various age groups the YM had to offer. My dad wanted me to be a senior player and he kind of pushed me towards this goal but I eventually found my own way and opted to take the business route in life. My ambitions obviously lay elsewhere. I have been quoted as being a player in my time and if you have the great fortune to be considered a 'player' in those days it really meant something because most of the lads in our team and area were players of great quality so I can be proud that I am regarded in this bracket. The two best players I ever played with were Bobby Russell and Chic Charnley. Two outstanding players of rare class and ability. In all, I grew up amongst many many great players – heard of or unheard of – nevertheless, truly great players.

Bobby Dinnie has contributed to my life in every positive respect. I am still in awe of Bobby and I still have a nervousness about me when I meet him. Throughout my life after my Possil YM days I always wanted Bobby to approve of what I was doing and in a way I have been followed by his very spirit. I wanted to let him know I was doing well and even today, nearly half-a-century old, I still feel like a wee boy in his company.

Frankie Anderson

I met Bobby in the 1960s when he managed Possil YMCA. At that time I was the founder member of Sighthill Boys´ Club.

Bobby and I go back a long way. Bobby's knowledge of young football talent was exceptional. Possil and Sighthill Boys´ Clubs met in the final of the U-15s cup in the Dunoon

Youth Tournament but my team suffered a 7-0 defeat, the best laugh was I told everyone it was 0-0!

Bobby had the honour of playing against Günter Netzer, who was present with a German youth team party in Dunoon, 1979.

Another funny story in regards to a Possil player, named Johnny Hamilton – he got his nickname 'Dinghy', as he went out on a boat but could not swim!

Bobby was Chief Commissionaire at Strathclyde Police's Glasgow Headquarters and was often heard proclaiming the fact that Scotland did in fact have youthful talent like the Kenny Dalglishs of today and that the area was not all vandals and hooligans.

Bobby was a true family man and often visited my family home, bringing his kids too. On one occasion, Bobby´s youngest son Robert took a shine to a jigsaw that was part completed, after three long years on the glass table...and let´s just say that after the visit, the jigsaw had to be started again!

Last but not least, Bobby´s finest hour was in 1998, when he was awarded the MBE from Her Majesty the Queen, which was truly well-deserved and justified.

Dougie Canning

Bobby Dinnie I have know for almost fifty years. Firstly, as a rival to his much loved Possil YMCA. As far back as the late sixties we strived to attract the best young players from the industrial West of Scotland, Bobby to Possil YMCA and the late great Douglas Smith and I to our beloved Drumchapel Amateurs – often targeting the same players.

Throughout the many years, and latterly working together scouting for Rangers Football Club, we have remained firm friends, and while there is little doubt in footballing circles he is continually talked about in reverence about the players whom he developed and progressed to the senior grade and international football. Bobby, to me, is one of a very few, very special people, who has dedicated his life to youth football.

Bobby did not only produce top-class players, by his presence and the respect he gained, also produced top-class citizens. Truly, one of football's gentlemen.

I can recall in the late sixties/early seventies, together with our boys, taking part in the Cowal Tournament in Dunoon during the summer recess and despite our determination and commitment to win, there was comradeship between the staff coaches in charge of the players. Although we all wanted to win, taking part and leading by example was also just as important to the development of the young players.

Understandably with the quality of players at Possil YM, like Drumchapel, we attracted scouts from clubs throughout the UK but with Bobby it did not matter how big or small the club, it was the the boy that mattered and I'm sure this reflects the respect he had not only from the players who made it to the top but to all who had the privilege of being a part of the Possil YMCA club.

I am delighted to make a small contribution to Bobby's biography and there is obviously not enough space to fully pay tribute to him, but little doubt others will do so. I trust that this quiet, gracious, unassuming giant to youth football will for many more years continue to contribute to the game we all love and some of his exceptional qualities rub-off on those fortunate to share his company.

David Moyes

I lived beside Bobby in Bardowie Street. The locals used to chap Bobby up for a loan of a ball now and again. Fathers of young boys would come to Bobby for a game of football because the team had great recognition and if your boy was good enough there was a chance he'd get snapped up by the many clubs Bobby's team were connected to.

Possil YMCA, as you know, fed the likes of Arsenal, Aston Villa and Rangers amongst many top profile teams throughout the UK.

I played in a band at that time called The Madcaps with Bobby Carrenduff, Freddy and Johnny Wyles. We'd play in front of audiences to help with the fund-raising events that the club held often. We played at the Mecca and we got ourselves some exposure in the city's media. It was a great time, a unique bond between all of the community and everyone did their bit for the team and the area. We dressed up as part of our gig and entertained. So long ago but still fresh in the memory.

Bobby kept everyone together. You can never forget the man. He was and still is a one-off. Of all the gigging, the entertaining, the media exposure and the local fame thing, it is Bobby who is the star. What he has done not only for the district but for humanity on a whole is incredible and fully deserves the recognition. A true father figure.

Possil YM, although never died, faded through time but I am very proud to know that just recently, steps have been made to put the great institution of Possil YM back up there where it belongs and my grandson, Henry Dunlop, has signed up to hopefully start the wheels of history in motion once again.

Charlie Rae

I first met Bobby sometime in 1981. Battlefield Boys' Club was the team I managed; where I took them from a school team to amateur status. We were sponsored by Billy Craig of Strathclyde Meats, a sponsor for twenty years, a rare loyalty it has to be said.

Some of our boys at Battlefield were given training facilities arranged by Bobby Dinnie, who was at Partick Thistle at this time. The lads trained at the Firhill complex and before long we had built up a big friendship with Bobby. We were mostly a South of Glasgow team but once word got out of our involvement with Partick Thistle we soon attracted boys from all over.

Our club enjoyed trips to Canada to play in the famous Robbie Tournament and in England – where we won an International tournament in Blackpool and of course far away parts of Scotland like Aberdeen – pipped by an Aberdeen team.

Battlefield were like most Boys´ clubs in and around Glasgow; we had terrific people that helped us raise the necessary funds that allowed us to take part in those major youth tournaments. Kids raised £5000 and Jim Shields, Glasgow Councillor, was monstrous in raising £12000 in ten months. He played a huge part in the club, coming to games with his wife and played a big part in the interest and welfare of the kids.

We had great times at our club where we formed friendships and links across the country. Perfect example of this was our annual games against Lytham.

Our best years, however, were with Bobby.

Bobby keeps his own council and not a man to be trifled with. He certainly doesn´t suffer fools gladly, that´s for sure. His knowledge of football is immense.

I would like to mention a few who contributed or were involved at some point with our own club besides Bobby Dinnie. Eddie Hunter, Robert Archibald, Gordon Blackwell, Arthur Chatfield, James Abraham and Kenny McLeod.

Ian McConachie

I first met Bobby when he arrived at Partick Thistle to organize the youth teams. Since that time I feel I have known him all my life. His whole life has been football and anyone who is involved in the game knows and respects Bobby.

A couple of cases I particularly recall from the youth team

days.

One. The way the boys reacted when Mr Dinnie appeared (in fact, I wouldn't be surprised if Her Majesty referred to him as Mr Dinnie when he received his MBE award).

Two. The time he spoke to a boy for turning up for Partick Thistle training wearing a certain other Glasgow team's strip. *IT DIDN'T HAPPEN AGAIN!*

Anyway, I have enjoyed all the times being involved with the Thistle youth teams under Bobby and wish him all the best in years to come.

Bobby Briggs

I grew up in the Possil YM family. My Uncle Johnny Hamilton, played for the YM then moved to Hibs. My father and grandfather, Thomas Hamilton, worked for the YM. My grandfather's involvement lasting over twenty years.

J. Wales was my manager, a fantastic person whom I enjoyed playing under. Also, visiting California in 1977, which I have lasting memories.

Bobby Dinnie was always the chief mentor for all YM players and officials and deserves all the plaudits for his continued support of the YM. I'll never forget the Cowal tournaments in Dunoon, they were fantastic times for me as a juvenile and have fond memories of my time at the YM.

Billy Reid

Billy Reid's playing career:

Possil YM	1975 - 1978
Petershill	1981
Ashfield	1981 - 1982
Queen of The South	1983 - 1987
Clyde FC	1988 - 1990
Hamilton Accies	1990 - 1993

Stirling Albion   1993

Billy Reid's managerial career:

Clyde FC   First team coach
                         Assistant manager
                         Manager

Hamilton Accies   Manager 2005 – 2006

I had many dealings and encounters with Bobby where a few young prospects passed through him. You always knew what you were getting from his kids in terms of quality and character and they all came with a very high opinion.

I wasn't at all surprised at the accolades and achievements he has been given, he's such a gentleman.

Bert Paton

I joined the YM when I was twelve-years-old and stayed with the club for ten years as it was one of the most established clubs in Scotland at that level; mostly because of the amount of work and effort my Uncle Bobby Dinnie put into the club.

I stayed until my time at U-21 level where we won several trophies under Jim Gillespie. I left the YM to join Baillieston Juniors where we had a great bunch of lads like Pat Cairney, Willie Dalziel and many more, including our crazy gaffer Tam Young.

From there I moved to Partick Thistle and played under Billy Lamont: a hard gaffer to please. I think I did okay for him; winning all nine awards, it was my first year as a professional. I spent two-and-a-half years at the Jags then I was lucky enough to get a move to the Premier League. I joined Dundee for £100.000. I had five great years there at Dens Park under tremendous management. Jim Duffy, Simon Stainrod and my 'auld' pal forever, Gordon Wallace. I will never forget what Jim Duffy did for me. He is so dedicated to the game and he deserves to be at the highest level of the game at all times.

I departed from Dundee and headed back to Glasgow, back to Partick Thistle and teamed up with another great character of the game: the one and only Mr John Lambie. I was blessed with playing alongside such great players and they don´t come any better than Chic Charnley. It was an absolute priviledge to be in the same team and on the same park with a magnificent player: the best player I´ve ever played with in my career. He was also a very close friend so I stayed for another five years.

Going back to Jim Duffy, I will always have so much respect for him. Through the good and the bad times that gentleman has been there for me. If it wasn´t for him I wouldn´t have made it back from my cruciate ligament injury. Jim forced me not to give up when I clearly was giving up so I will always be forever grateful to him as a friend and a leader, thank you, gaffer.

My career came to an end at the age of 34 when I wasn´t offered a new contract at Partick but Thistle will always be in my heart. There are a few I would like to thank for helping me to enjoy playing against the likes of Rangers at Ibrox and Celtic at Parkhead and all the other good teams in the Premier League: Billy Lamont, Jimmy Hughes, Billy McLaren, John Lambie, Gordon Wallace, Simon Stainrod, John McCormack, Jim Duffy and of course, all the good players I played with at Partick Thistle and Dundee.

Allan Dinnie

I had the honour and pleasure of working closely with Bobby Dinnie during the nine years or so he was with Partick Thistle. What he accomplished at Firhill will be documented elsewhere so I will leave that to others.

He was known everywhere we went and was greeted with

genuine pleasure and respect by everyone. His great ability to encourage every boy and offer good advice is to be admired. In his own way he is a strict disciplinarian: no strips outside shorts, no dirty boots and certainly no bad language!

His contribution to football in Scotland is unique and is unlikely to be equalled.

Thanks, Bobby, for all the good times we had together.

Alex Robertson

My Dad (far right) with his team Argyll Thistle, later to become Kilmun Thistle.

Brother Jim with the real Dinnie stones.

Alex Forsyth and I visiting Firhill, home of Partick Thistle Football Club.

Myself, flanked by (left to right) Robert Russell and Jim Mullin inside the youth kit room, Murray Park.

BOBBY'S BOOK PROJECT
In words ...

What inspired you to work on this book with Bobby Dinnie?
When I first logged on to the internet many years ago the very first name I typed into a search engine was 'Bobby Dinnie'. I was so sure he had a book already but it turned out he didn´t. His name appeared in various football journals, magazines and online news articles but no book came up. I wasn´t involved in the writing industry back then; not as much as I am now – and it never crossed my mind to suggest anything like a Bobby Dinnie book. It wasn´t until recently that this project idea came to fruition.

I am inspired by his wonderful character and the very essence of the way he goes about his football and personal life. The way he has given to others is incredible but I think the contributors have said it all much better than me.

Were you selected to work with Bobby on the book?
I may have beaten off stiff competition; I really don´t know but I do know a few people were interested in writing up Bobby´s memoirs. Being related to Bobby means nothing in terms of favouritism; just ask any of his relations that played under him. I made some suggestions for his book at the beginning and it kind of grew from there. There´s so much to write about so I wouldn´t be surprised if someone else writes another Bobby Dinnie book. Certainly the one you have in your hands right now is the authorized version; the official

book I suppose.

Would you consider working on another Bobby Dinnie book?
I wouldn´t hesitate. I had so much fun and the whole journey was quite exciting. Of course, I would love to do it all over again and the truth is this book has been compiled in such away that we´ve left some doors open should another Bobby project surface.

A book about a football talent scout does ring of something different about it. Did you research other football talent scouts´ biographies before venturing into Bobby´s book?
I´ve always had zest and a taste for off-the-cuff ideas and entities in almost anything (as long as it works) but a book about the life of a talent scout wasn´t in the forefront of my mind, nor Bobby´s. Bobby and I drifted quietly between an autobiography and this type of biography. It was always about Bobby as a person. It just so happens one of the great things he is is a top-class talent scout.

As for research; neither of us did any research other than delve into the past and present life of Bobby and his surroundings. For curiosity reasons Bobby, myself and some others on the team tried to source a book about a talent scout but to no avail, for some strange reason unknown to us. I am sure there is a book, or many, about a football talent scout but we didn´t find any on our curious search but certainly we wouldn´t dare claim that this is the first book about a talent scout. We just couldn´t find a book about a scout during our search. In any case it was just out of curiosity and to be honest it doesn´t make a difference whether there is a book about a talent scout or not. Research is mainly for facts and I don´t know what another talent scout´s book would have given us.

What I would say, however, is that there are plenty – and I mean plenty – of people out there all across the globe that have done great things for the game in a background sense. Coaches, scouts, committee members and even right down to the individuals who slice oranges at half-time. Football nowadays is like a giant circus and almost rock concert like but all the audience sees is the stage, the big lights and the performers. What goes on behind the tents and the big screens is pretty much like a football club. Scale it how you want but the beautiful game simply couldn't survive without the background people. Bobby has brought those background people to the front of the stage in this book to take a bow. They deserve it.

Do you hope to sell many books?

None of us have ever considered the quantity of books we might or hope to sell; it's not that kind of project. The main motivation behind this book was to honour what I and many others consider to be a truly great Scot. Bobby Dinnie is a legend, and thankfully a living one at that.

We are not concerned about how many books we sell but we are more keen to offer a positive message and hopefully advice when you read this book. There are many great tips and ideas that you'll find inside this book...that must be worth more than anything that finances can bring.

You have some big names in this book. How did you manage to pull all that off considering your logistics?

All the names are big, not just some. Every name in this book has played a huge part in Bobby's life. Every name in this book means a great deal to Bobby. Every name in this book has established themselves as local or International legends. It doesn't matter if you have a title after your name; as far as Bobby is concerned: everyone has a stamp and a proud brand at that.

The beauty of the internet allowed us to correspond quickly and easily. Chic Charnley – thanked at the beginning of this book – was very instrumental with our research. Everything was smooth. I don´t recall any time where we had to rush and we didn´t break sweat. The contributors made everything run like a Rolls Royce. The name 'Bobby Dinnie' was the key knock on many doors and I believe we came a way with a few jeely pieces.

I was amazed at the way I was treated. I was humbled by the very fact I was talking to some of my heroes. I´m not a person who separates fame from non-fame, too readily, but I admit it was quite daunting to get quotes from worldwide figures. It was certainly an experience, but a very memorable and enjoyable one I have to say.

On your many telephone conversations with Bobby did you discuss anything else apart from the book?

Yes, definitely. Absolutely. Bobby and I are very private people and we don´t readily disclose private conversations but we talked about everything; we still do. An hour on the phone with Bobby is the quickest hour anyone is likely to experience. I learned a lot about myself during my talks with Bobby. I learned more about Bobby than perhaps I had put the kettle on for. Not many will know this unless you are privileged to have spent precious time with him but Bobby can sing, he can have you in stitches with his humour and I can safely announce to all who didn´t know. It is said that it takes a talent to spot talent and Bobby is one of those unique all-rounders.

Did you ever play for Possil YMCA?

No. I had an offer from someone connected to Possil YM but I opted for Kilbowie Union. I played for Kilbowie against Possil YM where they gave us a terrific pummelling in a cup-tie. I must have played well because someone hollored to me on the way back to the dressing room, "D´ye want tae join a good team, son?"

I can´t complain. Kilbowie were good to me and although I only played one full season it was a great experience. I have to point out that I lived in East Kilbride by this time and I commuted by two and sometimes three buses to training and games. Strange, East Kilbride was awash with good teams but I was always proud to cling on to my Drumchapel roots as much as possible and Kilbowie Union kept my flame for the west firmly burning. I´ve always travelled to play football anyway so it wasn´t a big thing for me.

You have a lot of contributors on this book. Are there any that stand out for you?

All of them. I honestly couldn´t say who stands out more than any other. There are a few that surprised me in some ways, however. I didn´t think Sir Alex Ferguson would have the time to contribute as I had contacted him during the pre-season and prior to the World Cup. It couldn´t have worked out at a busier time but Sir Alex was incredibly sporting. All of us were extremely taken aback with his generosity and for taking the time out of what is obviously a busy schedule and I will always be in debt to him for his kindness. A supreme ambassador not only for football but for human kindness.

Bertie Auld is a gentleman. I wouldn´t like to have been on the other end of one of his tackles, mind you, but what a gentleman. I had to pinch myself after I took notes from Bertie; I couldn´t believe I had just spoken to a Lisbon Lion… and I´m not even a ´tic fan. What I learned from Bertie Auld is this: if you think you know a lot about football (as I thought I did) then you have to have a talk with this man. I will always be grateful for the trust he put in me to write down his verbal contribution. An incredibly lovely guy and no wonder he receives all those respected tributes.

Bert Paton also comes into the gentleman category: of the very highest order. A very knowledgeable man and was a pleasure to talk to. Indeed another true Scottish legend. He was very supporting of this book project and for me one of the nicest human beings around. Great character too.

Mae Walker – who originally didn't think she merited a place in this book as in her words said, "I've not done anything to deserve a place in Bobby's book." After some gentle persuasion and describing who else was in the book she was very quick to inform me that: "It's Mae spelt M.A.E., there's nae 'Y' at the end." Very humbling. After interviewing Mae it suddenly dawned on me what this book project was all about: the people. Bobby's people.

Sammy Smith came up with the most astonishing lyrics. He seemed quite shy about the whole thing at first but he was truly amazing. Bobby and I still talk about that interview with Sammy.

Derek Robertson and Robert Carrenduff for their courage. Both have battled with their own demons but thankfully they are here to tell their story. Unless you have been to the dark and come out of the other end it's quite difficult to comprehend what it's really like. Thankfully I haven't been to that place so I really don't know what it's like but nevertheless I applaud their sheer strength and for allowing themselves to be so open. I hope by reading their words it will inspire and help others who have gone to that 'wilderness' zone. When we asked contributors to this book to just be themselves that is exactly what those two brave men did and we are all very appreciative of their support for us with this book. Their open words describing their struggles with alcohol was a reminder that we are all humble and vulnerable. A player is only a tackle away from a career-ending injury, a working man is only a few days away from what could be his last wage, a manager of a club is just one point away from the sack and we are all only one block away from the unknown.

Kenny Dalglish and John Greig: two idols of mine, were pivotal in our contributions section. I still have King Kenny memorabilia. Life can be funny sometimes. Here I am, one minute I have Kenny posters on my bedroom wall and the next thing I´m swapping E-mails with him. And who was it that said: "it´s a funny old game?" John Greig is another perfect gentleman for his role in this book. It´s still quite hard to take it all in. The list of people who have given us their time and support is just one long list of legends.

Jim Duffy was tremendous to us. Very sincere and although we contacted him at an awkward time (I think he was clearing his desk after departing Hearts) he still found the time to send us his written contribution. Our debt to Jim will always be unmeasurable.

Gus MacPherson was another true sport. At a very critical point during pre-season preparations he kindly gave me his time, his kindness and he trusted me to write his verbal contribution. I found it remarkable because his team St. Mirren were newly promoted to the SPL at this time and Gus was clearly involved in all team affairs for the new season and he still made time for us. It´s no wonder he´s one of football´s well-liked guys.

Everyone involved in this book made an outstanding contribution. It´s impossible to single any out. Each contributor was unique in so many ways and everyone was supportive of this book project.

How did you and Bobby and all the contributors come up with this book given the fact that you are in Germany and Bobby lives in Glasgow?

Logistics aren´t a real problem these days. The internet allows us to correspond and Bobby and I have spent many many hours on the phone throughout this project. It isn´t as difficult as one would think. The publisher maybe in London, Bobby resides in Glasgow and I am in Germany but a few of the contributors hail from all over the world. We have people who donated their kindness over the phone and online from Canada, South Africa and Australia, so there´s no real logistics problem as such. It´s great education; I´m now familiar with world time zones (it´s amazing how you find these things out: by phoning a sleepy Scotsman on the other side of the world, *ouch!*).

Would you say the project has been a success?
We didn´t set out to be successful. The motivation was to honour a truly great Scot as I said and you don´t have to be the inventor of an energy instrument or an electrical appliance to gain the honour of being a truly great Scot. Let´s look at it this way: I´m not saying Bobby is ready to leave the building just yet and none of us are writing any obituaries. But, it´s all too easy to hang a plaque on a wall and draw a velvet curtain to honour a lost spirit. I feel it´s better to honour those greats when they are here. I firmly believe – and many others involved in this project agree – that it´s better to acknowledge a present being than to remember a soul that is lost to us.

It´s only right and fitting that we honour Bobby, now, for his almost six decades of uninterrupted work from the grassroots level to professional ranks. Not to mention the outstanding humanitarian work he did for the community of Possilpark and the North of Glasgow, and not forgetting the city´s surrounding areas. In fact, for mankind. He has been, and still is, an incredible figure, an icon and we should cherish his very presence on this earth because we most likely will never see another like him.

How and where did you start this project?

Bobby and I arranged to meet in the heart of Glasgow as friends who hadn´t seen each other in a while, as relatives who would swap family tales and as two guys hanging out who both have a passion for football and for the city of Glasgow in general. Here I was, an ex-player and aspiring author (or so I have been told – cheekily, on both accounts) and Bobby: The General, The Master, The Saint (as many have labelled him) sitting in a busy Cosmopolitan mall café corner, bantering away as if we´d never been apart. The setting for our meeting reflected more Millennium family rather than football fanaticism but it highlighted the contrasts of Glasgow that Bobby has lived in: The industrious and bellowing city that once thrived under a low charcoal sky to today´s more aquarelle with a slight tint of gold.

I have always been in awe of Bobby but he has this gentle way of assuring everyone who he meets that we are all just humble wee boys and there is no such thing as First or Second Division people, anywhere, that we are all the same. I think Jock Tamson´s bairns had a lot of input into his down-to-earth ways of thinking. I have been out of the country for many years and although I didn´t doubt the magnitude of Bobby´s well-known, it suddenly dawned on me as we sat there in stylish chairs how famous Bobby actually is. It all started in the heart of Glasgow before the project took a trip around the globe and it ended up under a wooden ceiling on the most western point of Germany. Shows you the sheer international flavour Bobby has.

Did you plan the book out in the café?
No. It was just the idea of the book. I did have a vision that we could write a book about Bobby´s life but we needed to talk about where we could take the project. If I was to be involved in the book project it would surely include some international theme giving my living status in Germany and if

the book was about Bobby Dinnie we really had to take Possilpark and Possil YMCA with us on the journey because that is what Bobby is; Possil the place and Possil the team. We decided that we would take the people of the two Possils with us on this trip and that's where we came up with the idea of interviewing and drawing quotes and references from the people that matter to Bobby, the real people of the area where Bobby was born and grew up.

Did you get much work done in the café?

It was merely a meeting as we hadn't seen each other in a long time. We swapped notes and planned out the route of the book but it was much too busy after a while.

As the tea flowed Bobby produced a humble plastic bag from underneath his duke to reveal personal items he accumulated from the likes of Pele, George Best, Kenny Dalglish and Sir Stanley Matthews. I couldn't be certain but I'm sure I could hear the squeaking of more chairs nearing and the feeling of more prying eyes on us and I wouldn't be at all surprised if the Royal Infirmary received some new patients that evening suffering from sore necks and twisted backs.

Passers-by would stare in our direction, pretending to be on mobile phones or pretend to be listening to their friends in conversation, or even worse; pretending to be on mobile phones whilst pretending to be in mid-conversation! When in fact, they were evesdropping in our blether which included names like Arsenal, Aston Villa, the two Glasgow teams that need no introduction whatsoever (Partick Thistle and Clyde). Some other distinguished greats like Ian Ross, Alex Forsyth and many many others cropped up between the clinking of spoons against the inside walls of ceramic cups. I could see our corner – which we purposely selected for its privacy – becoming strangely busier...it was obvious who they found the most interesting between Bobby and myself.

Do you feel important next to Bobby or are you humbled like most of the young men Bobby has mentored?

Bobby wants to be friends. He doesn´t really like to be considered as a mentor. He encouraged me to be his mate. He draws it out of you and before you know you are swapping jokes and stuff like you do with your buddies. Well, actually, Bobby is a buddy but I know what you mean. It is sometimes difficult not to be a mate of Bobby but he has done so much in the game and everyone looks up to him it is very hard not to think of him in such a high honour. I tell you what though: he is a great mate to have. Full of energy, honesty and just a great guy to hang out with.

Bobby is timeless; he doesn´t seem to age and with all the prominent names he knows and the ones who know him on a personal level have never fazed or changed him either. Although relatively quiet and unassuming, he oozes personality and charm and I couldn´t help but allow myself a small inner-smile with an enormous feeling of pride and importance sitting next to a legend (who is more notably famous for… well…producing legends). I am in awe of him but I am honoured to be considered his pal.

Getting back to the café…it was becoming more unsettling and noisy so we headed off out into the melee of festive shoppers, jugglers and impatient beeping drivers. As we navigated our way through the Christmas mayhem Bobby tripped over a loose slab in Sauchiehall Street but superbly regaining his balance with dignity, turned around for a perpetrator of his stumble and quickly claimed he should have had a penalty. It was the Bobby I knew from years past and it was refreshing to know that of all the great Glasgow things Bobby is – he still had that typical Glaswegian trait: the acceptance of allowing oneself to be the recipient of an unprovoked moment of embarrassment. Now that´s what I call a mate.

So when did you both start the writing of the book?

I returned to Germany where I proceeded to set out the plan and group together the necessary research. I was fully aware of the magnitude of the task in hand; taking into account the logistics and the amount of people we had to contact. I had never suffered from writer´s block but I feared somewhere during the writing process with Bobby that I was going to come unstuck; not once did this happen to me. Bobby wrote his memoirs and sent his diaries of daily events from way back. Slowly but surely Bobby and I built up a nice rhythm. Bobby would send tapes of recorded memories of his life, interviews with family, friends and well-known footballers and I would type the verbal contents of the tapes into a word document. We found ourselves constantly on the phone exchanging notes and anything that came into Bobby´s mind, or mine, – at any time – he´d call me and we´d go through the process all over again: phone conversations, recordings, wrapping parcels and shipping by International courier. I would receive the packages at the other end in Germany and I´d type the contents into the computer: full circle work with the repetition of an angle grinder´s blade.

The original plan of the book was altered smoothly. We had planned on an autobiography but Bobby has done so much in his life and has been credited for many great things in and out of football; there were a lot of medals and praise going on in his life but Bobby being Bobby, he refused to take credit and often passed his achievements onto others he felt deserved it more. His humbleness made us retake our shots and we came up with the idea of this type of bio you have in your hand right now. It is slightly different but not maverick or wayward. It is a book where Bobby has the stage to tell us about his life and the ones who made an impact in it; in return, we get to tell him about the influence he made on us. By constructing the book in this way we hope we can tackle the humility aspects:

a clean challenge of course, and outside the box, too.

How did all those contributors join in?
They didn´t need much persuasion.

After we accumulated the research and sorted out the material for the book we compiled a list of the people that have played a huge part in Bobby´s life whether it be via the football circles, Bobby´s places of work or amongst the community. Letters were sent, calls were made, E-Mail addresses attacked (literally) and before we knew it; the community had gotten wind of the book project. Soon after, we were bombarded by enthusiastic individuals who sent us their memories of their time with Possil YMCA, details of their association with Bobby as a scout, tales from working colleagues and anecdotes from community members. Photos from private collections and a host of other material were quickly offered to the book´s cause... incredible!

Bobby gave me the key to his private collection (his address book) and I was given the most wonderful privilege of contacting regarded members of the community, working-class citizens and famous players – past and present. All of whom were more than helpful and if it wasn´t for those people who were kind enough to donate a line or two (and in some cases even more) then I am sure this project could well have taken a different route to the terminus.

Apart from the distinguished members who are biro´d into Bobby´s phone book it is well-documented that none other than Chic Charnley played a tremendous part in helping group together a proportion of contributors who were superb and extremely supportive during the research process of this book.

What message would you most like to send out with this book?
It´s Bobby´s book. It does involve his life and we hope

people will not only enjoy the book and read about how this great Glaswegian became one of the most important figures in all of the Scottish game. I mean, there are many who are great in the professional side of the game and there are many who are great in the lower leagues and amateur status but Bobby has been great in all circumstances.

Too often, cities like Glasgow and their housing areas are stigmatized for the wrong reasons. In reading *The Scout: The Bobby Dinnie Story* we hope to promote the good that's evident amongst the communities that is all-too-often over-looked. The work that normal working-class individuals do sometimes never achieve acclaim by the second lamp post and their efforts go much un-noticed outside their own close.

Bobby himself will tell you that there are many great-minded citizens going about their work whilst the world takes almost little or no interest; much the fault of the spirited one as they give help and support because they want to and not to be rewarded for it – their reward for community work is seeing the fruits of it blossom for the good of the individual and for the benefit of their community. I don't know if we can stop the stigmatizing but there is a lyric I learned growing up in a sprawling housing estate before moving to a nice comfortable back-and-front door: the one's who have the less are often the one's who give more.

If any message can be taken from this book then I personally would like it to be those lyrics. Bobby would bless those lyrics as he is those lyrics.

Who would you like to thank most for this book?

I would say Bobby Dinnie, Mr Dinnie, and Bobby would say the people of Possilpark, the people of Possil YMCA, the people of the city and surrounding areas and the ones who have contributed not only to this book but the ones who have played a part in his life. Anyone who spreads good with

Christian and human values would be thanked by Bobby, I'm sure of that. For me, Bobby, for giving me the great opportunity to work with him on this book and definitely all the contributors.

In an article you tell it how it is about the 'trouble with our game'. How could and would you change about the way the game should be run in Scotland?

I am not qualified to make any bold statements that will be heard and I am definitely not profile enough to make a change but I do have feelings about being Scottish and how our game is; like a lot of people. I am very much in the shadows of guys like Bobby Dinnie but I do happen to live for over a decade in a country that has won three World Cups (Germany won it twice as West Germany and once as a unified country) and not forgetting their European triumphs on an international and club level. I am familiar with the German youth system and the reason why they produce a world-class player almost every couple of years as opposed to our ten to fifteen. Listen, I'm not going to tell anyone how the youth set-up should be run in Scotland, if they (the powers that be) don't know how it should be run then we have a problem. When you want to ask anyone what the trouble with our game is you'd do well to ask the guys who have run youth teams for decades. Ask them what it's like to fight to book parks that are on the verge of extinction. Ask the people who are involved in the game in the so-called sophisticated millennium environment who still run their clubs on a scratch-card basis and ask those great people about struggling to hire indoor school gyms for weeknight training sessions. Ask them what it's like when they trawl from pub to pub begging for donations so that they can purchase lightweight equipment for their boys' clubs.

Is there a way to change it?

Yes. I learned a lot from the Germans. I learned that they are actually quite similar in mentality to us but perhaps they are backed better by their governments. Brazilians and Argentinians will always produce more flair players than the Germans but the Germans utilize their strengths. Scots have strengths but we don´t utilize them as much as the Germans use theirs. They are supported…we are on our own. Probably a Celt thing but we seem to dwell or even relish being underdogs and we accept it. Scotland has enough talent by population to be relatively successful but the problem is we don´t realize nor do we believe it. We need to have a complete overhaul and a strict and structured plan. It could take years but Third World countries have started these plans so if we don´t sort it out we´ll be left behind. The 1978 World Cup disaster should have been our wake-up call.

Possil YM was renowned for the upbringing of many a great player. What was the secret?

Not so much as a secret but more of a recipe. Possil YM was situated in the industrial heartland and by nature that´s the kind of areas that produce great sportsmen. Jimmy Dinnie and a lot of the other guys mentioned in this book like Tam Young and Mr Hosie were pivotal in the success of the club. It´s worth pointing out that Possil YM not only produced great football players but some fine young men too. The club was, in Bobby´s words, 'an institution', and this is testimony today when you look at the success of former ex-members of the club. Some have gone on to become great fathers. Some have turned out to be good at their trade and in some cases some have beaten their demons; so this tells you that the club – or rather, the institution – was instrumental in the shaping of great young men….many now older…but still, the grooming of what was once a young man.

The book captures interviews from some great characters in the game. What was the thinking behind compiling these interviews and putting them out on print?

I received a tape from Bobby involving an interview with him and Alex Forsyth: another great Scottish legend. My work was to write the interview from Alex's words but the interview was so special and sincere I couldn't possibly touch it. Bobby had travelled out to Alex's pub in Hamilton and he whipped the tape recorder out and started interviewing Alex without any rehearsing. Not a note was discussed beforehand and the interview was quite something special. We decided that the interview be placed as an interview in the book, uncensored. The rawness of Bobby's book just captures everything really. I think if you dissect words, phrases, interviews and the true happenings of events then you lose the worth of what this project is about.

Did you meet Alex Forsyth on your interview and research trip?

No. But I did feel like an artist that recorded half a song across the Atlantic and the duet was recorded at home then the two mixed together.

I had one telephone conversation with Alex but that was just to thank him for his time and for his interview with Bobby. Alex was one of those guys we really had to have on board this book project. He typifies what this book is originated on: great player, ex-Possil legend, sincere, warm, plenty of memories about his time with Possil and in all he gave us lyrics that any up-and-coming youngster would do well to hear. I remember Alex as a player but I was a little too young to give my scouting assessment on him…I've heard he was a great player and Bobby rates him highly so he must have been a great player.

Do you think we'll ever see the tanner baw player again?
It's hard to tell. It's a different environment these days. Some say that the sheer gallusness has gone from our game; the Souness swagger, the Jinky jigging and Baxter's ba' keeping has died, gathering dust at the peripheral gravestone of our Scottish game. Will it ever return? Can we produce another Dennis Law? I believe that although the game has changed so much in the last twenty years or so, we have to get back to where and how these guys came about in the first place.

There is no reason why Scotland cannot blossom another few greats. The facilities appear to be better in today's society but are indeed sparse in comparison to the playing fields and council parks of yesteryear. Society has changed, some will argue for the better and some may even suggest that the young have more options available to them today like computers, other growing sports and pastimes. It could be argued that the young are not as active as once were, let's say, as the kids growing up in the seventies. One thing still remains though, football is still the most popular sport, hobby, pastime and way of life around the globe.

So how do we revert back to the old times, y' know, the good old days?
I suggest that talent is not in decline, it is merely case of the authorities must take some responsibility for our demise. There is a distinct and fundamental lack of school football – where once it ruled our roots in organized sport and talent. The facilities that are on offer have no real incentive for the kids to play these days and so we must get back to the absolute beginning to re-plant and reap what can rightfully be ours. I don't want to sound old but in my time there wasn't much else to do except play football and in all weathers, too. Nowadays, the kids have more options and you'd be hard pushed to find any of them slide-tackling on a rainy pavement

when they can easily curl up in front of a computer.

We should not kid ourselves that we can unearth the next Maradona, but what we can do is build upon the passion of what Scotland was formerly renowned for together with sublime talent and then, we may have a better chance of showcasing the next big-time player to come out of the country.

For years we have always listened to the so-called experts and media pundits about the tanner baw player. To an extent, reminiscing is acceptable as long as we can be realistic in dividing our expectations by reality. We need to get back to the old attitude and blend it with the modern technology of high-tech facilities and coaching methods. I don't believe that enough is being done about our situation and the quicker we realize our troubles as well as our potential, then I am positive about the future outcome.

We need to get back to the basics and compliment it with the modern day technology the Europeans use. We are not Germans or Dutch but we must blend our generic personalities with the same youth system they use; then we'll have something to shout about.

How do you become a scout for a top club?

Well, first you need to have a keen eye to spot a talented footballer. To gain a scouting position with a top club will most likely mean you have to be invited. If you've been invited it probably means that you have vast experience and a reputable track record in finding talent.

With the state of our national game (as many people would say) is there any real talented prospects coming through the ranks at clubs in Scotland?

Contrary to what many would assume; there is a vast array of talented players coming through their clubs' youth policies:

Not just the Old Firm but all around the country.

Do you see a bright future for the Scottish game with the scouting networks, the coaching and the present financial climate of our game today?

Certainly, as scouts, we are very confident. Take Rangers´ academy at Murray Park for example: there is a satisfying amount of young players now vying for a place in the first-team. Don´t forget, Murray Park is not that old, it is a relatively new project but already it is adequately functional to serve its purpose.

What advice would you give to young players and parents in particular to achieve the ultimate dream in becoming a professional footballer?

Do everything with a 100% attitude; that includes school, off the park and family duties. Train hard, work hard, listen hard and you will learn easy. Forget about the ratio on how many young players make it or not, there is a reason, a good reason why many do not make it; just believe in your abilities and do it with conviction that others will be certain too of your abilities. The rest as they say, is in the lap of the gods.

How can I get my son to be recognized by a scout?

It is a good idea that your boy is playing with a team, playing organized football. It is not necessary for the youngster to be playing in a top club but remember; good young players tend to want to play for the better sides (usually because there is a better chance of winning a medal, you know what kids are like). If your boy has talent then don´t worry, the chances of word getting around are greater than what you can probably imagine. Scouts trawl over to look at players and the slightest hint, even a whisper or even a small newspaper article with the lad´s name in it will surely attract scouts from various clubs.

Who would you say is the best player in the world right now?

There are a couple of great players right now like Ronaldinho and Henry but I like Juan Roman Riquelme. In my opinion he is the world´s best player. He is my type of player and the way he dictates games really excites me. Riquelme can slow a game down or speed it up; one of the very few players that can orchestrate a game at the highest level.

Was it difficult to compile this book and what did you learn most about the whole project?

This book for me has been great for my English as I conduct my business and most of my personal life in German so it was good for me to get back into English. I must admit, I am the type of person who thinks a semi colon is somewhere you want to be awarded a free-kick. In learning other elements I would say I learned more about myself as a person and I hope I can grow from here. Bobby gave me a chance in the professional football world and now he has given me another great chance to build my own platform in this world.

In one word how would you describe your time working with Bobby on his book?

Honoured.

TRIBUTES

Davie Cooper

I always wondered what the world would have seen in Davie Cooper had he been born into the favelas. Had he dawned the number ten shirt in Argentina or opted to show his sublime skills in the Mediterranean?

Coop was one of the last great geniuses and although it is over a decade since his untimely passing: it's still difficult to take in that we will never see that sweet left foot again.

Davie Cooper was a mix of all nations thrown into a pot of genius and brought to the boil on match-days for all to enjoy. There was that Brazilian body movement with slight of foot. The arrogance of a gifted Argentine, the efficiency of a well-drilled German topped up with the swagger of a confident Italian. He was, indeed, a very proud Scot and a superb advert for pure and elegant football of the highest degree.

To mark greatness in a player comes too easily these days. Some youngsters today can't split the difference between a pretty face advertising products to what he does on a field: Davie Cooper was not one of those manufactured types; he was a modest genius and I remember someone saying that Coop could open a tin of beans with his left foot. Well, I think he could stir the pan and put on some toast to boot.

He was a lovely man too. It was a pleasure to know him and I enjoyed his company. Davie was very witty and full of chat, a real warm and sincere man.

What a genius, what a man and what a loss.

Bobby Dinnie MBE and Stephen Hamilton Nicol

George Best

There is something about greatness that excites and invites bewilderment. There are some – the gifted ones – who are heaven sent purely to entertain. You are then taken by surprise when you find out that a player who can beat a string of opponents – from inside his own half – and in turn, turn out to be a very nice and friendly human being. Football on TV gives us the illusions but not like magic were most of the tricks are pre-rehearsed and planned...I mean, I'm sure they already have the rabbit in the hat before they pull the poor thing out.

I remember growing up in a football mad world where the only glimpses of such genius were shown for half-an-hour at lunchtime on a Saturday when the moderator would finish the other match viewpoints and take us straight to the circus arena where a certain George Best demonstrated his God-like expertise.

Those magical moments were imprinted in our minds and as often as we could catch a flick from the Irish genius: we couldn't wait to head out into our back greens to replay those wonderful swerves and dribbles.

George Best was the circus: the ringleader, the entertainer but sadly in many an eye: often the clown. But let this be known: no man can be judged on what he does, we all have our frailties and let me ask you this: how many human beings do you know, or have met or seen that can produce tricks – unrehearsed or planned? In George Best, he could pull a hat out of a rabbit – he really was that great.

DOWN MEMORY LANE

With John Wales and Jim Torrance

The YM hall was only a stone's through away around the corner from my home in Bardowie Street. I first began playing officially at the age of eight for the Lifeboys and progressed to the primary school team; aged ten/eleven, then onto Glasgow schools and Possil Secondary school teams at various age groups.

I first started with Possil YM when I was fourteen in 1965 in the U-15 side along with Alex Forsyth, Tom McAllister, Jamie Hughes and a number of others who went on to join the ranks of the professionals.

In my trials for Possil I scored a hat-trick (three goals in twenty minutes) and was duly signed. In my first three league games I score eight goals – two hat-tricks and a double. This was me starting on the crusade.

I played for a number of years before leaving and returning first as player/coach with the U-17 team playing in an open age league. Thereafter, I worked with various age groups as coach/manager and in my time represented the club on a number of association league committees and as chairman at YMCA meetings.

During my time at Possil with Bobby, the club were connected with Arsenal and Aston Villa when I was a player and when I came back they were with Sunderland and then Coventry City. Visits were made to these clubs and their training grounds which were well-ahead of the facilities in Scotland. It was good also having the Arsenal assistant manager Dave Sexton and the club captain Frank McLintock up in Possil doing coaching at the local junior ground of Perthshire. One hilarious moment came when Frank

McLintock made comment on how low the grass had been cut by the groundsman, (the 'Shire' at this time was still a black ash pitch) and the groundsman – who didn't click on to the joke – then began dialogue from his own wee world with Frank McLintock to see if he could get him a job as groundsman at Highbury. The joke was lost!

Also, Tommy Docherty, the then manager of Aston Villa, coming to see us play. Another memory is having practical jokes played on us by the Coventry captain Terry Yorath at their training ground. One bad incident at the time was when we were in transit to Coventry to play a match before a first-team game when early one winter morning our mini-bus skidded on black ice on the M74 and we crashed into the crash barrier. We were lucky that the worst injuries were a broken ankle and a cut head. We never made the game and the players missed the opportunity of being in the spotlight playing before a top English game.

Over the early years as a player there were many highlights, including:

- At school, standing in for Kenny Dalglish as centre forward in the older team whilst he was on international duty with Scotland.

- Playing at the highest level in Scottish youth football.

- Appearing in, scoring and winning cups and league titles.

- Playing alongside a number of players who went on to senior football at the highest level; gaining international caps for Scotland.

- Playing at Highbury in London against Arsenal youth team

before the Arsenal v Spurs match in September 1967; the Arsenal team contained a number of ex-Possil YM players who had made the step-up in the previous two years.

- Tour in London, summer 1968 and scoring three first-half headers against Welwyn Garden City. A double against Hatfield Town and a single goal against an Arsenal youth team at their training ground at London Colney. During this and the previous visit to London we stayed in the YMCA Hotel, off Tottenham Court Road in the West End. This had a gym, swimming pool, snooker room, café et cetera and was a short walk from the British Museum. Visits were also made to Buckingham Palace, Trafalgar Square and many other attractions and we enjoyed using the London Underground to get around the city.

There were very few disappointments: not making the grade and being left out of a cup final team where the venue was the local junior team´s ground.

During this time in the 60s when little was known about diet or playing conditions, games were played on black ash pitches at Torr Street or Cowlairs with the luxury of red blaes at some school pitches. At school we had the real luxury of a grass pitch at Liddesdale Road.

On the black ash many a skint knee was incurred and on occasions the white lime used for lining the pitch found its way into the wounds. Many an after-match clean up in the back room of the YM was spent with hot water and an old toothbrush scraping the muck out of the skint knee. The scars on my right knee are there to this day.

Many a Saturday morning was spent playing for the school team and then getting home as quickly as possible to get ready for the afternoon game with Possil. Jumping off the bus at Saracen Cross when it was stopped at the lights and going into Britton´s the butcher or Electric Bakery for one or two hot greasy pies before going off to play again. Injuries were sometimes picked up, but these were hidden and the boots were cleaned to hide the fact we had played earlier in the day. I remember one day when we had two Scottish Cup ties on the one day. I picked up a bruised foot in the morning for the school team and could hardly bare the pain, but camouflaged the knock to allow me to play. These were the days when one substitute had been introduced. I can still hear the bollocking and the trembling when Bobby whipped me off at half-time, when he realized I was carrying a knock. This experience stayed with me and gave me an early insight into man-management that is still with me to this day.

On another occasion in winter I remember going to an away game in East Kilbride in the winter, that was an eye opener! No-one bothered to phone Bobby about the ice station we were going to. The red blaes pitch – which was always hard – was covered in frost and ice. As we had travelled (in the sixties this was a long journey), and referees were not robots and wanted their fees, the game went ahead. With metal studs on the boots and on ice it was like ice-skating at Crossmyloof. I know we lost to the Eskimos; we could hardly keep our feet. I don't think I´ve played or seen a game in worse conditions to this date. Even the senior grounds in those days didn't have under-soil heating.

Changing facilities were sometimes primitive with the whole or sometimes both teams having to get changed in railway carriage sized spaces. Showering afterwards was non-existent with one bib tap for both teams and sometimes all teams at the venue.

This didn't deter a young enthusiastic lad from a tenement life in Possil.

After a few years away studying and playing amateur/junior football I returned as player/coach with the U-17 team playing in an open age league. In addition, I began training and assisting Bobby with the U-16 team. I then started working with younger players as we developed younger teams. At this time I started an U-12 team which became our first competitive team at U-13 age group. A number of the boys who started out at this age group remained with the club for a good number of years with some playing their entire youth football time with Possil. During this phase a good number of trophies were won but more importantly players developed and were given a chance with many senior clubs both in Scotland and England.

This time also introduced me to participating in a number of youth football tournaments both in Scotland, England, Europe and America, where we made many friends and reciprocal visits were made, with great memories.

Some of these include:

Cowal 1975, '76, '77, '78, '79 and '80
Teams we met were from St Louis USA, Hamilton Canada, Brann Norway, Djurgardens Denmark and Cologne (with German internationalists in the team) and Fankfurt from Germany. There were also many teams from throughout the UK. As well as the good football at the tournaments some highlights included the coaches games with the UK/USA v The rest of Europe. This included playing against coaches from Scandinavia with 40+ caps for their country. Another highlight was when three of our age groups won in the same year with Jock Stein – the then Scotland manager – doing the presentations in the Queen's hall.

A number of our players who took part in these tournaments went on to have very good senior careers.

From my first involvement we had Gordon Chisholm, Dennis McLeod and Jim McLean who all had spells at Sunderland. Chisholm also played for Manchester city before coming home to Scotland to play for Hibs, Dundee and Partick Thistle; he was recently manager at Dundee United.

As well as meeting other coaches and officials we met up with a number of Scotland´s up-and-coming young referees, Brian McGinlay, Gerry Evans, Andrew Waddell and Mike McKinley who all advanced to the highest level, started out at these tournaments on an annual basis. Some of them have remained friends to this day.

Bradford 1979, '80, '81

This tournament was over the Easter weekend for our U-18 team and involved a couple of games against local opposition. Accommodation was staying over with the local hosts.

Holland 1982

Trip involved three of our younger age groups who hadn't been to tournaments abroad. We based ourselves in a farm yard youth hostel in the small town of Teil, where we played a number of matches against the local club. Matches were also played in Amsterdam, Utrecht and close to the German border where we paid a sombre visit to a military graveyard and war museum before matches.

This trip was good for team bonding although the opposition wasn't what it could have been.

The weather was cold and we played during a snow storm in Amsterdam.

San Francisco 1981

This was by far a most memorable trip. An earlier trip in 1979 paved the way for this excursion, together with the YM´s first visit to the States in 1974 in New Jersey.

We took two teams: U-18 and U-16 together with some of the '79 squad who came with us to renew earlier acquaintances.

This squad contained a number of excellent players some of

whom had played all their youth football at Possil. These included Bobby's nephew Alan Dinnie who was an excellent full-back and he captained both Dundee and Partick Thistle in his professional career. Billy Reid was another who played in this team for six years and then went onto play for Clyde and Hamilton Accies. Ironically, Billy is now manager at Hamilton having had a spell as manager at Clyde following a number of years in coaching at the club.

Following this team finishing their U-18 season in USA '81, I looked after an U-17 team in the Glasgow Youth League. This was another fine squad of players who played in and won the Glasgow U-18 league and also won some other trophies.

This team included Robert Fleck (Rangers, Norwich, Spurs and Chelsea as well as representing Scotland at various levels) and Alan Moore who played for Dundee, Hearts, Partick Thistle and Stirling Albion, where he is currently manager.

Frankfurt 1982
Our U-18 and U-21 teams made this trip although not at the same time. The younger teams' tournament kicked off a week earlier; this was a mixture of our U-17 and U-18 squads; we narrowly lost the semi-final against Eintracht Frankfurt, whose team included German youth internationalists in their squad. Notably we beat Auchenbach Kickers. Overall a good experience for our young team who were up against some senior, older more experienced players.

Our U-21s arrived as Scottish Champions, having won the Scottish Cup the week earlier. Their winning continued as they won their tournament against some tough opposition and beat Sao Paulo from Brazil in a tight final. The Brazilians had brought their youth squads to Europe for experience prior to taking in the World Cup in Spain.

After a year out Bobby was invited to his first spell with Rangers and he invited me along to assist him. After a few months of settling in we were joined by Colin Stein onto the coaching staff.

We had many good players including full-timers from Ireland. We participated in a number of tournaments with success. There were a number of very good players; notably Brian Miller and Angus MacPherson. Gus remained at Ibrox for a number of years before being transferred to Kilmarnock where he had very good career before becoming manager at St. Mirren.

In 1999 whilst my son Gary was playing at Clyde, Bobby made arrangements for Gary to play the following season at PTFC as they would be starting a professional youth team with their boys' club team for the following season. In addition arrangements were made for me to come in to use my experience to assist with this team. Unfortunately during the close season Bobby severed ties with PTFC. I took up the post and continued; taking U-14 – U-19 teams before resigning at the end of season 2004-2005.

John Wales

Youth football in the fifties and sixties:
The fifties and sixties were arguably the high point for the footballing youth clubs.

At this time, the senior clubs did not yet have their own youth teams as they did on the continent. Our senior clubs preferred to develop their scouting system and through use of the 'S' (schoolboy) form, tended to leave the young lads with their youth team. In Scotland, we had not yet developed the senior nursery teams.

Schools' football and youth teams competed for the weekend services of their star players. Stamina? Boys played for their school in the Saturday morning, had their 'dinner' and played for their club in the afternoon!

In Europe – particularly in Germany and Scandinavia – the

nurturing of young players was already highly sophisticated. From as early as seven, young boys had an attachment to a senior club with first-team players coaching the youth teams.

The scouts would swarm around games involving Drumchapel Amateurs – sponsored and managed by wealthy patron Douglas Smith – Eastercraigs Amateurs and Glasgow United. To play for them was a recognized step towards the professional game.

Doon the Watter to Dunoon:

When I started Cowal Boys´ Club in 1968, one of the first visitors to play us in Dunoon Stadium was Possil YMCA.

The Stadium is famous for hosting the Cowal Highland Gathering but for the other 364 days of the year it lies underutilized. I still remember the impression when Bobby Dinnie brought his boys on the first of what was to be many visits to Dunoon, (I cannot recall ever having beaten any of his teams--but we must have at some time, surely!)

Possilpark is not the most salubrious of Glasgow´s districts so I did not know what to expect. But these lads from Possil YMCA were immaculately turned out in their blazers and proudly wore their club badge. It was a tremendous tribute to Bobby.

Not only did they look good, they behaved impeccably and played like wonder kids. Their discipline was first-class, both on and off the field.

It is almost forty years since I met Bobby and in that time I have come to know him as a friend and one of the most decent men you could hope to meet. Bobby Dinnie and Possilpark are synonymous. His YM teams reflect the character that is Bobby Dinnie.

Cowal '71:

Bobby helped me organize the Cowal tournaments.

As I said above: Drumchapel Amateurs and Eastercraigs were the trend-setters for foreign travel and youth tournaments. But neither had the setting of Dunoon Stadium in July. And it was with the help and contacts of Bobby that we tried to lure the foreigners to the Clyde coast. There is no doubt that the participation of Possil YM was a major factor in attracting famous clubs. Bobby knew so many people.

Sports writers such as Malky Munro of the Evening Times threw his considerable weight into publicizing the tournament. So did local lad Brian Wilson, in the Guardian. Brian went on to do something in government. But he might be even more noted as being the official biographer of Celtic FC.

The '71 tournament was won by the Icelandic youth side under the name of Faxafloi; who defeated our own Cowal Boys' Club 4-2, watched by an amazing 5,000 people, one glorious summer evening. Bobby Dinnie recommended two very young referees to officiate at the tournament. Andrew Waddell and Brian McGinlay stayed at my brother's house for the week and went on to better things. My brother Stuart tells me he was fascinated watching pathologist Andrew dissecting his fried egg!

Cowal '73, '75, '77 and '79:
It is impossible to quantify the wealth of experience that Bobby has opened to so many young lads.

The success of Kenny Dalglish is well-documented. But there are many, many more, who have achieved so much because Bobby opened the door. Maybe not on the soccer field but in many other aspects in life. And Bobby gave them that chance.

In my travels I come across so many people who took part in the Cowal tournaments in the seventies. In Gothenburg I had dinner with Glen Hyssen who came over with Djurgardens IF from Stockholm in 1973. He subsequently played with

Liverpool and now comments on Italian football for Swedish TV.

In Germany I renewed my friendship with Rolf Heller who brought Victoria Preussen from Frankfurt in 1973. Rolf organized our trip to the 1974 World Cup in West Germany and for some time became the President of Eintracht Frankfurt.

Bobby Dinnie's contacts were not restricted to players and referees. He was instrumental in getting a number of celebrities to visit Dunoon and meet the boys.

The great Jock Stein paid us a visit and I recall introducing Willie Waddell to Hubert Vögelsanger – who happened to kick him when Rangers played Vienna Rapide while on tour after the war. Brave man!

I recall walking over the Cowal golf course with the Icelandic Consul General Sigurstur Magnusson, the father of Magnus and grandfather of Sally. I never did take up his invite to visit in Edinburgh but I did go to Iceland the following year.

I also recall watching the early skills of (among many others) Alec Millar, John Wark, Neil McNab and one Robert Russell. The people who worked with these lads are special. Maybe not a dying breed but circumstances change and the times were right for these individuals.

Dougie Canning from Sighthill was like this. So was Davie Moyes (father of the current Everton FC manager). I had the pleasure of meeting with them at the Cowal tournaments.

These heady summer days were very special and meant a lot to many people. We learned thirty years ago that the Americans could play football! Bobby Dinnie knew this. Quiet, unassuming words which we all associate with Bobby, he was at the centre of it all. Always available for advice or just a chat. You knew what you would get from Bobby. And that's the truth! Like many others: I am grateful for his friendship.

Jim Torrance

REMEMBERING

As time passes we gain many new friends and family members but it is inevitable we lose some too. Sadly, this is part of life and we must accept it as there is nothing we can do about the circle of life and how it evolves.

There are have been many people from all walks of life that have come into our lives and my book could never be complete without paying my greatest respect to the following:

Mum and dad
John
Hugh
Jim
George
Catherine
Agnes
Betty

Dougie MacDonald, one of my great inspirations. Thanks to Dougie I have enjoyed every minute of my time with Possil YMCA. Greatly missed.

Paul Fitzpatrick – late brother of Tony Fitzpatrick – was a shining example to us all. Paul had the potential to be a star footballer but sadly he was stricken by a serious illness. He finally succumbed to this illness at a very young age. He is sadly missed.

Bobby Law, an assistant to the late Archie McKay. Both ran the U-21s in the 1950s. Bobby Law's son, also Bobby, was a left-back for the senior team.

Ben Gunn, the legendary comedian. He did a lot for us. He once made the joke that if the phone rang he hoped it wasn't me, he'd say, "If that's Dinnie, I'm no in, it'll be a free one he's after." Ben was a great guy and sadly missed. His jokes and patter thankfully live on.

Tommy Carnegie has played a true part as well as a humorous moment in the Possil YM history. As you know, Possil YM operated with a strict code of conduct policy and untidy hair was as unsuitable as dirty football boots. I arranged for all the boys to meet up and I gave them the belief that they were to be fitted up with blazers. I locked all the boys in the room and Tommy executed his barber's skills: he gave all the lads a cropping.... right intae the wid!

Alex Martin, synonymous for unearthing the late and very great Davie Cooper. People often mistook Alex and I. In our team we often collected jumble sale ware and on one occasion a lady in the neighbourhood approached Alex and offered him jumble sale goods to take away...she obviously got us mixed up as Alex was having none of it.

Davie Cooper. Coop was a very fine young man and apart from being a tremendous footballer he was a pleasure to be with; I enjoyed his company. Davie used to come to the White Horse Whisky Bond where I worked; he would bring his friends along too. Gordon Dalziel and Jim Stewart visited the distillers with Coop. They were lovely guys. Coop always had a smile on his face and could light up any room.

Walter Cameron

Robert Howat

Alex Jamieson

David Lowe

Jimmy Meikleham from the very fine Sandyhills Boys' Club.

John Scott and the late Frank Barratt from Morriston YMCA – real stalwarts in the football world.

Robert McPherson, who was a wonderful player for us and Ayr United. He was a fine left-back. Robert sadly passed away in Australia recently.

John Currie. An accomplished goalkeeper who has passed away. He was superb and instrumental when we won the

Scottish Amateur Cup in the 60s. He was also a really nice man.

Johnny Morrison, a real enthusiast and football-daft. Johnny was a committee man and his sons, Maxie and Tommy, played for the club with great distinction.

To the late Joe Hill who encouraged me into scouting, forty-eight years ago. Joe was Chief Scout of Arsenal at the time I met him in 1960. He then went on to Sunderland, Coventry and Aston Villa, and I went along with him which was a wonderful education

The late Davie Morrison who ran Possil YM U-21s. He was truly a wonderful man, a true source of information and knowledge. Unfortunately Davie died during a game his team were playing in. Davie´s brother-in-law broke the news to Davie´s wife whilst I was in their house. Davie´s brother-in-law was Allistair McNeil who assisted Davie. Davie´s wife, Mary, always invited you into her house with open arms. Davie´s three sons played for the YM. Jim, Joe and young David. Davie Morrison was a true friend to me, and a sad loss indeed.

Hector Cummings was a great physiotherapist. He was an officer in the Navy during the Second World War and was also Head Physiotherapist in Hairmyres hospital, East Kilbride. He treated all the players in the YM and at that time his son played for Arsenal. Gordon Cummings played for Glasgow United. Hector travelled with us on our many trips abroad with the boys, including the trip to America. He even treated boys in his surgery at his home in Eaglesham. A true gentleman indeed and one of our best signings.

Nellie McLeod, the 'mother' of the YMCA. She worked wonders in raising funds through dances, jumble sales and race nights. Nellie´s two boys Dennis and Norman were great servants to the YMCA. Dennis played for Sunderland. Nellie´s grandson, David McMillan, also played. David´s mother and father (Kay and David McMillan) also gave a big part of their lives with the wonderful work and dedication they gave to the YMCA, over many many years.

Allistair Rutherford for his unstinting work. He was the committee man and treasurer at times. His sons played a big part in the success of the YMCA: Jimmy; the late David and Allistair Jnr...a wonderful gentleman.

Tommy Hamilton, father of former Rangers player, Johnny Hamilton and grandfather of Billy Reid, the Hamilton Accies manager. Tommy was a real stalwart and a workaholic for the club. One time when we were over in Germany he got a bit upset because he couldn't find sticks of rock to bring back to his grandchildren.

Jimmy Brown who was trainer when I was a boy at the YM. His son, Jimmy Jnr ran a young team for quite some time. Jimmy Snr was a boxing trainer and he certainly put you through your paces. He also treated all the boys´ injuries. I remember he had an old heat lamp that seemed to work magic. We played in old black ash parks and you could get terrible rash and ash injuries; Jimmy would put on a kettle of hot boiling water and get the tooth brush out and scrub the wound until it bled.

MY ACKNOWLEDGEMENTS

My wife, Betty must surely take acclaim and honour because it can´t be easy being a 'footballer´s wife'. She has been through everything with me; thick and thin, supportive throughout my life and career and the highest praise to her could never be enough to make up for all that she has done for me. I believe I was put on this earth for a reason and the reasons have been all what I´ve been doing for all those years and thanks to Dougie MacDonald as well I´ve loved every single minute of it.

To my dad for making sandwiches for the boys for an away game. The bread was great but unfortunately the fillings? Real dog meat!

Robert Caven Snr and his wife Celia Caven. Both did marvellous work for the YM as did their two sons, Robert and Ross Caven. Mr and Mrs Caven always made sure their boys attended music lessons before training with our club. A very nice family.

Allan Fleck, brother of ex-Rangers player, Robert Fleck. Allan was a fine player for the YM and his son, John Fleck, has a bright future at Glasgow Rangers FC.

John Jnr Semple. Did a lot for Possil YMCA. We were seldom apart.

Danny Delaney at Maryhill Harp when I played there. He slipped me some pill for a cure and I was running around for a week. I don´t know what it was but I saved a penny running home from the ground. Thanks, Danny.

Willie Blain´s parents. Both drove the mini-bus for the

YMCA. On one occasion the mini-bus overturned at Ashgill Road; both got out, rolled the thing back on it's four wheels and drove off without a glitch...great character and spirit shown and typified what the people in the community were like.

John Grubb, past President of Possilpark YMCA and was a fine player and very good badminton player. He was a giant of a man in every sense of the word – all 6ft 4 of him. John has been ill recently and is now thankfully recovering – we wish him well. John and I played together in the same YMCA senior team.

Peter Weir, former Aberdeen and Scotland player who later became a coach at Rangers. Now Chief Scout at Aberdeen FC. A good friend since we worked together at Murray Park.

Jimmy Smith, who ran Somerville Church senior football team in the YMCA League. Jimmy and I played against each other in the late 1950s and we are still good friends to this very day. Jimmy is a life member of the Scottish Amateur Football Association in which he has been involved for numerous years.

John Robertson, has been a true friend to me for many years. John is also a member of the S.A.F.A. and has given a rather large part of his life to advance the future of football for the youth in Scotland.

A big thank you to Willie Fleeting for his unstinting work for the YMCA.

Jimmy Mearns, a wonderful player for the YMCA. I couldn't understand why he didn't go senior as he was one of the finest players I've seen. Jimmy's late brother, Hugh, also made a great contribution to the success of the YMCA.

Hugh McBride, was a super right-half and was Mr consistent over along period.

John Willock, who ran Barrhead Boys' Club with great success over many years.

Gilbert Baird, school teacher at Barrhead High school. He

also ran a fine team when he was in Glasgow – Colston Youth Club. Gilbert ran this club with great success. A true gentleman.

Willie Gunn for his outstanding service to Possilpark YMCA. Willie helped a number of young players to great success in their lives. Willie was ably assisted by my trusted friend John Hamilton. They are really a fine team indeed.

Allan Mann, former YMCA player and also a big thank you to his dad, John, who was a great help when anything had to be done – no question.

Brian Cairney done well for Possil YM. A really smashing bloke and I'm pleased to see him reach the director heights in football with Hamilton Accies.

Robert Dunn was a fine goal scorer for the YM. Enjoyed spells with Partick Thistle and Stirling Albion. Robert was a very good centre forward but sustained many injuries in his career. I wish him well.

Ronnie Gay. What a player he was. He could have gone on to great things in the football world; if he'd only apply himself a bit more. A good Possil boy.

Jim Halliday. Wonderful player. We felt that Jim had the talent. His illness curtailed what would surely have been a promising career.

Garry McDowall was a really wonderful player. He played in Australia before venturing into coaching. Gary is the brother of Kenny McDowall who is on the coaching staff at Celtic Football Club.

Bill Munro and I played together in our younger years. He was a lovely right-winger. A former and distinct manager of Clydebank FC. And of course, not forgetting an ex-Possil YM player.

Alex Carnegie was a great servant for Possil YM for many years. Now living in England.

Jimmy McGinlay of Leeds Boys' Club. He ran a great team

from the South of Glasgow many years ago and produced some quality players and brought them through the ranks. Jimmy worked very hard for youth football and was always a pleasure to be involved with.

Peter Jenkins, another great servant to the Possil YM cause.

Clarke Brown. The first guy I've ever known or heard of that went on to enjoy a career with computers. This was years ago, probably no-one, at least very few people anyway, would have any experience of a computer; I certainly never had any.

Joe Haldane. A terrific player and I feel another player who if applied a little bit more could have done more in the football world at a higher level.

We ran a wonderful concert party made up of footballers and some of their families and other members. We did Cinderella.

Alex Cameron, in full kilt dress, was a wonderful Scottish tenor.

The late Walter Cameron entertained with his accordion.

Willie Laing playing piano and his young cousin, aged 10, she also played the accordion quite beautifully.

Miriam Sutherland and Morag MacDonald, two beautiful singers.

The Scout Pipe Band from Lambhill, they were absolutely brilliant.

Joey Gibb, who featured in all aspects of the show. Nothing was ever a bother to him.

My wife, Betty, who has a fine voice and her late cousin, Audrey Laverty Bell, who played a major role in the shows.

To Maureen Downie, brother George's daughter.

Jack McCluskey, who was a great Country and Western singer and yoddler.

The late Robert Howat, he took part in Cinderella and also ballet which was a scream. The boys wore football boots for this.

Alex Hosie, played saxophone. He and Malky MacDonald

were the good fairies. When it was Malky's turn, a young girl shouted, "A fairy wi hairy legs!"

Charlie Rae and Bobby Carrenduff, who formed *The Madcaps*.

Theresa Riordan, the late Nan Soutar, Alice Rankine, Cathie Kerr and not forgetting the powerful singing vocals from Mary Hamilton.

David Kennedy from the Colour Copy Centre in the Savoy Centre, Glasgow.

John McGhee and Billy Adams were both tremendous players for the YMCA. John was manager of a number of junior clubs. Billy is now manager of Perthshire Juniors. John is now Billy's assistant. Billy's brother, Teddy Adams, also gave great service to the YMCA, as a centre-forward.

Joanne, Kate Miller and the staff at Possilpark library, Allander Street who have been wonderful throughout the photocopying process of the text drafts and photos.

Rowland's Pharmacy girls in Balmore Road: Sheila, Phyllis, Mari, Elaine and Karen.

Ruth Cargill for all her work and boundless energy in her part for my testimonial dinner evening. Her typing for this great occasion was magnificent and I am very very grateful to her for this.

Fiona, for presenting my wife, Betty with the most beautiful bouquet of flowers and all the staff at the RAC club for their terrific work in one of the greatest moments of my life.

To my close friend Ian Johnny Birkens who ran the YM senior team in the late 50s and his late wife, Nancy. Wonderful friends.

Alex Rae and Stephen Frail. Two lovely lads and fine footballers.

To Mrs Sandra West, Robert Russell's teacher. Robert went on to play for Rangers. Sandra ran Robert's school team in Easterhouse, Bishoploch. She also refereed the school team games. It was with her permission that I invited Robert to play for Possil YM when he was about ten-years-old. I met Sandra some time ago at a testimonial dinner for Robert in the Hilton hotel, Glasgow. It was lovely to see her again. She certainly knows her football.

Tommy Young was very special to the club with his dedicated and very professional manner in which he organized the fine training he gave to the boys, and of course, his strict code of discipline which he applied. He was instrumental in guiding our young players to very high standards, not only on the football pitch but in other parts of their lives. Tommy was a major influence in the success of this great club, Possilpark YMCA.

Jimmy Brown. Who could forget the medicine ball? Marvellous man for Possil YMCA. Remembered by many former YM players.

George Marshall, better known as 'Bloss' to all who knew him. Also, his brother Alex for their outstanding dedication.

Tommy O'Neil for his tremendous work over the long years in running his team and the great success he and his son, Stephen accumulated. The fine contribution his late wife, Helen, gave to the Possilpark YMCA.

Willie Henderson was one of the finest players to grace a football park but Willie just wanted to play. If he could have applied himself more he could easily have gone on to make a name for himself.

Thanks to George Coyle for his part in the success of the team that he ran for many years.

Thanks to Ronnie and Maureen Lewiss for their fine team that they fielded with great success. Their son, Stephen was selected to play for N.Ireland schoolboys. He was a fine player indeed. He played for St. Johnstone.

Colin Brodie, former goalkeeper with the YM and performed great feats for Clydebank FC when they were in the Premier League. Colin is now a civil servant.

Joe Dickson also went on to play for the famous 'Bankies'. A very good right-back and was a real fans' favourite with Clydebank FC. A smashing guy!

Rab McCafferty, corner of Bardowie Street and Carbeth Street.

For the hundreds of spools Munro-Klick developed for me. Football and personal prints. Great thanks to Nancy and Sophia.

Duncan Warren and sons Duncan, Colin, Andrew.

Eddie Henderson and his son, John.

Tommy Muir, ex-player and assistant manager to our senior team for quite a considerable amount of years.

Willie Black played for our U-21s team. He was also a very talented table tennis player and coached a number of boys at the YMCA. Unfortunately due to a serious illness, Willie lost both his legs but is now recovering with great spirit and we all wish him very well for now and the future.

Andy Healey, who played a huge part in our success. He now keeps goal for St Roch's Juniors.

Stevie Rankine, great thanks for his work with the YM. He is now manager of Ashfield Juniors.

Jamie and John Hughes were super contributors to Possilpark YMCA. Truly, they were players of great distinction. Both went on to play for Aston Villa. Jamie was a captain in every sense of the word and a fine ambassador to our club. John was also a magnificent player. He now resides in the Channel Islands. John played centre-forward for us and in one game he score ten goals in the first-half – he never scored any in the second!

To Dan McFarlane.

To Tommy Gibson.

FINAL WHISTLE

IT HAS BEEN INDEED a great honour to receive so many wishes and praise. I've said this so many times I've actually lost count, well, I lost count many years ago (several times) but it's true; without the people of Possilpark we could never have achieved the success we enjoyed over the great many decades. Medals, trophies and honours are great for any football team and some say the most important thing in the game of football but I've always considered the enjoyment first and foremost. Yes, the amount of trophies we won and the incredible influx of players that went from Possil YMCA to international stardom has been an incredible journey but let's not forget the reason the YMCA was built. For all the countries and the many fine people that I met during my tenure at the club; this surely has to be the pinnacle.

Way back during the YM's infancy it would probably have been regarded as the ultimate dream; to visit other countries, exchanging cultures and learning from each other across the globe and to do this at the expense of a simple game of fitba just shows what can be achieved when the young are given a chance.

The young members of the club have never let me down. I have always given faith to the young as we need their energy and drive and they certainly gave me that. A great many of the contributors in this book may have played for one of my youth teams all those years ago and the fact that they took the time to contribute to this book just typifies what a great bunch of people they truly are.

I've no regrets. I'd do it all over again. Even the dreams that didn't come true actually swayed me toward another piece of glory in my life. I only ever wanted to play for one junior club and that was Perthshire Juniors but somehow they passed me by. I signed for Greenock Juniors where I would eventually play against Perthshire in a cup-tie: I scored a hat-trick; so it does show you the twists of fate we come across in our lives.

To the foreign guy who, during my time working for Strathclyde Police as Commissionaire, checked in saying he was here to register his *rifle*. After leaning closer to him to see if I was hearing right, he was trying to say *arrival*..."I have come to register my arrival in the country." Thanks for the relief.

To the lad who steeped a Detol soaked toothbrush into a boiling kettle for hygiene purposes. The toothbrush was used to clean out any gravel scrapes and scores occurred during a game on the many black ash or red blaes pitches. Someone made a cup of tea with that very boiling water.

For Bobby 'Murphy' Macintosh, who rubbed condensed milk on his hands and even used emery paper as goalie gloves.

Thank you all for not only taking part in The Bobby Dinnie Story but for being a part of The Bobby Dinnie Story.

Robert Nicol Dinnie MBE

VERNACULAR INDEX

Ah	I	Ah haven't got a clue, sorry.
Aye	Yes	Aye, you can say that again.
Ba'	Ball	Please can we have our ba' back? *(also, baw)*.
Bob	Bob *(old currency)*	I've only got two bob to my name.
C'mon	Come on	C'mon over here.
Chin-wag	Chat, blether	We had a right good chin-wag down at the pub.
Close	Tenement's interior	The lights were out. We couldn't see a thing up the close.
Close-mouth	Tenement's entrance	The kids played peaver at the close-mouth.
Dork	Dark	We played until way after dork.
Duke	Underneath coat	He hid his newspaper up his duke (also juke)
Fitba	Football	We played fitba on Saturday.
Fur	For	What was that fur?
Glesga	Glasgow	We drove into Glesga the other day.
Guid	Good	He is a right guid runner.
Haw	Hey!	Haw! Where are you going?
Heids	Heads	We've got to keep our heids above water.
Humf	Lift/Carry	We had to humf four crates of milk ourselves.
Huv	Have	Huv you got a spare bucket you

The Scout: *The Bobby Dinnie Story*

		could lend me?
Huvnae	Haven't	No, I huvnae got a spare bucket.
Intae	Into	You'll have to go intae the shop and ask them for one.
Jist	Just	Jist hang on a minute.
Kip	Bed/Rest	I'm tired, I think I'll head off to my kip.
Leerie	Lamplighter	Here comes the leerie to light up the street.
Lum	Chimney	Santa came down the lum.
Ma	My	Ma car is in for its service.
Maw	Mum/Mother	I have to give my maw a hand with her shopping.
Middens	Bin shelter	Take that rubbish out to the middens.
Midgey-raking	Bin inspection	We go midgey-raking to see if there are valuables thrown out.
Noo	Now	I'm not ready noo.
Oor	Our	Oor wee house is nice and cosy.
Polis	Police	You need to be quick to run away from the polis.
Polisman	Police Officer	That big polisman chased me all the way down the street.
Punt	Bet	I'm going to punt on the horses today.
Reek	Smell	Is that cabbage you're boiling? It doesn't half reek.

Sling	Cross/Throw	The coach instructed his wee winger to sling in a good ball.
Stairheid	Stairwell	Mrs McCafferty took her turn to wash the stairheid.
Stooky	Plaster	He broke his arm; he wore a stooky for several weeks.
Tanner ba´	Tanner Ball	He learned all his skills with a tanner ba´.
Tatties	Potatos	Last night I had mince and tatties for my dinner.
Thoat	Thought	I thoat you were supposed to meet me yesterday?
Watter	Water	I got soaked. I fell into the watter.
Weans	Children/Kids	Are the weans not at school today?
Wid	Wood	Go down to the sawmills and get me a length of wid.
Ye	You	Ye can say that again, Mister.
Ye´d	You´d	Ye´d be better off wearing your warm jacket.
Yer	You´re	Yer kidding me, aren´t you?

The Scout: *The Bobby Dinnie Story*

A publication by Club Books

For more information please visit www.club-books.com

The Scout: *The Bobby Dinnie Story*

www.ingramcontent.com/pod-product-compliance
Lightning Source LLC
LaVergne TN
LVHW091248080426
835510LV00007B/159